THE 50 GREATEST PLAYERS IN PITTSBURGH PIRATES HISTORY

THE 50 GREATEST PLAYERS IN PITTSBURGH PIRATES HISTORY

David Finoli

ROWMAN & LITTLEFIELD

Lanham • Boulder • New York • London

Published by Rowman & Littlefield

A wholly owned subsidiary of The Rowman & Littlefield Publishing Group, Inc.

4501 Forbes Boulevard, Suite 200, Lanham, Maryland 20706

www.rowman.com

Unit A, Whitacre Mews, 26-34 Stannary Street, London SE11 4AB

British Library Cataloguing in Publication Information Available

Library of Congress Cataloging-in-Publication Data

Names: Finoli, David, 1961-

Title: The 50 greatest players in Pittsburgh Pirates history / David Finoli.

Other titles: Fifty greatest players in Pittsburgh Pirates history

Description: Lanham : ROWMAN & LITTLEFIELD, [2016] | Includes
bibliographical
    references and index.
Identifiers: LCCN 2015035507| ISBN 9781442258709 (hardcover : alk. paper) |
    ISBN 9781442258716 (ebook)
Subjects: LCSH: Pittsburgh Pirates (Baseball team)—History. | Baseball
    players—Rating of United States.
Classification: LCC GV875.P5 F55 2016 | DDC 796.357/640974886--dc23
LC record available at http://lccn.loc.gov/2015035507

This book is dedicated to two of the most passionate baseball fans
I've had the pleasure of knowing: Tom Aikens and Eddie DiLello.
You both touched many lives and were valued collaborators
as well as beloved friends and cousins.

Also to my aunt, Louise Finoli, who was an inspiration to anyone blessed to
cross her path. You will all be missed, and may you rest in peace.

CONTENTS

Acknowledgments   xi

Introduction   1

Rankings

1	Honus Wagner	5
2	Roberto Clemente	13
3	Paul Waner	21
4	Willie Stargell	27
5	Ralph Kiner	35
6	Dave Parker	43
7	Barry Bonds	49
8	Joseph Vaughan	57
9	Harold Traynor	63
10	Charles Adams	69
11	Andrew McCutchen	75
12	Max Carey	81
13	Bill Mazeroski	87
14	Lloyd Waner	95
15	Wilbur Cooper	101
16	Fred Clarke	107
17	Roy Face	113

18	Sam Leever	119
19	Deacon Phillippe	125
20	Hazen Cuyler	131
21	Ray Kremer	137
22	Vern Law	143
23	Bob Friend	149
24	Andy Van Slyke	155
25	Dick Groat	161
26	Clarence Beaumont	167
27	Tommy Leach	173
28	Al Oliver	179
29	Jesse Tannehill	185
30	Doug Drabek	191
31	Brian Giles	197
32	John Candelaria	203
33	Vic Willis	209
34	Manny Sanguillen	213
35	Kent Tekulve	219
36	Bobby Bonilla	225
37	Bill Madlock	229
38	Truett Sewell	235
39	Matty Alou	241
40	Frank Killen	247
41	Howie Camnitz	253
42	Glenn Wright	259
43	Elmer Smith	265
44	Jason Kendall	271
45	Gus Suhr	277
46	Tony Pena	283

CONTENTS

47 Frank Thomas   287

48 George Grantham   293

49 Steve Blass   299

50 Jason Bay   305

On the Outside Looking In: The Next 10
Pittsburgh Pirates   311

What Could Have Been: The 10 Pittsburgh
Pirates Who Became Stars after They Left   317

Notes   323

Bibliography   331

Index   333

About the Author   343

CONTENTS

ACKNOWLEDGMENTS

A project like this requires the support and assistance of a multitude of individuals, none whom are as important as my wonderful family—my wife Vivian and children Cara, Matthew, and Tony.

My extended family has also been a source of pride throughout the years, and their support during the completion of this project has been unwavering. My father Domenic; brother Jamie; sister-in-law Cindy; nieces Brianna and Marissa; sister Mary, brother-in-law Matthew; aunts Maryanne and Betty; and cousins Fran, Luci, Flo, Beth, Tom, Gary, Linda, Amy, Amanda, Claudia, Ginny Lynn, Pam, Debbie, Diane, Vince, and Richard have been essential in any success I've enjoyed in life. I'd also like to remember my mother Eleanor; cousins Tom Aikens and Eddie DiLello; Uncle Vince; grandparents Tom, Inez, and Maria; as well as aunts Louise, Norma, Jeannie, Libby, Mary, and Evie. They too made lasting contributions to my fortunes. Thanks also to my in-laws Vivian and Salvatore Pansino, as well as their daughters Sondra, Cindy, and Nancy, and my niece Teresa and nephew Nathaniel, for their continual support.

The bullpen of Bill Ranier, Chris Fletcher, Dan Russell, Bob O'Brien, Matt O'Brotka, and Rich Boyer has always been available for me to bounce around ideas or thoughts for my projects, as have the fine people at the Society of American Baseball Research, without whom I would have missed out on the incredible research opportunities they have made available to me.

Finally, thank you to Jim Trdinich and the Pittsburgh Pirates, who generously donated the pictures in this book, and my editor Christen Karniski, my production editor Andrew Yoder, and the fine people at Rowman & Littlefield, who have made this project a pure joy.

INTRODUCTION

Lists. In sports they are how we measure our favorite games, moments, and players. Making lists is also an important part of communicating with, or, perhaps more clearly, arguing among one another as sports fans.

I've made many lists during my career as a writer, including those for the players on the franchise I am most passionate about, the Pittsburgh Pirates. I've mostly done it with collaborator and close friend Bill Ranier, using a combination of agreed upon statistical ratings, as well as our own personal opinions. And while we have made many lists, we have always done so with the passion, difference in opinion, and thorough discussion that makes creating these compilations so enjoyable.

The rankings in this book follow a similar pattern, yet they were created quite differently. First I used the raw data and statistics I felt were most important in determining what makes a ballplayer most effective. Next I rated the statistics against the average time period each man spent playing the game, as well as how they ranked as leaders against their contemporaries in the various categories, along with awards garnered, achievements, and postseason success.

In addition to statistics, I used my own personal opinions and information gathered through extensive research on those who were stars long before I started following the game. I also employed one other factor—treasured conversations and opinions of the many Pirate faithful who I've had the pleasure of speaking with throughout the years—to determine if I felt comfortable with where I had a player ranked.

There were many conversations with my cousin Tom Aikens where he'd wax poetic about the Pirates of the 1970s. He would often lobby for his favorite player, third baseman Richie Hebner, whose model glove he owned as a kid, although I could never understand why someone would want a Richie Hebner glove, but he had one. Tom always brought up Hebner's clutch home run in the 1971 National League Championship Series, as well as other reasons why he felt Hebner is one of the great Pirates of all time. While Hebner is not included in this list, Tom was right in his assessment, and Richie Hebner deserves to be included in the discussion about rating the greatest Pirates in the history of the game.

My cousin Eddie DiLello was a devout New York Yankees fan, and every time we'd talk he would inevitably digress into how the 1960 World Series crushed him as a kid, reminding me that the Bucs were nothing more than lucky in their victory. After his bitter dissertation, he would always assure me how phenomenal Vern Law and Roberto Clemente were and that they were among the most special players he had ever seen; he was correct, of course, as they both rank high in this vaunted list.

Needless to say there have been many others, with Bill constantly talking about the amazing three-year stretches of Andrew McCutchen, Barry Bonds, and Kiki Cuyler. There is also my father Domenic, who will turn 100 in 2015, telling me about his favorite players from days of old.

Despite the various factors used to formulate rankings, a list is nothing more than the opinion of the person putting it together, in this case mine, and it doesn't mean that other opinions are invalid or incorrect; this is what makes the discussions about making these lists so enjoyable, with one fan contending that their special memories are more treasured than those of the next. Let the discussions begin!

RANKINGS

1

HONUS WAGNER

A local son of Pittsburgh from nearby Carnegie, Honus Wagner is widely considered one of the top 10 players in the history of the game and arguably its greatest shortstop.

Photo courtesy of the Pittsburgh Pirates.

When making a list of the greatest players to ever take the field for a particular franchise, there is usually a spirited debate as to who will receive the honor as the top player in team history; when it comes to the Pittsburgh Pirates, the discussion begins and ends with Honus Wagner.

Wagner wasn't an athlete with movie star looks; he was stocky, barrel-chested, and severely bowlegged, and had a face that only a mother could love, but he had an incredible baseball sense and natural athletic talent that turned an otherwise odd-looking man into one of the game's greats.

Compare the "Flying Dutchman," as he was called, to other short-stops in baseball history, and Wagner continually lands at the top of statistical lists. One of today's most important stats is WAR, wins above replacement players, and here Honus is dominant. His career total is 119.8,[1] 20.8 percent higher than Cal Ripken Jr., whose 95.5 is second on the list. Wagner captured eight batting titles in his 21-year career, including five in six seasons between 1903 and 1909, finishing second in 1905, with a .363 mark, to Cy Seymour. He also led the National League in the various offensive and defensive categories 139 times during the course of his career. The Flying Dutchman finished with a lifetime .328 average, including an eighth all-time best 3,420 hits and 723 stolen bases, the 10th-best figure in the history of the game for that category. Not bad for a severely bowlegged individual.

With these incredible totals—statistics that become even more remarkable due to the fact that he played his entire career in the Dead-ball Era—it is no wonder Pirates fans scoffed when it was recently suggested that Derek Jeter may arguably be at Wagner's level. It is also no wonder Honus was included in the inaugural Baseball Hall of Fame class in 1936, with 95.1 percent of the vote, the same total as the great Babe Ruth.

Impressive statistics aside, perhaps one of the most significant facts about the greatest player in Pirates history is that he was homegrown, born in Chartiers Valley, about six miles outside the Steel City. One of nine siblings, it was his older brother Albert who helped Wagner begin his professional baseball career, suggesting to management that they sign his younger brother while he was playing at Steubenville, Ohio, in the Inter-State League in 1895. Two years later, Honus had become a star third baseman for the Patterson (New Jersey) Silk Weavers of the Atlantic League, hitting .375, and the powers that be in the National League eventually took notice.

While playing against the Norfolk Jewels, Wagner's play so impressed Jewel outfielder Claude MacFarlan, a Louisville native, that he wired the president of his hometown entry in the Senior Circuit, Harry Pulliam, to extol the baseball virtues of his opponent. Phil Auten and manager Patsy Donovan of the Pittsburgh Pirates had also become interested in the young star and began a bidding war for his services. Pittsburgh had first offered $1,500, which Patterson had turned down, before Louisville topped them with a bid of $2,000, a generous amount for the time. Pittsburgh matched the amount before Pulliam increased it to $2,100. Auten was given the chance to match, but the request went unanswered by the Pirates, giving the Colonels the future Hall of Famer.

Wagner was an immediate hit, with a .335 average for Louisville in the final 62 games of the 1897 campaign. Two years later, he had his first breakout year, hitting .341, with 114 RBIs. It was at this point that fate interceded; after three years with the Colonels, Honus returned to his hometown, where he began the assault on the record books that would make him an icon.

It was actually a result of financial woes more so than fate that brought the shortstop to the Steel City. As the 19th century was coming to an end, it was decided that the 12-team National League would be contracted to eight, and Colonels owner Barney Dreyfuss was determined to stay in the game. With the probability that his team would be one of the four contracted, Dreyfuss began negotiations to invest in the Pirates with the promise that he would bring his young, talented core with him. He eventually negotiated a purchase of 47.3 percent of the Bucs and was named president of the team. He then worked out a "trade" with Louisville, bringing Wagner, Fred Clarke, Bert Cunningham, Mike Kelley, Tacks Latimer, Tommy Leach, Tom Messitt, Deacon Phillippe, Claude Ritchey, Rube Waddell, Jack Wadsworth, and Chief Zimmer to Pittsburgh for Jack Chesbro, George Fox, Art Madison, John O'Brien, and $25,000.

It was one of the most impressive deals in the history of the game, and one that would also include Chesbro when he returned to the

Pirates after the Colonels were in fact contracted. The agreement formed the core of one of the greatest teams in baseball during the first decade of the 20th century.

The impact of the new players on the franchise was immediate, with the team finishing second to the Brooklyn Superbas (Dodgers) in 1900, before capturing three consecutive National League pennants between 1901 and 1903. Wagner quickly established himself as the star of the team, with a career-high .381 average his first season in Pittsburgh, capturing his initial batting title before winning his second three seasons later, in 1903, while helping propel the Pirates to a spot in the first World Series against the champions of the upstart American League, the Boston Americans (Red Sox), that same year.

Wagner and his teammates were heavy favorites in the initial Fall Classic and started out well enough, with Honus singling in Tommy Leach for the first RBI in World Series history as the Bucs rushed to a quick three-games-to-one lead. They went on to lose the final four contests in the best-of-nine series and suffer a humiliating loss to the new world champions.

The loss was the low point of Wagner's career. Hitting only .222 in eight games, the future Hall of Famer's courage was called into question. In *Sporting News*, a Boston correspondent made the statement, "While Wagner is a fast, gingery player, he is not a wonder as regards courage. I am half inclined to think that old Honus has some yellow in him."[2] It was a charge that, while unfounded, would hamper the greatest player in Pirates history until he finally got his chance for retribution six years later, when the Bucs cruised to their long-awaited fourth National League championship in 1909.

It was a special season for the team; they not only opened the first concrete and steel stadium in the Senior Circuit, magnificent Forbes Field, but also treated their fans to a 110-win season, defeating Chicago by 6.5 games on their way to the pennant. Their opponents in the World Series were the three-time defending American League champion Detroit Tigers. The series was billed as a battle between good and evil, the quintessential good sportsman Wagner against one of the great villains in baseball history, Ty Cobb.

Wagner had been deeply affected by his failure in the 1903 World Series. Christy Mathewson explains in his book *Pitching in a Pinch* that "this was a real tragedy in Wagner's career. Notwithstanding his stolid appearance, he is a sensitive player, and this hurt him more than anything else in his life ever has."[3] After many tortured years, his burden would finally be lifted in 1909.

It was pure theater as the two clubs battled through six exciting contests leading to the first seventh and final game in World Series history at Detroit's Bennett Park. Cobb had not been at his best, exhausted from traveling the elongated route from Michigan through Canada and south to Pennsylvania, trying to avoid Ohio, where authorities were waiting to charge him for an incident at the Euclid Hotel in Cleveland during the season where he had stabbed and beaten a hotel detective in a fight instigated because Cobb was told he couldn't use the elevator after midnight.

Game Seven was all Pittsburgh, as the Flying Dutchman led the way with a triple and two RBIs in the Pirates' dominant 8–0 victory and first world championship. Wagner was anything but "yellow" in the series, hitting a team-high .333, with six RBIs, compared to Cobb's disappointing .231 mark.

The Chartiers native was on top of the world, his lone career embarrassment now erased. But for the Pirates and their hall of fame shortstop, it was also the end of the glory days. The Bucs would not win another title for 16 years, while Wagner only had a few good seasons left in him. He hit over .300 the next four campaigns, which included his eighth and final batting title in 1911, with a .334 mark. Wagner's final .300 year came in 1913, and he spent his final four seasons hitting at a level he hadn't seen since his second season in 1898, when he dropped to .299.

After hitting .265 in 74 games during the 1917 campaign, a year where he took over as acting manager for four games after Nixie Callahan was relieved of his duties before informing Dreyfuss that he did not enjoy the position, Wagner called it quits. Said the batsman,

> I did not drop out of major league baseball because I was all through. I was not released. There was a contract on the table for me to sign at increased salary. As I say, I never paid much attention to the money end. I wanted to stay home for a while. I had traveled around from city to city for twenty-eight

years and was weary of it—the traveling I mean. I was never tired of baseball.[4]

Honus never tired of the game, returning to the team in 1933, for a 19-year stint as a coach before passing away in 1955, only months after attending the unveiling of his famous statue outside Forbes Field. The statue traveled with the club to Three Rivers Stadium, before being transported to PNC Park, where it stands outside the main entrance.

Even though it has been more than 100 years since he starred in the game he loved, Honus Wagner continues to set records of a different kind. His 1909 baseball card, distributed by the American Tobacco Company—a card that legend has it Wagner insisted be pulled off the market because he felt it sent a bad message to children about smoking (although some say it's because he was angry he wasn't paid for it)—has become a legend of its own. One sold for $2.8 million in 2007, while another went for $2.1 million six years later.

While it's his card that keeps the legend in the news more than a century later, it's his incredible performance on the diamond that has maintained him as the unchallenged greatest player in Pirates history.

MOST MEMORABLE PERFORMANCE

Despite the fact that Honus Wagner had many productive performances in his career, Game Seven of the 1909 World Series was probably his most memorable one.

As stated earlier in the chapter, Wagner was accused of being yellow and a coward following his less-than-stellar outing in the 1903 Fall Classic. It was a stigma that would stand with the hall of fame shortstop for the next six seasons.

With the series tied at three games apiece, and Wagner facing a loss that could further damage his reputation, the hometown hero, along with pitcher Babe Adams, was at his best, with Adams winning his third contest of the event in a six-hit shutout and Wagner coming through in the clutch to help give the Bucs the win.

After walking in the first and fourth innings, Honus came up in the sixth with the Pirates holding on to a 4–0 lead and Tiger fans chiding him with chants of, "It's alright. The Dutchman has a yellow streak."[5] With two on and one out, the shortstop destroyed what fading hopes the Tigers had of winning their first world championship when he sent a long, high fly deep down the left-field line, scoring Fred Clarke and Tommy Leach. The throw to third by Davy Jones was wild, sending the Dutchman home for a decisive 7–0 advantage. While the Tigers argued to no avail that the ball went into the stands and should be a ground-rule double, the Pirates bench erupted. Looking defeated, Detroit fans were suddenly aware that Wagner's reputation for being yellow was gone forever.

NOTABLE ACHIEVEMENTS (YEARLY LEADERS AND AWARDS ARE AS PIRATES ONLY)

Elected to the Baseball Hall of Fame's inaugural class in 1936.

Had statue dedicated to him in 1955, at Forbes Field, which now stands at PNC Park.

Had the number 33, the number he wore as a coach, retired by the club in 1952 (since he wore no number as a player).

Part of four National League championship teams (1901, 1902, 1903, 1909).

Part of one world championship team (1909)

Won eight National League batting titles (1900, 1903, 1904, 1906, 1907, 1908, 1909, 1911).

Led the league in WAR four times (1905, 1906, 1907, 1908).

Led the league in on-base percentage four times (1904, 1907, 1908, 1909).

Led the league in slugging six times (1900, 1902, 1904, 1907, 1908, 1909).

Led the league in on-base plus slugging percentage eight times (1900, 1902, 1904, 1906, 1907, 1908, 1909, 1911).

Led the league in runs scored twice (1902, 1906).

Led the league in hits twice (1908, 1910)

Led the league in RBIs four times (1901, 1902, 1908, 1909)

Led the league in doubles seven times (1900, 1902, 1904, 1906, 1907, 1908, 1909).

Led the league in triples three times (1900, 1903, 1908).

Led the league in stolen bases five times (1901, 1902, 1904, 1907, 1908).

Led the league in double plays at shortstop four times (1903, 1906, 1909, 1912).

Led the league in fielding percentage at shortstop four times (1912, 1913, 1914, 1915).

Led the league in putouts at shortstop twice (1908, 1910).

Eclipsed 100 RBIs seven times.

Eclipsed 200 hits twice.

8th in most hits in major league history, with 3,420.

35th in highest batting average in major league history, at .328.

10th in career WAR in major league history, with 131.0.

9th in most doubles in major league history, with 643.

3rd in most triples in major league history, with 252.

10th in most stolen bases in major league history, with 723.

18th in most at bats in major league history, with 10,439.

23rd in most runs scored in major league history, with 1,739.

21st in most RBIs in major league history, with 1,732.

7th in most singles in major league history, with 2,424.

18th in most assists in major league history, with 6,782.

22nd in most assists by a shortstop in major league history, with 6,041.

4th in most putouts for a shortstop in major league history, with 4,576.

9th in Major League Baseball Elo Rating by Baseball-Reference. com, a rating that attempts to rate the all-time greatest players.

2

ROBERTO CLEMENTE

Roberto Clemente is the only Pittsburgh Pirate to have 3,000 hits while in a Pirates uniform. Winner of 12 Gold Glove awards, Clemente died in a plane crash on December 31, 1972, while trying to deliver relief supplies to earthquake-ravaged Nicaragua.

Photo courtesy of the Pittsburgh Pirates.

Honus Wagner may be remembered for his exploits on the field as the greatest Pittsburgh Pirate of all-time, but for Roberto Clemente, his greatness extends well beyond the diamond. He may not be at the top of this list, but when it comes to the most beloved Pittsburgh sports icon, Clemente has no peers.

It's one thing to amass 3,000 hits, with a career .317 average, and another to be a trailblazer as the first Latin American superstar, but dying a true hero's death before his playing career had a chance to conclude has made this Puerto Rican a legend. Clemente is still talked about with reverence five decades after he was killed in an overloaded DC-7 en route to earthquake-ravaged Managua, Nicaragua, with much-needed supplies.

There were reports that the supplies were being taken by the government headed by Anastasio Somoza Debayle. An incensed Clemente wanted to accompany them to ensure that they made it into the hands of the intended recipients. A fool's errand perhaps, but the hall of fame right fielder felt that the government wouldn't stop a Latin figure as popular as he and that he would be able to achieve his goal.

The plane, carrying more than 16,000 pounds of supplies and five people, did not go far, plunging into the ocean and killing all on board on New Year's Eve 1972. The tragedy stunned the world and devastated the people of Pirate nation, who had learned to love Clemente so. Years later the city still grieves.

It wasn't always that way though. When he began his career in Pittsburgh, Clemente was anything but a beloved figure, challenging racist attitudes as not only a man of color, but also one from a foreign land.

Born in Carolina, Puerto Rico, Roberto was a natural athlete who had become a successful javelin thrower, which helped him develop one of the strongest outfield arms in the history of the game. "He may not have known it at the time, but the footwork, release, and general dynamics employed in throwing the javelin coincided with the skills needed to throw a baseball properly," says author Bruce Markeson in his book *Roberto Clemente: The Great One*.[1]

Developing a reputation in Puerto Rico as a potential major league player, the Dodgers, Giants, and Braves made offers, but Clemente decided to sign with Brooklyn on February 19, 1954, for $5,000 plus a

$10,000 bonus. Because he was given more than $4,000 in salary and a bonus, the rules at the time dictated that he be placed on the major league team or be subjected to the Rule 5 Minor League Draft. With a championship team already in place in Brooklyn, the Dodgers tried to hide him on their Montreal farm club.

There were rumors that the Dodgers only signed him to keep him from the rival Giants and sent him to Montreal because there wasn't a chance that Brooklyn would have five men of color in their starting lineup—a fact that was disputed by Stew Thornley, who wrote the biography of Clemente on the Society for American Baseball Research website. He claims box scores showed he played often and was not being hidden at all.[2]

Whatever the issue, they did in fact send him to Montreal, where after the 1954 campaign, he was drafted by general manager Branch Rickey of the Pittsburgh Pirates. It allowed Rickey, whose tenure as Dodger GM did not end on good terms, to steal a future hall of fame player from his former employers.

Clemente began his major league career the following season, 1955, with the Bucs, hitting .255 before eclipsing the .300 mark for the first time with a .311 average in 1956. As he was becoming a fixture in the lineup, Roberto not only faced prejudice due to his nationality and skin color, but also a lack of respect from some of his teammates for his perceived complaints about his various injuries. The right fielder did not want to play if he was not at his best physically because he felt it would embarrass him and hurt the team, according to former Pirates hurler and announcer Nellie King. It was perceived as something different by the dugout. "It became kind of a sign that he was a malingerer or didn't have enough (guts) so to speak. He didn't want to play today because so and so was pitching, Gibson or Antonelli. It got whispered around that he didn't want to play, he was jaking it."[3] On top of the lack of respect from his teammates, he was made fun of in the media for the way he spoke. Various media outlets would often quote him with the imperfect English he spoke or call him Bob Clemente in an attempt to Americanize him.

In 1960, Clemente had a breakout season, with 16 home runs, 94 RBIs, and a .314 batting average, helping the team surprisingly win their third world championship, but he finished only eighth in the

Most Valuable Player voting, behind teammates Dick Groat and Don Hoak, who finished first and second, and even the Cy Young Award winner, Vern Law, who was seventh. The hall of fame right fielder felt this was a slight because of his nationality and color, and refused to wear his championship ring, instead opting for the ring he was awarded for being selected to play in the All-Star Game in 1961.

Despite the difficult issues he faced, Clemente quickly became one of the premiere players in the game in the 1960s, winning four batting titles, including a career-high .357 batting average in 1967. While receiving votes in the MVP race between 1960 and 1965, he never won the coveted award until 1966, when he showed what power he possessed, with 29 homers and 117 RBIs, finally capturing the MVP Award.

As the decade was coming to an end, the Pirates were beginning to add more players of color, as well as Latin American players, to the system, as the veteran, formerly the subject of scorn by his teammates, was becoming a leader in a young roster that would soon become one of the most powerful in the National League.

The team flourished under Clemente's newfound leadership. The Pirates won the National League Eastern Division in 1970 and followed that up with a memorable 1971 campaign, during which they took the Senior Circuit pennant and a spot in their first World Series in 11 seasons. Clemente was now on the national stage and, at 37 years of age, was about to show the country what the city of Pittsburgh already knew—what a special ballplayer he was.

Playing in the Fall Classic against the defending world champion and heavily favored Baltimore Orioles, who took a convincing two-games-to-none lead, the hall of fame right fielder put the team on his back. Roberto led the Bucs back into the series, winning the next three contests before dropping an exciting Game Six, which set up a seventh and final contest at Baltimore's Memorial Stadium.

Hitting safely in all seven games in the 1960 Fall Classic, Clemente continued his World Series hitting streak, stretching it to 13 games by hitting safely in the first six games. He made it 14-for-14 in the top of the fourth, when he hit a majestic home run to left-center field against Mike Cuellar to give Pittsburgh a 1–0 lead. The Pirates added one run in the eighth and held on for a 2–1 win and the world championship. Roberto was named MVP and the undisputed leader of the team.

After the issues he had faced earlier in his career, Clemente was on top of the baseball world. He went into the 1972 season needing only 118 hits to become the first Pirates player to get 3,000 hits in a Bucs uniform. He hit .312 for the campaign and battled through injuries, needing only one more hit coming into a game on September 30 against Jon Matlack and the New York Mets. After striking out in the first, he smacked a double to left. He stood proudly on second and scored soon thereafter, before being pulled in fifth, when Bill Mazeroski pinch-hit for him.

Roberto played in one more game, as a ninth-inning defensive replacement for Gene Clines in the final contest of the season, but the 3,000 hit proved to be his last at bat of the season, and unfortunately his career. Three months later he was dead.

Clemente became the second player to have the five-year rule waved for induction into Cooperstown, as he was enshrined in 1973, but the honor did nothing to lessen the devastation—grief is still felt today. He remains the most beloved athletic idol in Pittsburgh history, a symbol of greatness for Pirates fans.

MOST MEMORABLE PERFORMANCE

Roberto Clemente had many impressive clutch performances in his long career, including a MVP performance in the 1971 World Series and a National League-tying three triples on September 8, 1957, but his most memorable one had to be on September 30, 1972, against the New York Mets.

It was during this game that Clemente stood at 2,999 hits, needing one more to reach the historic 3,000-hit plateau. The night before, the Hall of Famer had hit a grounder up the middle that was bobbled by second baseman Ken Boswell. Roberto beat the throw. He thought he had his hit at that point, but scorer Luke Quay ruled it an error, much to the dismay of an irritated Clemente. Despite the fact that he felt he had been given an unfair decision, the ruling held, and Roberto had to wait another day.

After striking out in the third, Clemente came up in the fourth and this time made sure not to leave it up to the official scorer. He ripped a clean double to left field, as a meager crowd of 13,117 fans at Three Rivers Stadium stood to give their hero the adulation he deserved. It was perhaps his proudest moment, and unfortunately his last regular-season at bat. The picture of Roberto Clemente standing proudly on second, full in the knowledge he had done something no other Pirate had—3,000 hits in a Pittsburgh uniform—is one most Pirates fans remember when they recall the career of the second-greatest Bucco of all time.

NOTABLE ACHIEVEMENTS (YEARLY LEADERS AND AWARDS ARE AS PIRATES ONLY)

Elected to the Baseball Hall of Fame in 1973, the second player to have the five-year rule waved, Lou Gehrig being the first.

Had his number 21 retired by the Pirates in 1973.

Had statue dedicated to him in 1994, outside Three Rivers Stadium, which now stands in front of the left-field gate at PNC Park.

Had the Roberto Clemente Bridge in Pittsburgh dedicated to him.

Had the right-field wall at PNC Park constructed at 21 feet high in honor of his number 21.

Part of two Pirates National League championship and world championship teams (1960, 1971).

Part of three Pirates Eastern Division championships (1970, 1971, 1972).

Hit safely in all 14 World Series games in which he played for a career average of .362.

Played in 15 All-Star Games.

Won the 1966 National League MVP.

Won the 1971 World Series MVP.

Won the 1971 Babe Ruth Award.

Finished in the top 10 voting for the National League MVP eight times.

Won 12 consecutive Gold Glove Awards (1961–1972).

Won four National League batting titles (1961, 1964, 1965, 1967).

Led the league in hits twice (1964, 1967).

Led the league in triples once (1969).

Led the league in putouts for a right fielder twice (1958, 1961).

Led the league in double plays for a right fielder three times (1955, 1961, 1967).

Led the league in assists for a right fielder six times (1955, 1958, 1960, 1961, 1966, 1967).

Led the league in assists for an outfielder five times (1958, 1960, 1961, 1966, 1967).

Led the league in double plays for an outfielder twice (1961, 1967).

Eclipsed 100 RBIs twice.

Eclipsed 200 hits four times.

17th in most assists for an outfielder in major league history, at 16.

Holds the all-time major league record for assists by a right fielder, with 253.

2nd in most putouts by a right fielder in major league history, with 4,446.

29th in most hits in major league history, with 3,000.

39th in WAR in major league history, at 94.5.

59th in highest batting average in major league history, at .317.

30th in most singles in major league history, with 2,154.

27th in most triples in major league history, with 166.

Holds the all-time major league record for most games in right field, with 2,306.

15th in most games in the outfield in major league history, at 2,370.

Only player in Pirates history to have 3,000 hits while in a Bucs uniform.

3

PAUL WANER

Honus Wagner and Roberto Clemente have statues in their honor and are still revered by Pirates fans. The third-best player in Pittsburgh Pirates history, however, is mostly forgotten, except for his retired number, which sits above the second level at PNC Park—an honor that was severely delayed, not occurring until 2007. The third-best player is also perhaps the most underrated player in the history of the franchise: Paul Glee Waner.

It was said by Joe Tronzo of the Beaver Valley *News-Tribune* in 1971, the heyday of Roberto Clemente, that "Paul Waner, when he was sober, was the best right fielder the Pirates ever had. The second-best right fielder the Pirates ever had was Paul Waner when he was drunk."[1]

Born in Harrah, Oklahoma, the star right fielder was not considered a great prospect at that position as he attended East Central State Teachers College in Ada, Oklahoma, where Waner was a prized pitcher. In 1922, he was 23–4, with a 1.70 ERA, before pursuing a professional baseball career instead of one as a teacher, the career his parents were intent on him focusing his attention on.

Playing for the San Francisco Seals of the Pacific Coast League in 1923, the Hall of Famer hurt his arm, prompting manager "Dots" Miller, a former Pirates second baseman, to send him to the outfield. Miller eventually put Waner in a game, and a legend was born. Paul hit .369 in 325 at bats that season and never looked back.

After cracking the .400 plateau with a .402 average in 1925, the New York Giants and Pittsburgh Pirates were scouting the Oklahoma native when the Giant scout reportedly told manager John McGraw,

"That little punk don't even know how to put on a uniform."[2] Waner not only knew how to put on a uniform, but—after Pittsburgh owner Barney Dreyfuss paid San Francisco $100,000 for him and shortstop Hal Rhyne—also showed that he knew how to hit at the highest level.

In arguably the greatest rookie season by a Pittsburgh Pirate, Waner made his 1926 entrance into Major League Baseball a magnificent one. He led the league with 22 triples, while garnering 180 hits for a .336 average, good enough for fifth place in the Senior Circuit. If there would have been a Rookie of the Year Award given out in 1926, the hall of fame right fielder easily would have won it. Instead, Paul used his first season as a precursor to his greatest.

After slipping to third place in 1926, following their surprising world championship season the year before, the Bucs once again rose to the top of the Senior Circuit in 1927. Following a closely fought battle with Chicago, Pittsburgh overtook the Cubs for good with a 5–3 victory over the Cardinals on September 2. They built their lead to four and a half games after a doubleheader sweep of Brooklyn on September 17, for their 11th consecutive victory, but stumbled down the stretch, with a 7–7 mark to win the pennant by a game and a half over St. Louis.

Waner was the unheralded leader of the team, along with his brother Lloyd, who made his major league debut in Pittsburgh that season with a .355 average. The Oklahoman had an incredible season, leading the circuit with 709 plate appearances, 237 hits, 18 triples, and 131 RBIs, while winning his first batting title with what would prove to be a career-high .380 average. His 237 hits remains a franchise record 10 decades later. Perhaps the most impressive feat of his record-laden season was the fact that he had an extra-base hit in 14 straight games (12 doubles and four triples), a major league record that has yet to be beaten. For his efforts in his sophomore season, the older Waner became the Bucs' first winner of the National League Most Valuable Player Award and earned a spot on the *Sporting News* Senior Circuit All-Star Team.

The pennant was Pittsburgh's second in three years and their sixth in the first three decades of the franchise. After quickly falling to one of the greatest teams in the history of the game, the vaunted Murderers' Row (more commonly known as the 1927 New York Yankees), in a four-game sweep in the World Series, the Pirates would not win another for 33 years.

Despite the lackluster effort by his team, Waner played effectively in the Fall Classic, with a .333 average in the four games, with 5 hits and 3 RBIs in his first and last postseason appearance.

While the right fielder never made it back to the World Series, he went on to have one of the most spectacular hitting careers in the history of the Pirates. Winning two more batting titles, in 1934 and 1936, while leading the league in doubles twice, including 62 in 1932, which is not only the fifth-highest total in major league history, but also a figure that no Pittsburgh Pirate has eclipsed, Waner firmly established himself as one of the game's greats.

Between 1926 and 1940, Waner hit a team record .340 (with 2,868 hits), a franchise-high 558 doubles, 1,177 RBIs, a .407 on-base percentage, a .490 slugging percentage, and an .896 on-base plus slugging percentage. He achieved this while also being a heavy drinker, prompting many baseball historians to wonder just how much more impressive his statistics would have been had he been sober. Paul proudly stood next to his brother, who was in center for all but one season of his time in the Steel City, and the two compiled what remains an all-time best 5,611 combined hits by brothers. Dubbed "Big Poison" (Paul) and "Little Poison" (Lloyd), the men were staples in the city until after the 1940 campaign, when Paul was released and signed with the Brooklyn Dodgers.

After hitting over .300 in 13 of his first 14 seasons in Pittsburgh, season 15 was not kind to the future Hall of Famer. Paul hurt his knee and was eventually replaced in right field by future MVP Bob Elliott. The Oklahoma native took the situation well, however, simply saying, "When a young fellow comes along, somebody has to move over, and now it's me. I have no regrets."[3] Limited to 89 games and 261 plate appearances, both career lows, Waner finished the season below .300 for only the second time since entering the majors, with a .290 average. After the season, Pittsburgh tried in vain to deal the 37-year-old right fielder and eventually gave him his outright release.

Waner played for five more seasons, the majority during World War II, when older players were kept on to fill the spots of those who were in the armed forces. He bounced around between the Dodgers,

Braves, and Yankees, playing competitively but not at the level he enjoyed during the prime of his career. He finally called it quits in 1945, when he walked in his only plate appearance of the season.

By the time he was done, the hall of fame right fielder had amassed 3,152 hits, becoming only the seventh player in the history of the game to break the 3,000-hit barrier. While he failed in his first six attempts to be given the highest honor to which a baseball player can aspire—election into the Baseball Hall of Fame—Waner took his rightful place in Cooperstown in 1952, with 83.3 percent of the vote.

It was a phenomenal career, one that has strangely been forgotten for the most part by Pirates nation. It was only because members of Paul's family, including his grandson, Paul Waner III, brought a request to then–team owner Kevin McClatchy to honor their relative that the team decided to retire his number—67 years after he left the franchise.

In 2015, Major League Baseball had a fan vote to select the top four players in franchise history, a Mount Rushmore of the team if you will, with Wagner, Clemente, and Stargell rightfully making the list. Waner was left off in favor of Bill Mazeroski, a phenomenal player in his own right but never reaching the level of excellence displayed on the diamond by Paul Waner, the greatest forgotten player ever to put on a Pirates uniform.

MOST MEMORABLE PERFORMANCE

In a career full of memorable games, May 20, 1932, stands out as perhaps the most impressive for Paul "Big Poison" Waner. Waner was a doubles machine. Finishing with 605 two baggers, the 11th-best mark in the history of the game, the hall of fame right fielder had a phenomenal campaign in 1932, when he smacked 62 doubles, a tally eclipsed by only four other major leaguers and a team record that still stands. On May 20, Paul had an impressive afternoon, tying a major league mark as he became only the 13th player ever and 4th in the 20th century to hit four doubles in a game.

Pittsburgh was facing the St. Louis Cardinals that day and was off to a less-than-stellar start, standing at only 10–17. Big Poison proved to be the spark they needed, as he went 4-for-5, with all four hits resulting in doubles, propelling the Bucs to a 5–0 shutout win. It gave Waner

23 doubles on the young season in only 28 games, while raising his average to .378. The record of four doubles in a game has only been equaled 49 other times in baseball history and remains the all-time Pirates mark.

NOTABLE ACHIEVEMENTS (YEARLY LEADERS AND AWARDS ARE AS PIRATES ONLY)

Elected to the Baseball Hall of Fame in 1952. Along with Lloyd Waner, Paul is part of the only brother combination to be inducted into the Baseball Hall of Fame.

Had his number 11 retired by the Pirates in 2007.

Part of one Pirates National League championship team (1927).

Played in four All-Star Games.

Won the 1927 National League MVP.

Finished in the top 10 voting for the National League MVP four times.

Won three National League batting titles (1927, 1934, 1936).

Led the league in hits twice (1927, 1934).

Led the league in runs scored twice (1928, 1934).

Led the league in games played three times (1927, 1932, 1933).

Led the league in doubles twice (1928, 1932).

Led the league in triples twice (1926, 1927).

Led the league in RBIs once (1927).

Led the league in putouts for a right fielder four times (1927, 1931, 1933, 1936).

Led the league in assists for a right fielder and an outfielder once each (1931).

Led the league in double plays for an outfielder twice (1931, 1936).

Led the league in fielding percentage for a right fielder four times (1927, 1929, 1931, 1934).

Eclipsed 200 hits in a season eight times.

Eclipsed 100 RBIs twice.

Holds the all-time major league record for putouts by a right fielder, with 4,808.

2nd in most assists by a right fielder in major league history, with 238.

25th in most assists by an outfielder, with 241.

3rd in most double plays by a right fielder in major league history, with 54.

2nd in most games in right field, with 2,251.

26th in highest batting average in major league history, at .333.

Had a .340 career batting average as a Pirate, the best mark in franchise history.

45th in highest on-base percentage in major league history, at .404

11th in most doubles in major league history, at 606.

Had 559 doubles as a Pirate, the franchise record.

10th in most triples in major league history, with 191.

17th in most hits in major league history, with 3,152.

42nd in most at bats in major league history, with 9,459.

40th in most runs scored in major league history, with 1,627.

48th in most total bases in major league history, with 4,478.

22nd in most singles in major league history, with 2,243.

Had 62 doubles in 1932, a Pirates record and 5th highest in major league history, including four in one game on May 20, also a current Pirates record and tied as the best mark in major league history.

4

WILLIE STARGELL

The all-time franchise home run leader, with 475, Willie Stargell was famous for his long blasts, including hitting a ball out of Dodger Stadium, smacking four of the six upper-deck blasts at Three Rivers Stadium, and clearing the right-field roof at Forbes Field six times.

Photo courtesy of the Pittsburgh Pirates.

April 9, 2001 was supposed to be a day baseball fans in Pittsburgh would always remember, the day the city was set to welcome its newest sports venue, PNC Park, a stadium so spectacular that 15 years later it is still considered one of the best, if not the best, facilities in the game. It was a day that the city and the team also planned to honor one of its icons, the man who led the Bucs to its last world championship in 1979, Willie "Pops" Stargell.

While April 9, 2001, is always remembered by Pirates nation, it is not one that fans celebrate. Instead, it was the day their hero Pops passed away, the result of a stroke suffered after entering the hospital to have his gallbladder removed. Legendary pitcher and broadcaster Steve Blass said it best when he stated, "When we heard about Clemente's death at four o'clock in the morning, I went to Willie's house. I'm not sure where to go this morning."[1]

Before Stargell was the unabashed leader of the franchise in the mid-1970s, he was a talented young prospect born in Earlsboro, Oklahoma. He then moved to the Bay Area in Alameda, where he attended Encinal High School, a school that produced other major league talent, including Jimmy Rollins, Bernie Williams, Dontrelle Willis, Tommy Harper, and Curt Motton, the final two being contemporaries with Willie in the majors, as well as his teammates at Encinal.

While Stargell told stories of the minor troubles he had gotten into as a kid in the projects of Alameda, he also gave his mother credit for the leadership and toughness that eventually became a hallmark of his as he led the Pirates toward the end of his career. "Mom taught me that it's important how you treat people. When you grow up in the project, there's no reason to be thin-skinned. If you were they stayed on you. I've learned you've got to be able to take what you dish out."[2]

While high school teammate Tommy Harper received a $20,000 bonus to sign a major league contract, Stargell received only $1,500. Despite the fact that he received so little and had an offer from a Chevy plant in San Leandro for $1,200 a month plus a chance to go into a management training program, Willie chose to pursue his dream of playing in the majors, signing with the Pirates on August 7, 1958.

Playing his first minor league season with the San Angelo/Roswell Pirates in the Class D Sophomore League, Pops showed his potential

CHAPTER 4

with 87 RBIs in 118 games, while facing racial slurs wherever he went. "I gave that up (the offer from the Chevy Plant) for a chance to make $175 a month and face racial insults in the minors."[3]

But he wouldn't have to face the verbal assaults in the minors for long, as the power hitter quickly rose in the system, increasing his home run production each year, from 7 in 1958 to 27 in 1963, his final year with Columbus in the International League. Stargell was called up by the Bucs in September of that year and would never return to the minors.

After hitting 11 home runs during his rookie year in 1963, Stargell quickly showed that he had the potential to be one of the game's preeminent power hitters—even as his totals may have been hindered by the spacious ballpark he played in, Forbes Field. During his first seven seasons, all of which were played in the iconic facility, the Hall of Famer hit 165 home runs, an average of 23.6 a season, while cracking the 100-RBI barrier twice, once in 1965, when he had his breakout campaign, with 27 homers and 107 runs knocked in, and then a year later, with 33 long balls and 102 RBIs while breaking the .300 plateau for the first time, at .315. Even though his home run total was mostly in the twenties, Willie demonstrated pure power by clearing the right-field roof at Forbes 7 times, more than any other player in the 61-year history of the stadium.

Many would blame Forbes Field for the fact Stargell never eclipsed 500 home runs (Pops himself once claimed he may have become the fourth to reach the 600-homer level if not for Forbes). While it is difficult to quantify the number of hits that would have been home runs in another park but were outs at Forbes, the claim that it cost him several homers is brought to light by the reaction he had when the Pirates moved into the more hitter-friendly Three Rivers Stadium in July 1970.

Stargell and Three Rivers were immediately a perfect fit. His manager in 1969, Larry Shepard, understood the effect a new, smaller park could have on the slugger. Said Shepard, "Next year when he gets into the new park with its normal dimensions he'll challenge Ruth, Maris, and all the home run records."[4] He knew what he was talking about. Willie finished the 1970 season with 31, followed by his greatest campaign a year later, the season when the franchise once again rose to the top of the baseball world.

In 1971, the star left fielder led the National League in home runs, with 48, and had a career-high 125 RBIs, good enough for second in the Senior Circuit. Many felt that Stargell should have been given the league's highest honor, the Most Valuable Player Award, but he finished second to the St. Louis Cardinals' Joe Torre, who comfortably defeated the Pirate by 96 points.

Even though he didn't win the award, Willie had something that Torre would have treasured more than a MVP selection: a National League championship and a spot in the World Series against the Baltimore Orioles. Following a successful first foray into postseason baseball in 1970, with a .500 batting average against the Reds, Stargell was not at his best in 1971, going hitless in 14 at bats in the National League Championship Series and hitting only .208 with one RBI in his first Fall Classic. While playing poorly, he scored the winning run in the eighth inning of Game Seven, coming home on a double by Jose Pagan.

Poor postseason aside, Pops continued his remarkable three-year run in 1972 and 1973. He finished third and second, respectively, in the MVP race, while hitting 77 homers and knocking in 231 runs in the span of the two campaigns, including a National League-high 44 long balls and 119 RBIs in 1973, a year during which he grieved the loss of teammate and friend Roberto Clemente.

Stargell was on top of the baseball world by 1974, but he turned 34 that season, and while the Bucs would win two more Eastern Division titles, the Hall of Famer's career looked like it was beginning its decline. He hit only 25 homers in 1974 and was moved to first base a year later, missing time with a cracked rib. His worst season both personally and on the field came in 1976. His wife Dolores suffered a brain aneurysm, and Willie's thoughts were properly on her instead of the diamond. She managed a full recovery, but Stargell hurt his elbow in a fight with the Phillies and had the lowest home run total since his rookie year, with 13.

For all intents and purposes, Stargell's career seemed over at 38, but no one told the slugger that. Remarkably, and aside from the fact that he suffered from arthritis in his knees, Pops revived his career with 28 homers and a .295 average to capture the league's Comeback

Player of the Year Award in 1978. He proved that his resurgence was no fluke, when a year later he was even better in a season that placed him among the greatest Steel City icons and made him a first-ballot Hall of Famer. Willie took the team on his back, leading the Bucs to their first Eastern Division crown since 1975, hitting 33 homers and finally winning the MVP Award he had longed for, tying with Keith Hernandez of the Cards in the vote. He made up for his subpar 1971 postseason experience by hitting .455, with two homers, in the NLCS, before continuing his clutch performance with a .400 average in the Fall Classic with three long balls, the last of which gave the Pirates a lead in Game Seven that they would not relinquish. For his efforts, Stargell won the MVP Award in both series for a clean sweep of the three MVP Awards in 1979.

Nonetheless, it was the beginning of the end for Stargell, his age finally catching up with him. Hamstring and knee injuries ended his season a year later, and his career lasted only two more seasons. In 1982, the team retired his number on Labor Day, with Willie following suit after season's end. He appreciated his time in Pittsburgh, honoring the people who loved him so much. "Pittsburgh isn't fancy, but it's real. It's a working town, and money doesn't come easy. I feel as much a part of this city as the cobblestone streets and the steel mills. People in this town expect an honest day's work, and I've given it to them for a long, long time."[5]

He finished his career 25 homers short of the 500 plateau, but many of those he hit were prestigious: a record seven homers over the Forbes Field right-field roof, four in the upper deck of Three Rivers Stadium, two remarkable shots out of Dodger Stadium, and the longest home run ever into the upper deck of Philadelphia's Veterans Stadium. While he may not have had the impressive career marks of other famous sluggers, Pops was a first-ballot Hall of Famer in 1988. He was a coach with the Pirates and Braves for a few years and remains one of the most beloved sports icons in the Steel City. Even though many are still saddened by the remembrance of his death on what should have been a celebratory day, they have a smile on their face when they remember the great gift he helped bring to the city in 1979.

MOST MEMORABLE PERFORMANCE

In a season that proved to be Willie Stargell's most heroic, his final game of the 1979 campaign is the one most Pirates fans cherish. After leading the Bucs to an Eastern Division championship and the National League crown, the Pittsburgh Pirates faced their nemesis from the 1971 Fall Classic, the Baltimore Orioles.

Following a split of the first two games in Memorial Stadium, the visiting Orioles took control of the series in Game Three and Game Four at Three Rivers Stadium, all but ending Stargell and his teammates' dream season. Pittsburgh fought back thanks to clutch pitching performances by veteran Jim Rooker and John Candelaria to force an unexpected seventh and deciding game in Baltimore.

Regrettably for the Bucs, Rich Dauer homered off Jim Bibby in the top of the fourth to give the home team a 1–0 advantage. Willie singled and doubled in his first two at bats, but as the game entered its final three innings, the Orioles still clung to a one-run advantage. With time running out, as was the Pirates magic in 1979, in came Pops for one last chance to be a hero.

With Bill Robinson on first and one out, Stargell took a Scott McGregor offering deep over the right-field fence to give Pittsburgh a lead it would not relinquish. In the eighth inning, the Hall of Famer put an exclamation point on his four-hit evening with a double, as the Bucs tacked on two more runs an inning later to claim their fifth—and to this point final—world championship, with a 4–1 win.

NOTABLE ACHIEVEMENTS (YEARLY LEADERS AND AWARDS ARE AS PIRATES ONLY)

Elected to the Baseball Hall of Fame as a first-ballot Hall of Famer in 1988

Had his number 8 retired by the Pirates in 1982.

Had statue built outside PNC Park, dedicated in 2001.

Part of two Pirates National League championship and World Series championship teams (1971, 1979).

Part of six Eastern Division championship teams (1970, 1971, 1972, 1974, 1975, 1979).

Played in eight All-Star Games.

Won the 1979 National League MVP.

Won the 1979 NLCS MVP.

Won the 1979 World Series MVP.

Won the 1979 *Sporting News* Player of the Year Award.

Selected as the 1979 *Sports Illustrated* Sportsman of the Year.

Won the 1978 National League Comeback Player of the Year Award.

Won the 1974 Lou Gehrig Memorial Award and Roberto Clemente Award.

Finished in the top 10 voting for the National League MVP seven times.

Won two National League home run titles (1971, 1973).

Led the league in on-base plus slugging percentage twice (1973, 1974).

Led the league in doubles once (1973).

Led the league in RBIs once (1973).

Led the league in slugging once (1973).

Led the league in assists for a left fielder four times (1966, 1967, 1968, 1970).

Led the league in assists for an outfielder once (1970).

Led the league in double plays for a left fielder three times (1965, 1971, 1973).

Led the league in fielding percentage for a left fielder once (1971).

Eclipsed 40 homeruns in a season twice.

Eclipsed 100 RBIs on five occasions.

29th in most home runs in major league history, with 475.

48th in slugging percentage in major league history, at .529.

72nd in most total bases in major league history, with 4,190.

45th in most RBIs in major league history, with 1,531.

42nd in most at bats per home run in major league history, at 16.7.

36th in most games in left field, with 1,229.

61st in most putouts by a left fielder, with 1,858.

68th in most double plays by a left fielder, with 12.

71st in OPS in major league history, at .889.

Holds the all-time Pirates record for home runs, with 475.

5

RALPH KINER

Ralph Kiner (left) and Johnny Mize (right) tied for the National League home run title in 1947 and 1948. Kiner would go on to lead the Senior Circuit in homers in eight consecutive seasons for the Bucs, finishing his career with the fifth-best mark in at bats per home runs, with 14.1, in the game's history.
Photo courtesy of the Pittsburgh Pirates.

Most of the players who are in front of Hall of Famer Ralph Kiner on the list of the all-time greatest Pittsburgh Pirates are more complete players than the Santa Rita, New Mexico, native; in fact, Kiner was somewhat of a one-trick pony. But when that one trick is more impressive than just about any player in his era, it's enough to include him high on a list of the franchise's all-time immortals.

Kiner grew up eight miles outside of Los Angeles in the San Gabriel Valley in a town called Alhambra, where he chose an offer from the Bucs over the New York Yankees, convinced that he'd have a better chance to crack the Pirates lineup.

After a relatively unspectacular three-year stint in the minor leagues, the future slugger went into the U.S. Navy as a pilot during World War II. While many ballplayers played military ball for the morale of the troops, Kiner spent his time in the South Pacific, flying missions in search of enemy subs and battleships. Others may have found it unfair to be in the middle of action while some got to play baseball, but the future Hall of Famer was not one of them. Kiner commented,

> Though I rarely got on the field myself, I wasn't jealous of
> those who did. Everyone who volunteered for the service pos-
> sessed a singular focus on saving this country. I never felt like
> I was missing out on anything because I was doing exactly
> what I was supposed to be doing. For all of us ballplayers in
> the service, our duty to our country was always more impor-
> tant than playing baseball.[1]

After the war ended in 1945, Kiner returned home to California to prepare for the upcoming season. At 23 years of age, out of the game for three seasons, the young slugger aggressively attacked spring training the following season, hitting 13 homers in 30 exhibition games. Even though he hit a less-than-stellar .247 during his rookie season in 1946, the New Mexico native tied a franchise rookie record with 23 home runs. Thanks to the fact Giant superstar Johnny Mize was out with a broken wrist for part of the season, Kiner also captured his first home run title by one over the injured veteran.

The following season the new Pirates ownership, led by the Gal-breath family, wanted to aggressively pursue better talent, so they signed Detroit Tigers slugger Hank Greenberg to baseball's first $100,000 salary. While the 36-year-old Greenberg had seen his better days, he was coming off a 44-home run season, and management was hoping he would influence and combine with Kiner to form a danger-ous lineup.

Knowing Forbes Field was not exactly friendly to hitters—Kiner only hit eight of his 23 homers there in 1946—the Pirates moved the right-field fences in, creating a bull pen area and making a home run to right a more manageable 335 feet instead of 365. It was nicknamed "Greenberg Gardens" in honor of the newest Pirate, but it was the 24-year-old who, by year's end, would truly take advantage of the new fences.

Kiner got off to a slow start, so slow that manager Billy Herman wanted to demote the second-year player. Greenberg, who Kiner considered his biggest influence in the game, talked the team out of it. The young batsman went on a rampage unseen by a Pirates power hitter before or since, smacking eight homers in four games on his way to becoming the first and only Pittsburgh Pirate to eclipse the 50-home run mark, tying Mize for the league lead, with 51.

By 1948, Greenberg had retired, but Kiner had learned his lessons well and was about to become a true superstar in his own right, both on and off the field. While he was ripping home runs on the field, he became popular off the field, dating many of the biggest Hollywood stars of his day, including Elizabeth Taylor and Janet Leigh, while be-friending such luminaries as Jack Lemmon and Lucille Ball.

Ralph's third season would be one of the most memorable of his career. While his home run total dipped to 40, he once again tied with Mize, one ahead of Stan Musial, who had his 40th wiped out due to a rainout. The team also did much better, finishing in the first division with a surprising 83–71 record. Even more impressive was the Bucs' attendance, which topped the Senior Circuit, crushing their former team record, as 1,517,021 fans entered the turnstiles at Forbes Field. Kiner was now perhaps the greatest drawing card in the game.

What should have been the beginning of a great run for the franchise turned out to be the start of one of its most embarrassing eras. During the next nine years, the club finished in either seventh or eighth place in the National League in all but one season, 1949, when they were sixth. Despite the incredibly poor performances, Kiner remained one of the preeminent sluggers in the game.

Perhaps his greatest season was in 1949, when he led the Senior Circuit in both home runs and RBIs with career highs in both, 54 and 127, respectively. He also hit .310 and was the leader in the National League in on-base plus slugging percentage with another career best, 1.089, beating Musial by .29 and third-place finisher Jackie Robinson by 129 points.

The Hall of Fame left fielder continued his assault on Senior Circuit pitching throughout the next three seasons, stretching his run of consecutive National League home run crowns to seven by 1952, even though he had his lowest total since his rookie campaign, with 37. While the team continued to lose on the field, they won in the box office thanks to Kiner, drawing more than 1 million customers in both 1949 and 1950, and pulling in slightly less than 1 million in 1951 but remaining in the top half of the circuit. Once the Ralph would take his final at bat late in the game, fans would quickly file out of Forbes Field.

As the losing continued, Kiner was not enough to keep fans in the building. His drawing capability was not enough for management, which now included Hall of Fame general manager Branch Rickey among its ranks. The New Mexico native was looking for a raise after leading the league for the seventh consecutive time, and Rickey was not keen on spending a lot of money for a player he was losing with. Interested in rebuilding with younger players, the legendary general manager uttered the famous phrase, "We finished last with you, and we can finish last without you."[2]

Rickey sent his slugger to the Chicago Cubs with Joe Garagiola, George Metkovich, and Howie Pollet for Bob Addis, Toby Atwell, George Freese, Gene Hermanski, Bob Schultz, Preston Ward, and $150,000. The $150,000 the Pirates received was the only positive part of the deal.

Even though Kiner was only 30, back issues quickly derailed his career. He hit 35 homers between Chicago and Pittsburgh in 1953, before dropping to 22 a year later and 18 with the defending American

League champion Cleveland Indians in 1955. He had the option of back surgery to hopefully correct the problem but instead chose to retire and become GM of the Pacific Coast League's San Diego Padres.

The Pirates great went on to have a second memorable career in baseball starting in 1962, when he was hired as a broadcaster with the expansion New York Mets. He made the claim the Mets were interested because "they looked at my background with the Pirates and saw I had losing experience."[3]

In 1975, Kiner was given his rightful place in baseball history when he was finally elected into the Baseball Hall of Fame by the baseball writers, making it in by the slimmest of margins, with 75.4 percent of the vote, only .4 percent higher than the minimum vote needed. He was further honored by the team he starred for in 1987, when the Pirates officially retired his number. The franchise later dedicated a statue of his hands and bat with his home run titles on the cement below, located on the bottom level of PNC Park—a monument to a man who is not only fifth all-time with one home run per every 14.1 at bats, but also a player who Hall of Fame pitcher Warren Spahn once claimed could "wipe out your lead with one swing."[4]

After a long and distinguished career in the game, Ralph Kiner died on February 6, 2014, at 91 years of age; gone but not forgotten, he will always be the greatest one-trick pony in Pirates history.

MOST MEMORABLE PERFORMANCE

The 1947 season saw second-year Pirate Ralph Kiner go from a prospect with potential to one of the best sluggers in the game. After a slow start, the young left fielder caught fire, hitting home runs at a record-setting pace that made many wonder if Babe Ruth's record of 60 was in serious jeopardy. Ralph fell short, but on August 15 and 16, he put his name in the record books, tying two marks by hitting home runs in four official at bats and five in two games, while also setting the mark for seven in four games, which he broke a month later.

Kiner had homered in each of the two prior games before smacking a two-run shot in the bottom of the first to give the Pirates a temporary 2–0 lead. The Cardinals eventually scored seven runs, but the slugger made it closer when he hit another two-run shot, once again knocking in Frankie Gustine, in his last at bat in the eighth, making the final 7–4 St. Louis.

In the following contest on August 16, Kiner became the first Pittsburgh player to hit three long balls in a single game. After walking in the first inning, the Hall of Famer hit the first of back-to-back homers with Hank Greenberg in the third to give the Bucs a 6–4 advantage. Two innings later he smacked a three-run shot, making the score 9–5.

Kiner walked in the sixth and then put his name in the history books for a third time that day when he hit his third of the game, fourth in four consecutive at bats, fifth in two days, and seventh in four days off Johnny Grodzicki in the bottom of the eighth to put the final touches on a 12–5 victory.

Almost a month to the day later, Kiner once again set a new record when he hit eight home runs in four consecutive games between September 10 and 12, a mark that has yet to be equaled.

NOTABLE ACHIEVEMENTS (YEARLY LEADERS AND AWARDS ARE AS PIRATES ONLY)

Elected to the Baseball Hall of Fame on his last chance in 1975.

Had his number 4 retired by the Pirates in 1987.

Had statue built inside PNC Park, dedicated in 2003.

Played in six All-Star Games.

Finished in the top 10 voting for the National League MVP five times.

Won seven consecutive National League home run titles (1946, 1947, 1948, 1949, 1950, 1951, 1952).

Led the league in OPS three times (1947, 1949, 1951).

Led the league in RBIs once (1949).

Led the league in slugging three times (1947, 1949, 1951).

Led the league in on-base percentage once (1951).

Led the league in runs once (1951).

Led the league in at bats per home run seven times (1946, 1947, 1948, 1949, 1950, 1951, 1952).

Led the league in assists for a left fielder once (1950).

Led the league in putouts for a left fielder twice (1947, 1948).

Led the league in putouts for an outfielder twice (1947).

Led the league in double plays for a left fielder twice (1949, 1950).
Led the league in fielding percentage for a left fielder once (1948).
Only Pirate to eclipse 50 home runs in a season, twice.
Eclipsed 40 home runs in a season three times.
Eclipsed 100 RBIs on six occasions.
5th in most at bats per home run in major league history, at 14.1.
67th in on-base percentage in major league history, at .398.
25th in slugging percentage in major league history, at .548.
23rd in OPS in major league history, at .946.
78th in most home runs in major league history, with 369.
29th in most games in left field in major league history, with 1,307.
27th in most putouts in left field in major league history, with 2,560.
Tied a major league record for four home runs in four consecutive at bats (1947).
Tied a major league record for five home runs in two consecutive games (1947).
Holds the major league record for eight home runs in four consecutive games (1947).

6

DAVE PARKER

Pittsburgh Pirates fans know that Dave Parker was one of the greatest players to ever don a uniform for the franchise; however, his career was stunted by injuries and well-publicized drug use during his later years with the team. Drafted in the 14th round of the 1970 amateur draft out of Courter Tech High School in Cincinnati, the Cobra, as he was known, quickly rose through the Bucs' system, being promoted to their Double-A team in Waterbury in only his second season. Parker stalled with a .228 average that year with no home runs in 30 games before being returned to their Class A team in Salem the following year. It was in Salem that the Cincinnati native began to show his potential, smacking 22 home runs with a .310 average.

The young slugger jumped two levels to the Triple-A Charleston Charlies in 1973, hitting .317—ironically the same career average of Pittsburgh great Roberto Clemente, the man who Parker would eventually replace following his tragic death on New Year's Eve 1972. The right fielder was called up to the big-league team in July 1973, hitting an impressive .288 in 139 at bats his first season. He continued to impress management and fans alike in a reserve role in 1974, with a .282 average, before finally getting his opportunity to start in right field a year later.

Several moves happened in 1975, to free up a space in the lineup for Parker. Willie Stargell was moved from left field to first base, replacing Bob Robertson, who was never able to live up to the potential he showed during the Bucs' 1971 championship season. Richie Zisk was shifted to left field, opening up the starting spot in right.

Parker immediately became the most damaging hitter on a team that was affectionately referred to as the Lumber Company. The 24-year-old budding superstar eclipsed the .300 mark and 100 RBI plateau for the first time that season, hitting .308 with 25 home runs and 101 RBIs. His breakout season did not go unnoticed among the writers, with the outfielder finishing behind Joe Morgan and the Phillies' Greg Luzinski in third place for the Most Valuable Player Award. While successful in the regular season, Parker struggled during his first two postseason experiences, going 1-for-18 in the 1974 and 1975 National League Championship Series.

It would be three years before he would get another chance to perform in the postseason, but what a three-year run it was. The right fielder slumped a bit in 1976, with only 13 home runs, although hitting .313, but Parker ascended to the top of the game a year later, capturing the first of two consecutive batting titles in the Senior Circuit in 1977, with what proved to be a career-high .338 average, again finishing third in the MVP race.

As good as that season was, 1978 would prove to be one of the best for the Cobra, now 27 years old. Parker always played the game aggressively, and he demonstrated his toughness during a bad collision with catcher John Stearnes of the Mets, during which he broke his jaw, an injury that only kept the right fielder out of the lineup for two weeks. When he came back he wore a batting helmet that was half of a football facemask to protect his jaw, but it didn't slow him down, as he went on to capture his second consecutive batting championship, this time with a .334 mark, while collecting 30 homers and 117 runs knocked in. It was enough to win the league's MVP, as Dave easily outdistanced Steve Garvey with 21 of 24 first-place votes.

While 1979 may not have been as successful for Parker personally, he was still one of the best players in the league. He took a backseat to teammate Willie Stargell as the Pirates had a phenomenal season that culminated with the team's fifth World Series championship. The Cobra's finest moment in 1979 was perhaps not with the Bucs, but for the National League in the All-Star Game, after which he was honored with the MVP Award for his lethal arm in right field. In what is considered one of the 10 greatest throws in the last 40 years by SportsOnEarth.com, Parker took a ball on a bounce and threw a strike on the fly to catcher Gary Carter, who tagged out Brian Downing of the California Angels, stunning the crowd at Seattle's Kingdome.

In 1979, Parker also made history when he became the game's first million-dollar player. As big a contract as that was for the time, the Cobra looked like he was worth it in the postseason, when he made up for his poor showings in earlier playoff appearances by hitting .333 against his hometown Reds in the NLCS and .345 against the Orioles in his first World Series appearance. He also made a clutch catch against Eddie Murray in the eighth inning of Game Seven with two outs and the bases loaded with the Bucs clinging to a precarious 2–1 lead.

With a world championship in hand and Parker seemingly at his peak, it looked as though the good times would go on in Pittsburgh during the 1980s; however, unfortunately for the team and its superstar right fielder, 1979 proved to be the beginning of the end for championship baseball in the Steel City.

The Cobra appeared out of shape and overweight, and had issues with some fans, prompted by a battery-throwing incident that forced Parker to wear a batting helmet while on the field. His stats began to suffer, with his average falling below .300 for the first time since 1974 and his homer count to 17. Things got worse throughout the next two seasons, as injuries began to take their toll, despite the fact the former top player in the league was just entering his 30s. He played in only 140 games during the two seasons, hitting only .264, with 15 home runs.

Rebounding moderately with a 12-home run, .279 campaign in 1983, Parker's days in the Steel City, which had looked so promising just four short seasons earlier, were over. He signed a free agent contract with his hometown Cincinnati Reds in 1984, and it was there that he eventually found his power stroke again a year later. It was also during that season, in the midst of the infamous Pittsburgh drug trials, that fans found out that Parker's disappointing performance had been the result of his drug habit, which had affected his play on the field. Although he went on to find success with the Reds, A's, and Brewers before ending his 19-year career with the Angels and Blue Jays, Dave was no longer welcome in Pittsburgh by the fans.

Drugs not only hurt Parker on the field, but they also may have cost the former Pirate a spot in the Hall of Fame. While not a certain candidate, the Cobra's stats should have warranted more serious consideration for Cooperstown. Famed sabermetrician Bill James had rated him similarly to such Hall of Fame members as Billy Williams and Tony Perez, but the baseball writers, perhaps influenced by his drug use, gave him little support, as he garnered no more than 24.5 percent of the vote in his 15 years on the ballot.

While Dave is not a Hall of Famer, his relationship with the city of Pittsburgh has thawed, as he has been a regular at autograph shows and various Pirates events in the city, despite suffering from Parkinson's disease. Pirates fans now celebrate Parker's accomplishments during his Pittsburgh career rather than lament the greatness he could have shown without the drug use. He truly is one of the franchise's great players no matter how his time in the Steel City ended.

MOST MEMORABLE PERFORMANCE

Dave Parker's finest moment did not come at Three Rivers, but in Seattle's Kingdome, as a member of the National League's All-Star Team in the 1979 Midsummer Classic.

Offensively the Cobra was not bad, but he was not at his best, with a single and a sacrifice fly that brought in a run during the Senior Circuit's 7–6 victory over the American League. It was his incredible throwing arm in right field that made it a magnificent evening for the Ohio native.

Parker had taken over the right-field spot for the great Roberto Clemente, a man who arguably had the strongest arm for a right fielder in the history of the game. While perhaps not as good as Clemente, Dave demonstrated his excellent throwing ability.

In the top of the seventh, Boston star Jim Rice doubled down the right-field line and challenged Parker's arm, trying to turn a double into a triple. It turned out to be a foolish move, as Dave rifled a perfect throw to third, nabbing Rice as he was sliding into the bag.

As great as that throw was, it wasn't as memorable as the one that ended the bottom of the eighth inning and kept the game tied at six. With two out and Reggie Jackson on first and Brian Downing in scoring position at second, Graig Nettles hit a line drive that dropped in front of the Pirates right fielder. Failing to learn his lesson from the prior inning, Downing decided to take a shot at scoring to give the American League the lead. The Cobra was again on the mark, sending a perfect throw on the fly to Gary Carter at home. Carter caught the ball and tagged Downing out as he was trying to touch the plate on an inside slide. Parker's two assists likely saved the game for the Senior Circuit, making him perhaps the only player in the history of the game to be named MVP because of his defense.

NOTABLE ACHIEVEMENTS (YEARLY LEADERS AND AWARDS ARE AS PIRATES ONLY)

Played in four All-Star Games.

Won the 1978 National League MVP Award.

Part of one National League championship and one world championship team (1979).

Part of three Eastern Division championship teams (1974, 1975, 1979).

Won the 1979 All-Star Game MVP Award.

Finished in the top 10 voting for the National League MVP three times.

Won three Gold Glove Awards (1977, 1978, 1979).

Won two National League batting titles (1977, 1978).

Led the league in on-base plus slugging percentage once (1978).

Led the league in slugging twice (1975, 1978).

Led the league in hits once (1977).

Led the league in doubles once (1977).

Led the league in assists for a right fielder once (1977).

Led the league in putouts for a right fielder four times (1975, 1976, 1977, 1983).

Led the league in putouts for an outfielder once (1977).

Led the league in assists for an outfielder once (1977).

Led the league in double plays for a right fielder once (1977).

Eclipsed 200 hits once.

Eclipsed 100 RBIs twice.

66th in most games played in major league history, with 2,466.

63rd in most hits in major league history, with 2,712.

53rd in most total bases in major league history, with 4,405.

DAVE PARKER

96th in most home runs in major league history, with 339.

42nd in most doubles in major league history, with 526.

54th in most extra-base hits in major league history, with 940.

55th in most RBIs in major league history, with 1,493.

14th in most games in right field in major league history, with 1,792.

25th in most double plays for a right fielder in major league history, with 28.

12th in most putouts for a right fielder in major league history, with 3,633.

20th in most assists by a right fielder in major league history, with 137.

7

BARRY BONDS

Barry Bonds had a controversial career not only in
Pittsburgh, but also with the Giants. Winning the
National League's MVP in 1990 and 1992, his greatness
was often overshadowed by his abrasive personality.
He became the all-time home run champion, with 762,
while being accused of steroid use.
Photo courtesy of the Pittsburgh Pirates.

Barry Bonds should have ended his career in glory, with statistics that would have been inconceivable only a few years before. Seven-time Most Valuable Player; all-time home run king both for a season (73) and career (762); walked more than any man in the history of the game (2,558 times); grandson to Willie Mays, the greatest living player. The list goes on. It would have been the perfect ending for a player who was the best of his generation, except for one thing—accusations of steroid abuse, which would have inflated his numbers.

But it wasn't that way early on. Drafted as the sixth overall pick by the Pittsburgh Pirates in the first round of the 1985 Major League Baseball Draft out of Arizona State, Bonds was the man Pittsburgh baseball fans hoped would lead them out of the doldrums they had been suffering in the mid-1980s. His minor league career was brief, playing one season of Class A ball in Prince William before jumping two levels a year later, where he hit .311, with seven home runs in 44 games, for the Hawaii Islanders. At that point he was brought up to the major leagues, making his debut on May 30, at Three Rivers Stadium, against the Dodgers, going hitless in five at bats, with three strikeouts.

After struggling through his first five games, Bonds showed what limitless potential he had against the Atlanta Braves on June 4, when he had four hits, four RBIs, and his first major league home run in a 12–3 victory.

The 21-year-old budding superstar had a season mixed with disappointment and hope. He hit what would become his career low, with a .223 average, with 102 strikeouts in only 413 at bats, yet stole 37 bases, hit 16 home runs, and had 45 extra-base hits, while finishing sixth in the National League Rookie of the Year vote. It was a meteoric rise through the system, one current general manager Neal Huntingdon probably never would have allowed, but Barry was a special player and seemed to adjust to major league pitching just fine.

Bonds improved throughout the next two seasons, while moving from center field to left in 1987, after the team acquired Andy Van Slyke, where he would become a Gold Glove recipient. Barry was a leadoff hitter early in his career and proved to be one of the most powerful ones. Improving his average from .261 to .283, while hitting 24 and 25 homers in 1987 and 1988, respectively, with his number of strikeouts dropping each season, the Arizona State alum continued to show baseball that superstar status would soon follow. He had a setback in 1989, during which time his average fell to .248, with only 19 long balls, but it was a momentary lapse before embarking on one of the greatest three-year stretches in franchise history, lifting the team to championship level, something it hadn't experienced in 11 seasons.

With a solid squad in place, manager Jim Leyland inserted Bonds into the middle of the lineup, and the results were spectacular. The slugger joined the 30–30 club, hitting 33 homers and stealing 52 bases, eclipsing the 100-RBI plateau for the first time, with 114, as well as hitting .300, coming in at a .301 mark. For his efforts, Bonds became the sixth Pittsburgh Pirate to be awarded the league's MVP Award. His play in left field was also exceptional, as he captured his first Gold Glove.

The Riverside, California, native entered his initial postseason in 1990, beginning a streak of three less-than-stellar performances that became as noted during his time in Pittsburgh as his magnificent regular-season play, hitting a paltry .167 against the Reds.

Barry's 1991 season began as poorly as the 1990 one had ended. During spring training, he had his infamous run in with one of the Pirates' communication people, Jim Lachima. The controversy surrounded Bonds not wanting to be told who would take his picture. He got in Lachima's face, ripping him apart. He then started screaming at spring training instructor and former Pirates great Bill Virdon. Leyland had finally had enough and took Bonds to task, all of which was caught on camera for the world to see. Bonds did not appear in a positive light, yet he went on to have another strong season for the team, with a .292 mark and 116 RBIs, finishing second to Terry Pendleton of the Braves in a close vote for the MVP, where he was only 16 points behind, while once again being honored with the Gold Glove Award for his work in left field. As he had done in 1990, the star, now 26 years old, was anything but spectacular in the National League Championship Series against the Braves, going 4-for-27 for a .148 average.

The 1992 campaign marked the end of Bonds's contract with the Pirates, and with a good season he could demand his desired salary, with many teams ready to sign him. Inspired with a huge free agent contract looming, Barry once again led the Pirates to an Eastern

Division championship with his second MVP season in three years, the only Pirates player to win the award twice, as well as his third Gold Glove. He once again became part of the 30–30 club, with 34 home runs and 39 stolen bases, to go along with what at the time was a career-high .311 average.

In the postseason, he improved over his previous two performances, with a .261 average and his first playoff home run, but with the Pirates clinging to a 2–1 lead in the bottom of the ninth inning of Game Seven, it was his last play in a Pittsburgh uniform that signaled a bad ending to an otherwise spectacular career with the Bucs. With two outs, pinch hitter Francisco Cabrera smacked a line drive at Bonds. Before the at bat, Gold Glove center fielder Andy Van Slyke had reportedly directed Bonds where to play, with Bonds refusing to move. The ball dropped in the vicinity of where Barry had been instructed to move, which at the least would have put him in position to keep Sid Bream from trying to score. Bonds followed his poor positioning up with a weak throw, and Bream scored the winning run, handing the Pirates a heartbreaking defeat. Van Slyke remembers the play to this day, still with irritation. "He turned and looked at me and gave me the international peace sign. So I said, 'Fine, you play where you want.'"[1]

Unable to sign Bonds beyond the 1992 season, the Pirates had actually tried to trade him to Atlanta before the season began. According to former Braves GM John Schuerholz in his book *Built to Win*, the Bucs and Braves had finalized a deal sending Bonds to Atlanta in exchange for pitcher Alejandro Pena, Keith Mitchell, and a prospect. As the two teams were about to announce it, Leyland got word of the agreement and talked team president Carl Barger into cancelling the trade.[2] Instead they would keep Barry and win a third-consecutive division title, before losing him to the San Francisco Giants in the off-season and beginning a streak of 20 consecutive losing seasons, which has never been equaled by any other team in major North American sports.

After he left Pittsburgh, Bonds continued to succeed, winning the 1993 MVP, as well as placing in the top 10 for MVP voting in four of the next five seasons. When he turned 35 in 2000, when most players are in the twilight of their careers, Bonds went on an incredible streak, hitting 49, 73, 46, 46, and 45 home runs in the next five seasons, while capturing an unprecedented four consecutive MVP Awards. He hit .339 during that time period, with an incredible .535 on-base percentage.

The slugger should have been on top of the world, posting numbers as he approached 40 that no one else ever had, but accusations of steroid use followed him wherever he went. As Bonds zeroed in on breaking Hank Aaron's all-time home run mark, onlookers outside San Francisco were tepid, as most felt he achieved those numbers through the use of illegal performance-enhancing drugs. When asked why his power had improved so significantly as he got older, Bonds once said, "Call God, ask him, it's like, wow. I can't understand it, either."[3]

On August 7, 2007, Bonds finally passed Aaron, hitting his 756th home run; as his reward for such a magnanimous accomplishment, a federal jury indicted him three months later on charges of perjury and obstruction as part of an investigation into steroid use in baseball. Four years later, he was convicted for obstruction of justice, sentenced to two years of probation, and fined $4,000, a conviction that was overturned in April 2015, by the Ninth U.S. Circuit Court of Appeals.

In the proceedings, it was revealed that the all-time home run champ had used two PED's called "the cream" and "the clear," both undetectable at the time by testing. Bonds denied knowing he had taken them, stating, "When he (personal trainer Greg Anderson) said it was flaxseed oil, I just said, 'Whatever.'"

Barry has never admitted to knowingly using steroids, but his reputation for suspicious behavior has tainted his career and kept him far from the Hall of Fame. To this date, he has received no more than 36.8 percent of the vote, far short of the 75 percent needed for induction, as of his third year of eligibility in 2015. All this for a career that should have been highly celebrated but is now shrouded in controversy.

MOST MEMORABLE PERFORMANCE

While he went on to have many incredible moments in a Pittsburgh uniform, it was the sixth game of Barry Bonds's Pirates career that could be considered his most memorable moment.

The city of Pittsburgh was looking for a baseball hero while mired in a bad period of Pirates baseball, and fans were looking to Bonds to be their savior. He came up to the majors on May 30, in only his second season of professional baseball, and had performed poorly in his first five games. Then came Game Six, on June 4, 1986, a day when everything changed as the Pirates took on the Atlanta Braves.

Leading off the contest, the young slugger struck out in the first inning, giving no hint of what was about to come. In the top of the second, Bonds singled in two runs to help the Bucs to a 4–0 lead. Two innings later, another single knocked in another run as part of a six-run frame to increase their lead to 10–2.

In the fifth it came, a long shot to left field off of Craig McMurtry, the first of a record 762 home runs in his career. Bonds doubled three innings later to complete his breakout four-hit performance, not only giving Pirates nation hope, but also showing the baseball world his incredible potential.

NOTABLE ACHIEVEMENTS (YEARLY LEADERS AND AWARDS ARE AS PIRATES ONLY)

Played in two All-Star Games.

Won the 1990 and 1992 National League MVP Awards.

Finished in the top 10 voting for the National League MVP three times.

Part of three Eastern Division championship teams (1990, 1991, 1992).

Won three Gold Glove Awards (1990, 1991, 1992).

Won three Silver Slugger Awards (1990, 1991, 1992).

Led the league in on-base percentage twice (1991, 1992).

Led the league in on-base plus slugging percentage three times (1990, 1991, 1992).

Led the league in runs once (1992).

Led the league in at bats per home run once (1992).

Led the league in assists for a left fielder three times (1989, 1990, 1991).

Led the league in putouts for a left fielder four times (1989, 1990, 1991, 1992).

Led the league in double plays for a left fielder once (1987).

Led the league in double plays for a center fielder once (1986).

Led the league in assists for an outfielder once (1990).

Eclipsed 100 RBIs three times.

Holds the all-time major league record for home runs in a single season, with 73.

Holds the all-time major league record for home runs, with 762.

Holds the all-time major league record for walks, with 2,558.

Holds the all-time major league record for intentional walks, with 688.

4th in most RBIs in major league history, with 1,996.

4th in most total bases in major league history, with 5,976.

3rd in most runs scored in major league history, with 2,227.

4th in OPS in major league history, with 1.051.

5th in slugging percentage in major league history, at .607.

6th in on-base percentage in major league history, at .444.

4th in wins above replacement in major league history, at 162.4.

2nd in most extra-base hits in major league history, with 1,440.

8

JOSEPH VAUGHAN

He was the other famous number 21 in Pittsburgh Pirates history—the number he wore for the majority of his career with the Bucs, and he ironically died tragically trying to help others, just like another 21 did 20 years later. While Joseph Floyd "Arky" Vaughan's Pirates career wasn't as long as Roberto Clemente's, it was nonetheless spectacular, warranting his inclusion in the top 10 on this list.

Born in Clifty, Arkansas, where he picked up his famed nickname, Vaughan's family moved to Fullerton, California, where he was a star halfback on the Fullerton High football team, as well as an exceptional baseball player. He was signed by the club in 1931, and sent to the Wichita Aviators of the Western League that year, where he was remarkable, hitting .338 in 132 games, while smacking 21 homers, all at the young age of 19. Seeing the shortstop's potential and incredible talent, Pittsburgh brought him up in 1932, and Arky quickly became a star.

He started the season on the bench, hitless in two pinch-hit appearances his first 13 games in a Pirates uniform. He got his first start in the team's 14th game, after starter Tommy Thevenow broke his finger. Vaughan made the most of the opportunity, with two triples in four at bats with three RBIs and two more hits the next day. Thevenow quickly became a former starting shortstop.

The 20-year-old rookie continued to have an effective offensive season in 1932, hitting .318, with 61 RBIs, but Arky had some flaws in his game, mainly his defense. Vaughan not only led the National League in errors for a shortstop that first season, with 46, but also had more errors than any player in the Senior Circuit regardless of position. He repeated the feat a year later with the same number of miscues but continued to impress at the plate, leading the league in triples, with 19, while increasing his RBIs to 97 and maintaining a fine average, at .314.

The team was concerned with his defensive misgivings, however, and hired as a coach the one man who they thought could fix it: Honus Wagner. As it turned out, Wagner would be the only man in franchise history who could claim to have been a greater shortstop than Vaughan, and he did his best to try to turn the youngster into a shortstop of his ilk.

Wagner monitored his student closely, rooming with him on the road, and while he reportedly was not the best instructor, he seemed to have somewhat of an effect on Arky in the field, as his errors dropped slightly, to 41. While errors still may have been an issue, Vaughan's offense continued to improve; he finished fourth in the league, with a .333 mark, while leading the circuit in on-base percentage, with an impressive .431. He also showed increased power, hitting double-digit home runs for the first time, with 12.

In a three-year span, Vaughan established himself as one of the best offensive forces in the National League at short. In 1935, he took his performance to the next level, not only becoming one of the best offensive players at any position, but also having one of the greatest seasons in team history, setting a single-season record for batting average that has never been broken and rarely approached.

Arky had what would become career highs in both home runs (19) and RBIs (99), leading the National League in four offensive categories—on-base percentage (.491), slugging (.607), on-base plus slugging percentage (1.098), and batting average (.385, winning his one and only batting title with a team record). As late as September 10, Vaughan was hitting over .400 with a .401 average after a 2-for-4 performance versus the Cards. He unfortunately slumped the rest of the way, hitting .250 the remainder of the campaign, costing him a spot in the history books, as he would have been the last player in the National League to eclipse the .400 plateau.

Following up his marquee season with a .335 average in 1936, a campaign where he led the Senior Circuit for the third consecutive year in on-base percentage, at .453, Arky continued his consistency, maintaining a .300 average during the next four years, including a .322 mark in 1938. During that season, he helped lead the club to within one week of the National League pennant and his first chance at playing in a World Series, but they lost their lead to the Cubs on September 28, 6–5, in the infamous Homer in the Gloamin' game, during which Gabby Hartnett smashed a walk-off home run in the darkness at Wrigley Field. Vaughan walked twice that day, with a single in two at bats and two runs, but had one of four Pirates miscues. Pittsburgh went on to lose four of their final five games to finish two games behind Chicago.

Arky was still young, but his days in the Steel City were numbered, as he played only three more seasons for the Pirates. In his final campaign in 1941, at only 29 years of age, he hit .316 and played in his eighth consecutive All-Star Game, a contest where he hit two home runs and drove in four in a 7–5 National League defeat.

According to writer Frederick Lieb in his history on the Pittsburgh Pirates, manager Frankie Frisch had not necessarily been a fan of Vaughan, sitting him 50 games in 1941, despite the fact that he was seemingly still effective.[1] While it wasn't a surprise, he was still inexplicably dealt to the Brooklyn Dodgers in the off-season, much to the dismay of Pirates fans, for Pete Coscarart, Luke Hamlin, Babe Phelps, and Jimmy Wasdell.

Arky played poorly for the Dodgers in 1942, and retired for the first time following the 1943 campaign, a season where he had argued with Brooklyn manager Leo Durocher about criticism the manager had delivered to the press about a teammate, almost resulting in a players' strike. The shortstop, now 35 years old, returned in 1947 after three years away from the game, hitting .325 in a reserve role, while finally playing in his first World Series. He quit for good in 1948, after a season where he hit .244 for the Dodgers and then .288 for the San Francisco Seals in the Pacific Coast League.

Vaughan retired to his ranch in California and, in 1952, went out fishing on a nearby lake with a friend. The boat capsized, and Vaughan tried to save his friend who could not swim. They swam toward shore but didn't make it, drowning within a reported 20 feet from land.

It was a tragic end to Vaughan's life, who, by all accounts, was a quality person. Following his death, the local paper stated that the main reason Vaughan probably wasn't considered more of a superstar was because "[h]e lacked only one thing—a colorful personality." The paper continues, "Those who knew him best believe he would have been one of the game's greatest heroes had he been endowed with the sparkling personality that made lesser players great."[2] His lack of personality might explain the lack of respect for his play among his contemporaries. When Bill James examined the stats to rank players by position in the *Bill James Historical Baseball Abstract*, he chose Vaughan as the second-best shortstop in the history of the game behind Honus Wagner.[3]

Perhaps also because of his personality, Arky was bypassed for the Hall of Fame until the Veteran's Committee elected him in 1985, and even then he wasn't given his due respect, as they misspelled Vaughan on the commemorative envelope issued to inductees.

While he may not have had an electric personality, Vaughan is still considered one of the greatest players in team history and the second-best number 21.

MOST MEMORABLE PERFORMANCE

Although never playing in a postseason game for the Pittsburgh Pirates, Arky Vaughan's greatest moment in Pirates uniform was still in the national spotlight, in his final season in Pittsburgh, 1941, during the All-Star Game.

Arky had fallen out of favor with Pirates manager Frankie Frisch, who had sat him quite a bit during the season, but he was still selected to play in his eighth consecutive All-Star Game. It would be his final one for the Bucs, but he went out with a blast.

After fouling out in the second inning, Vaughan's big day started off innocently enough in the top of the fifth, with a two-out infield single. With the National League down 2–1 in the seventh, Enos Slaughter was on first base when the Pittsburgh shortstop launched a home run that gave the Senior Circuit a 3–2 advantage.

An inning later, Arky did something that no man had ever done in an All-Star Game when he hit a second home run, another two-run shot that also plated Johnny Mize with two outs.

Vaughan was a quiet man, never gaining the respect and notoriety that he probably deserved, and in the 1941 All-Star Game it was no different. While becoming the first man to hit two homers in a Midsummer Classic and knocking in four with three hits, it was Ted Williams who stole his thunder with a three-run walk-off homer to win the contest, 7–5, for the American League.

NOTABLE ACHIEVEMENTS (YEARLY LEADERS AND AWARDS ARE AS PIRATES ONLY)

Elected to the Baseball Hall of Fame by the Veteran's Committee in 1985.

Played in eight All-Star Games.

Finished in the top three voting for the National League Most Valuable Player twice.

Won the 1935 National League batting title.

Led the league in on-base percentage three times (1934, 1935, 1936).

Led the league in OPS once (1935).

Led the league in slugging once (1935).

Led the league in runs twice (1936, 1940).

Led the league in triples three times (1933, 1937, 1940).

Led the league in assists for a shortstop three times (1938, 1939, 1940).

Led the league in double plays for a shortstop once (1938).

57th in batting average in major league history, at .318.

43rd in on-base percentage in major league history, at .406.

84th in most triples in major league history, with 128.

63rd in most games at shortstop in major league history, with 1,485.

61st in most double plays at shortstop in major league history, with 850.

85th in most assists in major league history, with 5,119.

57th in most assists at shortstop in major league history, with 4,780.

44th in most putouts at shortstop in major league history, with 1,485.

Holds the all-time Pirates record for batting average in a single season, at .385.

9

HAROLD TRAYNOR

Nicknamed for his affection for pie as a child, Harold "Pie" Traynor not only became the franchise's greatest third baseman, but a successful manager who almost led the Bucs to the 1938 National League pennant. Hitting .320 for his career, Traynor was elected to the Baseball Hall of Fame in 1948.

Photo courtesy of the Pittsburgh Pirates.

There may be no player in the history of the game who varies so greatly in the all-time ranking of players than Harold "Pie" Traynor. During his day, he was considered the greatest third baseman of all-time; contemporaries of his time, including Ty Cobb, Rogers Hornsby, and Paul Waner, agreed that no one was better at the hot corner.

In 1969, the baseball writers named Traynor the greatest to ever play the position in an all-star selection celebrating the game's centennial. His wife Eve said, "I'm so happy for Pie. Some of the writers today didn't see him play, some of the young writers, but they still voted for him."[1] And therein was the problem as time went on. While many universally agreed that more modern players like George Brett and Mike Schmidt were better, sabermetrician Bill James took it one step further in reevaluating the players and their positions; his ratings for Traynor weren't kind, dropping him to 15th.

While James points out that he was one of only four third baseman to average more than 200 hits per 162 games, he also claims that Traynor was only rated the greatest of all time at third base after 1955. He adds that Connie Mack didn't mention him in the all-time list he put together in a book in 1950, nor did Edward Barrow or writer Bob Considine when they compiled their lists in the early 1950s.

Regardless of where Traynor has ranked in the all-time third base picture, there is no doubt that he was a phenomenal player and one of the best to don a Pittsburgh Pirates uniform.

Born in Framingham, Massachusetts, in 1898, Harold Joseph Traynor was given the nickname Pie by an older friend of his whose family owned a convenience store. Traynor would always request a piece of pie, and a legend was born.

Following a stint with Falmouth in the Cape League after a failed tryout with the Boston Braves, Traynor tried out for the Red Sox. While he impressed them, it was reported that shortstop Everett Scott, afraid of the competition, talked manager Ed Barrow into sending him to a minor league team in Portsmouth they were affiliated with. The Red Sox didn't have a binding contract with Portsmouth, and after a fine rookie season in 1920, owner H. P. Dawson wanted to sell Traynor for $10,000. Thinking he had a deal with Washington, who then decided to cut their bid to $7,500, the Pirates decided to pay the $10,000 fee for the third baseman.

After spending 17 late-season games with the Bucs in 1920, Pittsburgh owner Barney Dreyfuss sent his expensive purchase to Birmingham in the Southern League for some seasoning, especially defensively. After he hit .336 for the Barons, Harold returned to the Bucs in September, this time sticking with the major league team in 1922.

Pie was impressive in his official rookie campaign of 1922, and after spending time at both second base and shortstop, he was given the third base slot he would become famous for when Bill McKechnie took over as manager from George Gibson. It was his sophomore season, however, where he really showed the damage he could unleash on National League pitching. Leading the league in triples with 19, Traynor hit a career-high 12 homers—the only time in his career he hit double digits in home runs—and broke the 100-RBI plateau for the first time, while finishing seventh in the league with a .338 average.

He continued to assault major league pitching and, in 1925, helped lead the Bucs to their first National League pennant in 16 years, becoming recognized as possibly one of the greats at his position. Such legendary managers as Hughie Jennings and John McGraw were putting him in the same class as some of the best third baseman at that time. Harold hit .320, with 106 RBIs, and was involved in 41 double plays at third, a major league record that stood until 1950.

While Pie was effective in the regular season, it was his first experience in the World Series where he was phenomenal. Hitting .346 for the series, including a Game One home run against Walter Johnson and many exceptional plays in the field, Traynor proved to be one of the key elements in an exciting Game Seven 9–7 victory. The Bucs were down 6–5 when he hit a clutch triple to right field with two out in the bottom of the seventh, scoring Max Carey to tie the game, before being thrown out at the plate trying to stretch it into an inside-the-park home run.

Two years later, in 1927, Harold was once again a key factor in a pennant-winning season by Pittsburgh with a career-high .342, which he later surpassed, that was the fifth best in the Senior Circuit, while knocking in a National League-best 106 runs. According to Pie it was a particularly grueling season, and by the time he got to the Fall Classic against the legendary 1927 New York Yankees, he weighed 20 pounds less than his normal 170. The Bucs went down meekly in a four-game sweep, with the Hall of Fame third baseman hitting only .200.

Even though the Pirates would not seriously compete for a pennant during the next four seasons, except for a second-place finish in 1929 (although they were 10½ games out of first), Traynor continued his remarkably consistent play, with a .337 average during that period and an average of 114 RBIs per season. Perhaps his best performance came in the 1930 season, when he was suffering from a serious eye infection. That year he hit a career-high .366 and had arguably his best day as a major league player against Philadelphia, with game-winning homers in both ends of a doubleheader on July 23. While he was superb, he surprisingly did not receive a vote for the Most Valuable Player Award after finishing in the top 15 the previous five seasons.

George Gibson returned to the Pirates in 1932, replacing Jewel Ens as manager, and helped vault the team into contention with two consecutive second-place finishes, ending the 1932 and 1933 seasons only four and five games out, respectively. After dropping to .298 in 1931, his first time below .300 since 1924, Pie rebounded with two fine seasons, hitting .329 and .304.

In 1934, the team faltered, changing the course of Traynor's career. Fifty-one games into the season, Gibson was relieved of his duties, and Pie was handed the reins of the team as manager. He played the rest of the season as a regular, with a .309 mark, and then bowed out, appearing in only 57 contests in 1935, before making 12 plate appearances two years later. As manager, the infielder was successful his first four full seasons, leading the team to winning records in each one, including an exciting yet heartbreaking second-place finish in 1938. But as *Pittsburgh Post-Gazette* editor Al Abrams points out, he was perhaps not suited to manage a major league team: "Pie's tactics would have gone over great with a high school or college athlete, where he would have been looked up to as a hero and leader, but with a gang of thoroughly hardened, grown-up men, driving leadership is sometimes required."[2]

Dick Bartell, who was a shortstop with the Bucs between 1927 and 1930, was not a fan of Traynor in general and also questioned his leadership. "He was an agitator, he started many things that people knew nothing about."[3] Bartell further commented on his managerial issues, saying, "His players didn't respect him. When one got into a brawl and wound up in the police station, Pie would bail him out and keep it quiet. No fines. No suspensions. No leadership."[4]

After a sixth-place finish in 1939, following the epic collapse the year before, Traynor was out of a job. He remained a Pirate scout the rest of his life and was elected to the Baseball Hall of Fame in 1948. He also worked as a recreation and parks supervisor for Allegheny County, a wrestling announcer, and a sportscaster on KQV-Radio. In March 1972, Traynor died of emphysema, the result of many years of smoking; the Pirates retired his number 20 later that year.

Whether you go with Bill James claiming Pie Traynor was an over-rated entity or Bill Burgess, who writes on Baseball-Fever.com that Traynor is properly rated, putting him behind Mike Schmidt, George Brett, and Ron Santo,[5] there is no denying that he is one of the best to ever play the position and a true franchise treasure.

MOST MEMORABLE PERFORMANCE

Playing the Philadelphia Phillies on July 23, 1930, at the Baker Bowl, Pie Traynor had a day of clutch hitting that many major league players dream of but few achieve, hitting game-winning home runs in both ends of a doubleheader.

In the first contest, Adam Comorosky singled in a run in the first game to give the Bucs a 1–0 lead. Lefty O'Doul scored the tying run in the bottom half of the frame, and the score remained tied until the Phils' Snipe Hansen faced Traynor in the top of the ninth. Pie drove a Snipe offering for his third home run of the season and a 2–1 Bucco lead. Heinie Meine kept Philadelphia off the board in the bottom of the frame to give Pittsburgh the win.

The nightcap of the twin bill was a slugfest, with the Pirates blowing 7–0 and 10–5 leads. After once again going ahead 11–10 in the top of the ninth, Philadelphia tied it in the bottom of the frame, sending the game into extra innings, which turned out to be like the rest of the contest. Pittsburgh took a 13–11 lead in the 12th, before Philadelphia tied it.

Traynor was having a brilliant day, going 4-for-6, when he came up in the top of the 13th. He smacked his second round-tripper of the day, a three-run shot that gave Pittsburgh a 16–13 advantage, as the club held on for a 16–15 win.

NOTABLE ACHIEVEMENTS (YEARLY LEADERS AND AWARDS ARE AS PIRATES ONLY)

Elected to the Baseball Hall of Fame in 1948.

Had his number 20 retired by the Pirates in 1972.

Part of two National League championship teams (1925, 1927).

Part of one world championship team (1925).

Played in two All-Star Games, including the inaugural one in 1933.

Finished in the top 10 voting for the National League MVP six times.

Finished in the top 10 for the National League batting title six times.

Led the league in triples once (1923).

Led the league in assists for a third baseman three times (1923, 1925, 1933).

Led the league in putouts for a third baseman seven times (1923, 1925, 1926, 1927, 1931, 1933, 1934).

Led the league in fielding percentage for a third baseman once (1925).

Led the league in double plays for a third baseman four times (1924, 1925, 1926, 1927).

Eclipsed 100 RBIs in a season seven times.

Eclipsed 200 hits in a season once.

51st in batting average in major league history, at .320.

30th in most triples in major league history, with 164.

79th in most singles in major league history, with 1,823.

51st in most sacrifice hits in major league history, with 231.

37th in at bats per strikeout in major league history, at 27.2.

5th in most putouts by a third baseman in major league history, with 2,289.

23rd in most assists by a third baseman in major league history, with 3,521.

27th in most double plays by a third baseman in major league history, with 303.

19th in most games played at third base in major league history, with 1,863.

10

CHARLES ADAMS

Charles "Babe" Adams was a 27-year-old rookie with the Pittsburgh Pirates who had a good season in 1909, but it was still a shock when he was called on to start Game One of the 1909 World Series. Adams was not only up to the challenge that day, but also for the entire series, winning three games in the Fall Classic and helping the Bucs to their first world championship.
Photo courtesy of the Pittsburgh Pirates.

Born Charles Benjamin Adams in Tipton, Indiana, on May 18, 1882, few fans of the game would remember the name on his birth certificate. Stories vary on how he was given the nickname he would be known by for most of his adult life, but suffice it to say the game's first player of note named "Babe" was thought to be quite good looking by the opposite sex.

Unlike Arky Vaughan, who precedes Adams on this list, Babe did not begin his major league career until in his later 20s. The hurler was born left-handed but learned to pitch with his right hand when he injured a finger on his left hand as a child. Adams was taught a new grip on the baseball by the shortstop on a team that had just beaten him. That grip turned into a devastating curveball that would help him garner success in the minor leagues.

Babe pitched well in the minors, highlighted by a 21–9 mark in his first professional season with the Parsons Preachers in the Missouri Valley League in 1905. He won more than 20 games twice in the next three seasons, getting two opportunities to pitch in the majors, where he had little success. He started one game with St. Louis in 1906, giving up six earned runs in four innings, while losing his first contest in the big leagues, and then had three unsuccessful starts with the Pirates a year later, going 0–2, with a 6.95 ERA.

Out of the majors in 1908, Adams had a fine season with Louisville, winning 22 contests, and he earned another opportunity with the Pirates in 1909, taking advantage of that one better than anyone could have imagined.

In 1909, the Bucs had a veteran squad and an impressive starting rotation that consisted of Deacon Phillippe, Vic Willis, Lefty Leifield, Nick Maddox, and Howie Camnitz. The team also had a new ballpark, Forbes Field, the first concrete and steel facility in the National League, and used their amenities to put together perhaps the most impressive campaign in the history of the club. They won 110 games on their way to their fourth National League pennant and second trip to the World Series.

Even though Adams didn't get many chances to crack the rotation, appearing in only 25 games, including 12 starts, the rookie more than took advantage of them, with a 12–3 record and sparkling 1.11 ERA. While not receiving many opportunities to take to the mound during the regular season, Babe got his shot when it mattered most, in the first game of the 1909 Fall Classic.

Camnitz had been the team's best pitcher, winning 25 contests during the season, but an attack of quinsy, an infection that is a complication of tonsillitis, left manager Fred Clarke looking for a replacement as they faced the three-time American League champion Detroit Tigers. Clarke unleashed Adams on the Tigers, reportedly choosing him because league president John Heydler said Babe's style reminded him of Dolly Gray of Washington, who had shut Detroit down during the season. Many historians have since discounted that story, claiming Clarke chose him simply because he had pitched well down the stretch. Regardless of the reason, Adams was the proper choice, winning three games during the World Series, 4–1 in Game One, 8–4 in Game Five, and an 8–0 shutout in the seventh and deciding game, to give the Bucs their first World Series championship. It would be more than 100 years before the Pirates would see rookies win three more games in the postseason, with Tim Wakefield capturing two in 1992 and Gerrit Cole winning one in 2013.

The Indiana native became a fixture in the Pirates rotation in 1910, going 99–69 between 1910 and 1915, on some less-than-stellar Pittsburgh teams, including two 20-win campaigns in 1911 and 1913. On July 17, 1914, he had probably the best game in his major league career against the New York Giants, battling Rube Marquard in 21 innings, finally losing, 3–1, in a contest where he did not allow a walk. It remains the longest game a pitcher has thrown without allowing a walk, a record that will certainly never be broken. The contest illustrated Adams's greatest attribute as a pitcher: pinpoint control with a walk rate per nine innings of 1.292, the 18th-lowest mark in the history of the game. He also had a walks and hits per innings pitched of 1.092, again the 18th lowest in major league history.

In 1916, Adams suffered a sore shoulder, which led to a 2–9 record, with a 5.72 ERA, the poorest showing of his career up to that point. Adams spent the next year and a half in the minor leagues working on getting back to the big leagues. He was unhittable in 1917, with St. Joseph/Hutchinson of the Western League, where he was 22–14, with a miniscule .903 WHIP, before a turning in a 14–3 campaign in 1918 with Kansas City.

The fact that Babe still demonstrated his effectiveness, coupled with his age, which was 36 (any person older than 35 was exempt from the draft in World War I), gave him an opportunity as he returned to the Bucs in 1918. After pitching well in his three starts in 1918, he went 48–28 his next three seasons in Pittsburgh, with an impressive 2.20 ERA and even more remarkable .972 WHIP.

Turning 40 in 1922, Babe's age began to catch up with him, although he pitched until he was 44, which included a scoreless inning of relief in the 1925 World Series. In 1926, he was part of the infamous ABC episode in the Pirates dugout, where he and Carson Bigbee objected to former manager Fred Clarke, who at that point was a bench coach under Bill McKechnie, criticizing Hall of Fame center fielder Max Carey's play in center and trying to convince McKechnie to pull him. Bigbee mentioned what he had heard to Carey, as well as Adams, who was incensed, creating a potential insubordinate situation on the bench. An irritated Barney Dreyfuss sold Carey to Brooklyn, let Clarke and McKechnie go, and released Bigbee and Adams.

After retirement, Adams returned to farming before becoming a sports reporter and war correspondent covering the Pacific Theater in World War II, as well as the Korean conflict. He passed away in 1968, at the age of 86, and has a portion of Route 136 in Missouri, near Mount Moriah where he lived, named after him.

For Babe, while he was honored later in life with the Babe Adams Highway, it was an unfortunate way to end a 19-year major league career, one where he had not only established himself as one of the greatest control pitchers in the history of the game, winning 194 games in a Pirates uniform, but became arguably the best pitcher in the history of the franchise.

MOST MEMORABLE PERFORMANCE

It was a close call in selecting Babe Adams's most memorable moment in a Pirates uniform. Even though he tossed an 8–0 shutout in Game Seven of the 1909 World Series during his rookie season to give the Bucs their first World Series title, his 21-inning no-walk performance against the New York Giants on July 17, 1914, which remains the most innings pitched in a single game by a pitcher without allowing a walk, is the best.

It was a strange game that the Pirates could have won in the regulation nine innings, as Honus Wagner appeared to score what should have been the go-ahead and eventual winning run in the sixth. As the hall of fame shortstop was going into third, an errant throw went up Wagner's sleeve. He went home on the error, but when the ball was discovered, he was called out on interference. Ironically, had the run been allowed, Adams may have won the contest but would have been cheated out of his eternal spot in baseball history.

Battling the Giants' Rube Marquard, the hurlers matched one another pitch for pitch for 21 innings. After giving up only 11 hits in 20-plus frames, New York's Larry Doyle got the 12th hit, a two-run homer that gave the Giants a 3–1 victory.

To add to the strangeness of the afternoon, New York outfielder Red Murray was struck by lightning after catching the final out of the contest. He recovered to play the next day, but Marquard did not. The 21 innings he tossed took so much out of him that he lost his next 10 starts and finished 12–22. While losing, Adams fared better in the long run as holder of one the game's most unbreakable records.

NOTABLE ACHIEVEMENTS (YEARLY LEADERS AND AWARDS ARE AS PIRATES ONLY)

Had a portion of Route 136 near Mount Moriah in Missouri named after him.

Part of two National League championship and world championship teams (1909, 1925).

Led the league in WAR once (1913).

Led the league in winning percentage once (1921).

Led the league in WHIP five times (1911, 1914, 1919, 1920, 1921).

Led the league in shutouts once (1920).

Led the league in strikeouts per bases on balls four times (1919, 1920, 1921, 1922).

Led the league in bases on balls per nine innings four times (1919, 1920, 1921, 1922).

Led the league in fielding percentage for a pitcher five times (1912, 1914, 1915, 1919, 1921).

Eclipsed 20 wins twice.

18th in bases on balls per nine innings in major league history, at 1.292.

18th in WHIP in major league history, at 1.092.

35th in most shutouts in major league history and best in Pirates history, with 44.

129th in most wins in major league history and second in Pirates history, with 194.

Had an ERA below 3.00 eight times.

Had an ERA below 2.00 twice.

Won three games in the 1909 World Series.

11

ANDREW MCCUTCHEN

Andrew McCutchen, pictured in the middle, is the face of the resurgence of Pittsburgh Pirates baseball in the 21st century and quickly becoming one of the franchise's greatest players. Winning the MVP in 2014, McCutchen has helped the club not only break its string of 20 consecutive seasons of losing baseball, but also lead them to two consecutive playoff appearances.
Photo courtesy of the author.

It takes a consistent, solid farm system for a franchise to survive and prosper in the major leagues. To have an effective minor league system you have to draft strongly. Taking a look at the top draft picks of the Pittsburgh Pirates throughout the past three decades, one can understand exactly why the team went through a miserable stretch of 20 consecutive losing seasons.

The list of draft choices the first 10 seasons of the streak, between 1992 and 2002, is a potpourri of legendary first-round busts. While Jason Kendall and Kris Benson did well, the rest included Shon Walker, Charles Peterson, Andy Rice, Mark Farris, Chad Hermansen, J. J. Davis, Clint Johnson, Sean Burnett, John Van Benschoten, and Brian Bullington, all of which helped contribute to the team's miserable showing.

Despite the fact that things improved in 2003 and 2004, as the Bucs took Paul Maholm and Neil Walker in back-to-back drafts, it wasn't until 2005 that the foundation was laid for the eventual end to the record-setting losing streak (which came to a close in 2013)—the year Pittsburgh took a young outfielder out of Fort Meade High School by the name of Andrew McCutchen.

When he entered the organization in 2005, it was barren, void of anything more than players of below-average major league potential; McCutchen soon filled that void. Hitting .310 his first season in professional baseball, playing between the Gulf Coast Pirates and the Williamsport Crosscutters, where he hit .346 in 52 at bats, Andrew began his meteoric rise through the system.

In 2006, the young center fielder attended his first major league spring training, and while it was only his first, fans could see a remarkable difference in the talent he possessed compared to what Pirates nation had been used to seeing for the better part of a decade. He took that experience and continued to succeed, this time showing some power with 14 home runs in 114 games before making the move to Double-A. There, he hit .308 with the Altoona Curve for the remainder of the season and was named the organization's Minor League Player of the Year.

McCutchen experienced the first slump of his professional career the next season in Altoona, hitting only .258. He rebounded by reaching base in his final 20 games with the Curve, which prompted the organization to promote him to the Indianapolis Indians late in the campaign. Finishing the season hitting .313 for the Indians, the 22-year-old rising prospect spent the entire 2008 campaign in Triple-A. He was not only a midseason International League All-Star, but was also named Most Valuable Player of the Triple-A All-Star Game and played in the Futures Game at the major league All-Star Game.

While most people expected the young center fielder to make the Bucs out of spring training in 2009, it never happened, as there was a new regime in charge in Pittsburgh, headed by Neal Huntington, who had taken over at the end of the 2007 campaign. They felt Cutch needed a little more seasoning, so he once again started the season in Indianapolis. His time in the minors was brief indeed, as he was brought up to the majors on June 4, after the Bucs traded All-Star center fielder Nate McClouth to Atlanta, opening the way for Andrew to take over the starting spot—a position he held on to.

McCutchen took over with a vengeance, going on a 13-game hitting streak between June 11 and 25, and he went on to have three 10-game or better streaks during the season, the first Pirate to do so in 26 years. Among everything else he did, including becoming the first Pittsburgh Pirates rookie since 1940 to triple in three straight games and leading Senior Circuit rookies in extra-base hits, the Florida native's most impressive feat was perhaps hitting three home runs in a game against Washington on August 1. For his efforts, he was named the Major League Rookie of the Year by *Baseball America* and finished second for the official National League award.

After matching .286 seasons his first two years in a Pirates uniform, Cutch's average slumped to .259 in 2011, although he showed an increase in power, smacking what was then a career-high 23 home runs, while knocking in 89. He also stole 23 bases, making him the eighth Pirate to eclipse 20 home runs and 20 stolen bases in a season.

During the losing streak, the Bucs had a few players who enjoyed successful careers with the team, for example, Jason Bay, Brian Giles, and Kendall, but none had the pedigree of McCutchen, a player who had the potential to be one of the most dominant players in the game. As he entered his peak in 2012, potential became reality.

Before the season began, knowing that he wanted to continue his career in the Steel City, Cutch signed a six-year, $51 million contract that made him a member of the franchise through the 2018 campaign. It is not uncommon to see a downturn in a player's statistics after he signs a long-term deal, either because he tries too hard to live up to the deal or simply relaxes after achieving financial security, but in the case of Andrew McCutchen, he has more than lived up to the contract, becoming one of the game's best.

The first-round pick hit a career-best .327 average, with 31 home runs and 96 RBIs. He was also spectacular in the field, almost leading the Bucs to their first .500 record in 19 years. Pittsburgh ran out to a 63–47 mark on August 8. The end of the losing streak looked like it was near, until the team suffered a historic collapse, ending the year 16–36 to finish at 79–83. It was a disastrous ending, but Cutch still won the Gold Glove and Silver Slugger awards. In addition, he was named the National League's Most Outstanding Player, as voted on by the players, and finished third in the official MVP race. Individual awards aside, it was not a satisfying campaign for McCutchen.

In 2013, he was once again among the best players in the game, with a .317 mark, while breaking the 20-home run and 20-stolen base plateau for the third consecutive season. This time the team did not falter, ending their futile streak at 20 years when they not only finished with a 94–68 record, but also qualified for the postseason for the first time since 1992. Going 2-for-3 in the Wild Card matchup at PNC Park against the Reds with two walks, Cutch had another impressive performance in the postseason awards circuit, becoming the first Pittsburgh Pirate to win the MVP since Barry Bonds in 1992.

After another impressive performance in 2014, during which time the team again played in the Wild Card contest, McCutchen had a difficult start to the 2015 campaign but began breaking out by the middle of May. By the All-Star break, he had not only topped the .300 plateau, but also hit one of the most memorable regular-season home runs in Pirates history, ripping a two-run walk-off shot that defeated the division-leading Cardinals in 14 innings, 6–5, on July 11. He also added to his lofty achievements with a home run in the All-Star Game in Cincinnati.

It is true that a franchise is only as strong as its farm system, a fact that the Pittsburgh Pirates now fully realize, as they finally have one of the strongest players in the game, a feat they began 10 years prior when they made Andrew McCutchen the first piece of their new winning era.

MOST MEMORABLE PERFORMANCE

Since 1992, when the Pittsburgh Pirates last had a winning campaign, they had looked long and hard for the player that would lead them out of the doldrums of losing seasons. That player finally appeared in 2009, in the form of Andrew McCutchen. On August 1, 2009, he showed his potential and then some.

Early on, Cutch showed the 26,855 in attendance at PNC Park that it would truly be a special night when he cracked a leadoff home run in the bottom of the first to cut a 2–0 National lead to a single run. After a single in the third, where he scored the go-ahead run to make it 3–2, the Fort Meade native ripped a two-run shot over the left-field fence to extend Pittsburgh's lead to 7–2. Two innings later, another long ball flew into the left-field stands, this time for a three-run homer, making it 11–4 and McCutchen the 10th man in team history, and the first in eight years, to hit three-home runs in a single game.

Fans were on their feet in the ninth inning as McCutchen came up with one out and one on and a chance to tie a major league record with four home runs in one game. He hit into an inning-ending double play but nonetheless gave Pirates fans hope, hope that would be realized four years later when the young rookie became a veteran and led the franchise to the postseason.

NOTABLE ACHIEVEMENTS (YEARLY LEADERS AND AWARDS ARE AS PIRATES ONLY)

Part of three National League Wild Card teams (2013, 2014, 2015).
Won the 2013 National League MVP.
Won the Silver Slugger Award three times (2012, 2013, 2014).
Won the Roberto Clemente Memorial Award (2015)
Won the Gold Glove Award once (2012).
Played in five All-Star Games, starting in two.
Finished in the top 10 voting for the National League MVP three times.

Finished in the top 10 for the National League batting title three times.

Led the league in on-base percentage once (2014).

Led the league in on-base plus slugging percentage once (2014).

Led the league in hits once (2012).

Led the league in putouts for a center fielder and outfielder once (2011).

Led the league in double plays for a center fielder twice (2011, 2013).

Led the league in double plays for an outfielder once (2011).

96th in most games in center field in major league history, with 957.

115th in highest slugging percentage in major league history, at .496.

80th in highest OPS in major league history, at .884.

12

MAX CAREY

In looking at the career of Pittsburgh Pirates center fielder Max Carey, one gets the impression that he was a very good player—but perhaps not one of the top 12 in the history of the franchise. It is necessary to look closely at what the man accomplished and delve deeper into to his stats to see what an innovator the speedster from Terre Haute truly was.

Perhaps one of Carey's greatest features was that he gave strategy to base stealing at a time when many just took off for second or third base and hoped with blind luck that they would make it safely. Max studied the pitcher, knew his moves, seemingly knew the best time to take off, and found himself safe a high percentage of the time.

The 1922 season is a prime example of this. That season runners in the National League attempted to steal 1,389 times, achieving success in 755 of their attempts, a success rate of 54.5 percent. Carey was remarkable, with 51 steals, 6.8 percent of the total steals in the Senior Circuit, in only 53 attempts, a 96.2 percent success rate. It was a season where he also swiped 31 consecutive bases without being thrown out.

The Hall of Famer stated that the secret to stealing bases was the "art of picking up little things, like a spitball pitcher who never threw to first if he was going to throw a spitter."[1] He also wore sliding pants to reduce the wear and tear of stealing. The pants were sewn by his mother, and Carey later patented the slacks. It was this attention to detail that helped make the man they called "Scoops," for his defensive prowess, so successful.

Born Maximillian Carnarius, a last name that meant "handler of meat," the center fielder attended Concordia College in Fort Wayne,

Indiana, before heading to Concordia Seminary in St. Louis in 1909, hoping to become a Lutheran minister, a career that his parents wanted their young son to pursue. When he returned to Terre Haute for the summer in 1909, a team from South Bend, which was playing his hometown, was looking for a shortstop, and Maximillian persuaded the team to use him. Not wanting to jeopardize his amateur status, he told the manager of the team to use a different name for him. The manager told the umpire the player's name was "Max Carney or Carey or something like that."[2] The umpire chose the last name Carey for the scorecard, and a baseball Hall of Famer was born.

After a less-than-stellar first year, Carey played again in 1910, moving to left field. It was during that season for South Bend that he showed what an electrifying a player he could be, swiping 86 bases in only 96 games and prompting the league president to suggest that Pittsburgh Pirates president and owner Barney Dreyfuss purchase the speedy player. Impressed, Dreyfuss took Carey for the team, and he went on to become a fixture in the outfield for the next decade and a half.

Entering Forbes Field for the first time in 1910, Max positioned himself at short, since he enjoyed playing there more than the outfield. Soon thereafter, Honus Wagner, the greatest player in Pirates history, walked up to him, irritated that someone was in his position. According to the story Wagner used to tell, he went to manager and starting left fielder Fred Clarke and told him if he was interested in keeping the Indiana native that perhaps he should play Clarke's position. Ironically, within two years, that's exactly what happened.

After finishing the abbreviated 1910 season with the Bucs, going 3-for-6, Carey hit .258 during his official rookie season in 1911, before really showcasing his potential a year later. The Hall of Famer broke the .300 plateau for the first time, with a .302 mark, and a year later showed off what would be his trademark, leading the National League in steals for the first time, with 61 thefts.

Throughout the next eight seasons, he led the National League in steals five more times, garnering 348 during that period, while hitting .276. He was also becoming one of the best center fielders in the game, topping the Senior Circuit in putouts six times in his first 11 full seasons.

CHAPTER 12

As the young player was becoming a grizzled veteran, rather that start a decline, Carey's career began to peak. In 1922, he hit .329 and garnered double digits in home runs for the only time in his career, with 10. He also had a National League high in steals, swiping 51, and walks, with 80. It was during that campaign that he also had perhaps his greatest game, reaching base nine times in a single contest.

Max continued his fine play throughout the next two years and, at age 35, had his marquee campaign in 1925, helping lead the Pirates to the National League pennant. He was seventh in the National League with a personal best .343 average, while swiping 46 bases, for his 10th and final National League crown. In his first and only World Series, Carey was at his best, especially when the Bucs needed him most. He hit a team-high .458 in the seven-game series and most likely would have been named the Fall Classic's Most Valuable Player had they named one in 1925.

In the seventh and deciding contest, the man from Terre Haute had four hits, including a third-inning single that gave Pittsburgh their second run after falling behind 4–0 in the first inning, a fifth-inning leadoff double that led to a run, and a double in the seventh that made it 6–5, before scoring the tying run after Pie Traynor smacked a two-out triple.

Like Willie Stargell 54 years later, the championship season should have been the veteran's ascension to idol status in Pirates nation, but an ugly incident in the dugout would prove to be the end of his Pirates career a year later. Carey was struggling mightily, and Clarke, who was an investor in the team and would sit on the bench, kept telling manager Bill McKechnie he should bench the man who helped lead them to their second World Series. The players were upset at the interference by Clarke, and Carson Bigbee and Babe Adams were at the forefront of a move to ask management to ban Clarke from sitting in the dugout. As captain, Carey became the leader of the revolt. In the end, everyone involved was cut loose by the team, including Max, who was eventually picked up by the Dodgers. He toiled in Brooklyn for four seasons, retiring in 1929, at the age of 39.

Pirates fans were happy when their hero returned to the team in a coaching capacity in 1930. Carey was given the job as manager of the Dodgers in 1932, lasting there for two seasons before taking on a role that he would later say was his greatest time in the sport, as manager and then president of the All-American Girls Professional Baseball League. He tried to teach the girls his disciplined, fundamental style of baseball and amazed those who saw them play with the qualities he had instilled in them. He stayed with the league until 1950.

Eleven years later Carey was given his highest honor when he was elected to the Baseball Hall of Fame by the Veteran's Committee in 1961. It was a great moment for him, as the committee recognized the fact he was not only perhaps the greatest base stealer in the game to that point, with his 738 stolen bases, but also one of the sport's greatest defensive players at center.

MOST MEMORABLE PERFORMANCE

On July 7, 1922, center fielder Max Carey gave the performance of a lifetime, setting a mark that remains a franchise, as well as a major league, record, as only three men in the annuls of Major League Baseball have ever reached base nine times in a single game.

The Bucs were playing the New York Giants at Forbes Field. It was a back and forth affair that saw the Giants take an 8–6 lead going into the bottom of the ninth. Pittsburgh tallied two in that frame, the first scored by Carey after a sacrifice fly by Ray Rohwer with the bases loaded.

Unfortunately for the Bucs, there would be no other scoring in the next nine innings, with the Giants picking up a run in the 18th to win, 9–8. While it was inconsequential who eventually won the game, the long contest allowed Max to have his incredible day. He had six hits in six official at bats; walked three times; stole three bases, including home; and scored three runs. It was his most incredible performance in a career of incredible acts.

NOTABLE ACHIEVEMENTS (YEARLY LEADERS AND AWARDS ARE AS PIRATES ONLY)

Elected to the Baseball Hall of Fame by the Veteran's Committee in 1961.
Part of one National League championship and one world championship team (1925).

Finished in the top 20 voting for the National League MVP three times.

Finished in the top 10 for the National League batting title twice.

Led the league in runs scored once (1913).

Led the league in triples twice (1914, 1923).

Led the league in stolen bases 10 times (1913, 1915, 1916, 1917, 1918, 1920, 1922, 1923, 1924, 1925).

Led the league in assists for a center fielder six times (1916, 1917, 1918, 1922, 1923, 1925).

Led the league in putouts for a center fielder seven times (1916, 1917, 1918, 1921, 1922, 1923, 1924).

Led the league in double plays for a center fielder five times (1916, 1917, 1918, 1921, 1922).

Led the league in putouts for an outfielder nine times (1912, 1913, 1916, 1917, 1918, 1921, 1922, 1923, 1924).

Led the league in assists for an outfielder four times (1913, 1916, 1918, 1923).

Led the league in double plays for an outfielder five times (1912, 1915, 1916, 1918, 1921).

Eclipsed 200 hits in a season once.

Eclipsed 100 runs in a season five times.

Eclipsed 50 stolen bases in a season six times.

Tied the major league record for most times on base in a single game, with nine.

9th in most stolen bases in major league history, with 738.

49th in most at bats in major league history, with 9,363.

42nd in most triples in major league history, with 159.

3rd in at bats per strikeout in major league history, at 44.9.

2nd in most assists by a center fielder in major league history, with 215.

7th in most assists by an outfielder in major league history, with 339.

4th in most putouts by an outfielder in major league history, with 4,639.

18th in most putouts by a center fielder in major league history, with 4,369.

Holds the all-time major-league record for most in errors by a center fielder, with 172.

3rd in major league history in both double plays by a center fielder, with 55, and an outfielder, with 87.

Holds the all-time major league record for runs scored in a season by a switch hitter, with 140.

Holds the all-time major league record (tied) for two hits in an inning in a game, twice.

Holds the all-time major league record (tied) for reaching base nine times in a game.

Holds the National League record for fastest player to reach 2,000 hits, in 1,468 games.

13

BILL MAZEROSKI

There is no greater moment in the history of the Pittsburgh Pirates than on October 13, 1960, when Bill Mazeroski, rounding third base as seen here, hit a home run to win the 1960 World Series. Also considered one of the greatest defensive second basemen of all time, Maz was elected to the Baseball Hall of Fame in 2001.

Photo courtesy of the Pittsburgh Pirates.

Many baseball historians and fans alike claim that there are two reasons Pittsburgh Pirates second baseman Bill Mazeroski is in the Hall of Fame. One is the fact that he is widely considered the greatest defensive second baseman in the history of the game. The second is a certain home run he hit in 1960 against the New York Yankees—no, not the one he hit in the first game—in the seventh and deciding contest, in the bottom of the ninth, to win the game and the World Series for the Bucs, the only time a seventh and deciding game has ended on a walk-off home run. Saying that Maz is in the Hall of Fame for these two reasons has merit, but while his offense prowess never would have been the reason the Veteran's Committee elected him in 2001, it is nonetheless a highly underrated part of his game.

In the 1960s, the Wheeling, West Virginia, native was at the top of the list in most offensive categories for National League second basemen. He hit more doubles (199), extra-base hits (333), and hits (1,385) than anyone else in the league. He also hit more home runs (93), a stat that, despite the fact he played in cavernous Forbes Field, was significantly higher than Julian Javier, who was in second, with 71. He also led the circuit in RBIs, with 600, a full 176 more than Javier, who again was second. Bill did all this while having the eighth-highest batting average among second basemen, at .268, and the fifth-best slugging mark, at .368, behind such luminaries as Joe Morgan and Pete Rose.

While these stats may not seem impressive when compared to other eras in the game, one must remember that the decade was dominated by pitchers, making it one of the worst hitting decades in the modern era. It's not to say that Bill Mazeroski was a terrific offensive force in the history of the game, but that he was a better hitter than most people give him credit for.

That being said, there was arguably no better defensive second baseman in the game than Maz. He didn't impress people with his athleticism like the great Ozzie Smith, but his positioning, technique, and incredible knowledge of his position was without peer. When asked about Maz, the young second baseman who was waiting for him to retire to take over his starting position, Dave Cash, also credited his cool, calm demeanor for his success. Said Cash,

I learned a lot from Mazeroski. He's a real man, and one of the things he taught me was to keep things in perspective. Maz didn't make many errors, and he hardly ever made any bad plays, but when he did, he didn't let it bother him. He was always the same whether things were going good, bad, or indifferently.[1]

These attributes allowed the smooth-fielding second baseman to accumulate the seventh-highest putout total in major league history, with 4,974, and the fifth-best assist total, with 6,685. No second baseman has been involved in more double plays than his 1,706. It also led to Bill being awarded the Gold Glove at second base eight times in his 17-year career

After being signed by the Bucs following his graduation from Wilton Consolidated High School in Tiltonsville, Ohio, Maz looked like anything but the game's greatest defensive second baseman; in fact, he started out as a shortstop with their Williamsport farm club in the Eastern League in 1954, having a subpar first season in professional baseball.

Despite his poor start, in spring training the following season he was playing second base and caught the attention of Pirates Hall of Fame general manager Branch Rickey for his ability to turn a double play. By 1956, Mazeroski had been sent to the club's top team in Hollywood, of the Pacific Coast League, where he was impressive, with a .306 average, while turning an incredible 70 double plays in 80 games. His success during his half-season in Hollywood prompted a promotion for the second baseman in 1956. Bill was given the starting spot for the Bucs and held on to it for the next 15 years.

He played his first season under Bobby Bragan, who was an aggressive manager, doing such unique things as pinch-hitting for his young rookie, sometimes as early as the second inning. The next year, 1958, Danny Murtaugh replaced Bragan, and Maz, along with the rest of the young squad, took to his tutelage, giving the team their first winning record in 10 years.

Mazeroski's performance warranted Rickey's enthusiasm. He hit a career-high .283 in 1957, and 19 home runs a year later, setting a franchise record for homers by a second baseman that held until Neil

Walker, who Maz helped adjust to second base as a spring training instructor for the team, finally broke 56 years later in 2014. It was also during the 1958 season that the Hall of Famer was recognized for his defensive excellence at second base with his first Gold Glove Award. Moreover, he finished eighth in National League Most Valuable Player voting and was selected to play in his first All-Star Game.

After slipping a bit in 1959, Mazeroski had a fine 1960 campaign and one that turned out to be one of the most memorable in franchise history, when the Bucs won their seventh National League crown and first in 33 years. As well as he played, it paled in comparison to what he was about to accomplish in his first World Series. Hitting .320 in the Fall Classic, the Wheeling native hit the team's only long ball in the first six games.

In the final contest he was 1-for-3, with a run and a single, when he came up to bat in the bottom of the ninth with the score tied at nine. At that point in his career he was known as a fine second baseman but nothing more than a piece in the Bucs' championship squad, not a superstar and certainly not a legend. Statues dedicated to him, a retired number, and a spot in the Hall of Fame were not even in the thoughts of the most optimistic people. That all changed at 3:36 p.m. on October 13, 1960.

Ralph Terry was on the mound for the Yanks and missed with his first pitch to the Pirates second baseman for a ball. His second pitch was to the liking of Mazeroski, who drove it over the left-field wall, with Yogi Berra watching helplessly as Bill gave the Bucs a dramatic world championship win over the heavily favored Yankees. It was the day he became a Steel City icon.

Maz was now being looked upon in a different light. He was honored as *Sporting News* Player of the Year in 1960, and given the Babe Ruth Award, which, while not the official World Series MVP Award, which was awarded to New York's Bobby Richardson, is given to the MVP of the series, as voted on by the New York Baseball Writers' Association of America.

Bill was consistent between 1961 and 1968, hitting .262, while winning seven more Gold Gloves and leading the league in double plays seven times, including a record 161 for a second baseman in 1966 that still stands. In 1967, he pulled muscles in both legs and continued to have issues with them until the injuries finally got the best of him in 1969. He played in 112 games in 1970, but by 1972, he had been forced into retirement, hitting .188 in 64 at bats that final season.

He has spent his retirement being celebrated as a Pittsburgh hero, spending many spring trainings as a special infield instructor for the team. In 2001, the Veteran's Committee elected him into the Hall of Fame. The 65-year-old team icon gave a memorable, if short, speech, telling how defense should be honored in the hall as much as pitching and hitting. He then broke down into tears. Maz quickly ended his speech at that point, but fans, especially those in Pirates nation, will remember his words for a long time and are pleased that baseball rewarded perhaps the greatest defensive second baseman in the history of the game with his rightful spot in Cooperstown.

MOST MEMORABLE PERFORMANCE

Mention the name Bill Mazeroski and only one game comes to mind, October 13, 1960, the day the 24-year-old infielder went from a good player to a Pittsburgh Pirates legend.

The 1960 World Series had been a strange one for sure, the Pirates winning their three games by 6–4, 3–2, and 5–2 counts, while the Yankees captured their wins by incredibly lopsided scores of 16–3, 10–0, and 12–0.

Maz was having a fine series, one in which he would hit .320, including the only home run for Pittsburgh in the first game. Game Seven looked like it would be an easy victory, with the Bucs leading the game 4–0 going into the top of the fifth at Forbes Field, including a run by Mazeroski, after he singled in the fourth and was driven in by a Bill Virdon single to right.

But an easy win was not to be. New York came back strong, plating seven runs in the next four innings to take a 7–4 advantage going into the bottom of the eighth. The Bucs then took a 9–7 lead going into the ninth thanks to a couple of fluke hits and a dramatic three-run homer by backup catcher Hal Smith, the single most memorable home run in Pirates history at that point. The Yanks tied it up with two runs off Bob Friend and Harvey Haddix, giving the Wheeling native his chance at history.

Mazeroski hit a 1–0 pitch over the left-field wall to become the only player to win a World Series on a seventh game walk-off home run, making Hal Smith's home run the second-greatest homer in team history.

NOTABLE ACHIEVEMENTS (YEARLY LEADERS AND AWARDS ARE AS PIRATES ONLY)

Elected to the Baseball Hall of Fame by the Veteran's Committee in 2001.

Part of two National League championship and two world championship teams (1960, 1971).

Part of three Eastern Division championship teams (1970, 1971, 1972).

Had his number nine retired by the team in 1987.

Had a statue erected in his honor outside the right-field gate at PNC Park in 2010.

Won eight Gold Glove Awards (1958, 1960, 1961, 1963, 1964, 1965, 1966, 1967).

Played in seven All-Star Games.

Won the 1960 *Sporting News* Player of the Year Award.

Won the 1960 Babe Ruth Award.

Finished in the top 10 voting for the National League MVP once.

Led the league in assists for a second baseman nine times (1958, 1960, 1961, 1962, 1963, 1964, 1966, 1967, 1968).

Led the league in putouts for a second baseman five times (1960, 1961, 1962, 1966, 1967).

Led the league in fielding percentage for a second baseman three times (1960, 1965, 1966).

Led the league in double plays for a second baseman eight times (1960, 1961, 1962, 1963, 1964, 1965, 1966, 1967).

Led the league in overall assists five times (1958, 1961, 1963, 1964, 1966).

5th in most assists by a second baseman in major league history, with 6,685.

7th in most putouts by a second baseman in major league history, with 4,974.

10th in most games at second base in major league history, with 2,094.

19th in most assists in major league history, with 6,694.

21st in defensive wins above replacement in major league history, at 23.9.

Holds the all-time major league record for most double plays turned by a second baseman, with 1,706.

Holds the all-time major league record for double plays turned by a second baseman, with 161.

Only player in the history of the game to hit a walk-off World Series home run in Game Seven.

14

LLOYD WANER

Paul Waner, left, and his brother Lloyd, right, are the only brother combination to be elected to the Baseball Hall of Fame. Rising up in the shadow of Paul in 1927, Lloyd had a phenomenal rookie season, hitting .355, with a league-high 133 runs.

Photo courtesy of the Pittsburgh Pirates.

Playing in the shadow of an older brother can be an intimidating, thankless endeavor, especially when the big brother is highly respected as one of the best in the game. Lloyd Waner played in the shadow of one of the finest hitters in the history of the game, his brother Paul, an undertaking that would be too much for most. The man they referred to as "Little Poison" to his brother's "Big Poison" was not daunted, however, excelling to the point that it gave the Bucs one of the greatest outfields in the Senior Circuit for more than a decade.

The famed nicknames came from a New York Giant fan at the Polo Grounds who referred to the Waners as "Big Person" and "Little Person." He did so in a thick New York accent that made it sound like poison instead of person, and the names stuck. The irony is that while Lloyd was eight pounds lighter than Paul, he was actually listed as being one inch taller. But when one saw their different hitting approaches, Paul with solid gap power, while Lloyd was more of a slap hitter, the names were most appropriate.

The one sabermetric statistic that emphasizes Lloyd's hitting style is his secondary average. A secondary average is a statistic created by Bill James to measure the productivity of a player's at bats, independent of batting average. The formula takes walks plus total bases minus hits plus stolen bases minus caught stealing and divides that sum by at bats. Of the top 100 center fielders James rates in the newest edition of his historical baseball abstract, Waner has the lowest secondary average of the group, with a .140 mark.[1] While this highlights that he had little power (his 27 homers in 18 seasons also does a good job of that), Lloyd was nonetheless an effective player and the preeminent defensive center fielder of his era in the Senior Circuit. His batting eye was such that he struck out only 178 times in his 18-year career. To put this into perspective, the major league record for strikeouts in a season is held by Mark Reynolds, who whiffed 223 times in 2009, a full 45 times more than Waner in his entire career.

Little Poison played three semesters at the East Central Teachers College in Oklahoma, as well as for an independent team called the Ada Independents after a stellar high school career at McCloud High School. His father Ora Waner was a decent player himself but knew his sons were special. He once recalled, "Now I was considered a mighty good hitter myself, but when I saw those kids cracking away at corncobs (the boys would throw corncobs instead of baseballs on the farm) I knew I was never in their class."[2]

Big brother Paul was the first to make it to the majors, beginning his career with the Bucs in 1926, and he set out to convince Pirates management to sign his little brother. He played with Paul for the San Francisco Seals in the Pacific Coast League in 1925, hitting .250 in 31 games, before his big brother's efforts paid off, as Pittsburgh signed him in April 1926.

Lloyd spent 1926 with the Columbia Comers of the South Atlantic League, joining the Pirates a year later. While 1927 proved to be one of the great seasons in his brother's Hall of Fame career, during which time he captured the league's Most Valuable Player Award, Little Poison most likely would have been named rookie of the year had they given the award at the time.

Lloyd led the circuit in runs and singles, with 133 and 198, respectively, while hitting what turned out to be his career high as a starter, with a .355 average, finishing third in the National League. Both his runs scored and singles represented major league records for a rookie in a season. For his efforts, he finished sixth in the National League MVP race.

As effective as his rookie campaign was in helping lead the Bucs to their sixth National League pennant in 26 years, his performance in what would be his only World Series was one of the lone highlights for the team. In their four-game sweep at the hands of the New York Yankees, Lloyd hit .400, with five runs scored.

While never reaching the lofty heights of 1927, Waner continued to be one of the most consistent hitters in the league; for a five-year period between 1928 and 1932, he hit .336, averaging 190 hits per season. To show he just wasn't an offensive threat, James estimates that Little Poison would have won eight Gold Gloves in center field between 1927 and 1937.[3] Perhaps his best season in that five-year period came in 1929, when he had a .353 average, leading the league with 20 triples and finishing fifth in the MVP race.

The center fielder stumbled in 1933 and 1934, falling below the .300 plateau for the first two times in his career, with .276 and .283 averages, respectively, but he soon rebounded, pulling himself back above .300 the next four seasons, including 1938, when the team made a surprising run at the National League pennant, only to have a disastrous collapse in September.

Despite the fact that the season ended so miserably, it was still a memorable campaign for the younger Waner. He was selected to play in the only All-Star Game of his career and hit .313. Little Poison also had the distinction of reaching the 2,000-hit mark faster than any player in National League history, doing so in 1,453 games, a record he still holds. That same year he and Paul also became the first Pirate brothers to hit back-to-back home runs in a game, a feat not repeated until 71 years later, by the LaRoche brothers in 2009.

The 1938 campaign proved to be the beginning of the end for Little Poison, however. He struggled again in 1939 and 1940, hitting a career-low .259 the latter season. A year later he was highly disappointed, as the Bucs sent him to the Boston Braves in exchange for Nick Strincevich. Said Waner, "I can tell you the saddest day of my career. It was the day in 1941 when the Pirates traded me to Boston for pitcher Nick Strincevich. I never thought I'd get over it."[4]

While disillusioned, Lloyd did set a record of note with the Bucs, Braves, and Phils in 1941, coming to the plate 219 times without a strikeout. He played sparingly the next two seasons, retiring in 1943, at 37 years of age. With players at a premium, as most were serving in World War II, Paul talked his little brother into coming back in 1944, to play with him in Brooklyn. By midseason the Dodgers had released him, paving the way for a return to the Pirates, where he ended his career in 1945, with a .316 average.

After retirement, the younger Waner spent four years with the Bucs as a scout, eventually becoming a field clerk with the Oklahoma City government for 17 years, retiring in 1967.

In the years following his baseball career, he was never given serious consideration for the Hall of Fame, as the highest voting percentage he ever received was 23.4 percent in 1964, far short of the 75 percent needed for induction. Finally, three years later, the Veteran's Committee endowed him with baseball's highest honor, and Lloyd joined Paul to make them the only brothers to be honored at Cooperstown.

Lloyd Waner may have had a big shadow to contend with in his brother Paul, but when your career ends with a trip to the Hall of

Fame, it's safe to say you've overcome anything that may have stood in your way.

MOST MEMORABLE PERFORMANCE

The contest played on June 15, 1930 was the game of a lifetime, one that would have been easily forgettable for any pitcher who would have taken to the mound that afternoon.

Eleven pitchers came in and eleven went cowering away after being pelted by one batter after another. It took 14 innings, 4 hours, and 17 minutes—a long game for that time period—but thanks to eight runs in the top of the 14th by the New York Giants, it was a 20–15 victory by the visitors at Forbes Field over the hometown Pirates. But it was also a day that Lloyd Waner had perhaps his greatest game in a Pirates uniform.

The Giants broke out to an 11–4 lead in the top of the sixth before Pittsburgh started chipping away at their advantage. They scored two in the sixth, one in each of the seventh and eighth innings, and three in the bottom of the ninth to tie the score. Each team plated one in the 11th to send the game into the 12th inning tied at 12. New York finally ripped the Pirates pitchers for eight runs in the top of the 14th, seven off reliever Larry French for the 20–15 win.

While his team inked a loss, Waner was the star of the game, picking up four singles, a double, and a triple in eight at bats for an impressive six-hit performance, one short of the National League record of seven set by Wilbert Robinson in 1892, but tied for the most since 1900 in the Senior Circuit—truly a spectacular day for the youngest Waner on the Pittsburgh roster.

NOTABLE ACHIEVEMENTS (YEARLY LEADERS AND AWARDS ARE AS PIRATES ONLY)

Elected to the Baseball Hall of Fame by the Veteran's Committee in 1967.

Part of one National League championship team (1927).

Played in one All-Star Game.

Finished in the top 10 voting for the National League MVP twice.

Finished in the top 10 for the National League batting title four times.

Led the league in hits once (1931).

Led the league in runs scored once (1927).

Led the league in triples once (1929).

Led the league in at bats per strikeouts five times (1932, 1933, 1936, 1937, 1938).

Led the league in assists for a center fielder twice (1929, 1931).

Led the league in putouts for a center fielder and outfielder four times (1929, 1931, 1932, 1934).

Led the league in fielding percentage for a center fielder three times (1935, 1937, 1938).

Led the league in double plays for a center fielder twice (1929, 1931).

Eclipsed 200 hits in a season four times.

67th in highest batting average in major league history, with .316.

42nd in most singles in major league history, with 2,033.

3rd in at bats per strikeout in major league history, at 44.9.

12th in most assists by a center fielder in major league history, with 141.

14th in most putouts by a center fielder in major league history, with 4,531.

Holds the major league record for runs scored by a rookie, with 133.

Holds the major league record for singles by a rookie, with 198.

Holds the National League record for fastest player to reach 2,000 hits, in 1,468 games.

15

WILBUR COOPER

Wilbur Cooper is the only man in the history of the Pittsburgh Pirates who won more than 200 games in his career while wearing the Pirates uniform. Garnering 202 victories in his 13-year career in the Steel City, Cooper was a 20-game winner four times for the Bucs, including three seasons in a row between 1920 and 1922.

Photo courtesy of the Pittsburgh Pirates.

There is an impressive array of hitters that dot the all-time greatest players list in the history of the Pittsburgh Pirates, a true cornucopia of offensive talent that ranks among the best in the game. When it comes to Pirates who have taken the mound, however, we have a collection of hurlers who have been mostly forgotten. Ask the casual Pittsburgh baseball fan how many hits Roberto Clemente had and most will confidently say 3,000, but ask them who the all-time leader in wins by a Pirate is and you will most likely get a blank stare. The answer is the 15th player on this list: Wilbur Cooper.

Rated as the 55th best pitcher in the history of Major League Baseball by sabermetrician Bill James in the *New Bill James Historical Baseball Abstract*, James quotes *Pittsburgh Post-Gazette* writer Harvey J. Boyle in describing Cooper's effortless pitching motion and defense. "He had a wonderful control of his deliveries, and he tossed a ball to the plate with less effort than any hurler in the league. . . . His gloved hand moved with the quickness of a cat's paw. He was one of the best fielding pitchers."[1]

The southpaw had an effective array of pitches, including a fastball, curve, and changeup, but he also significantly altered the ball, which was common during that era. According to United Press International writer John Carroll, "(Cooper would) chew tobacco during a game. Somehow tobacco juice would get into the pocket of his glove and then on the ball. After an inning or two the ball would get very dark."[2] The hurler was also known for his quick delivery, wasting little time in between pitches.

Spitball aside, when looking at his qualifications for the Hall of Fame, Cooper deserves a much closer look by the Pre-Integration Era Committee at its next meeting. His 216 victories are impressive—although perhaps less so when compared to other hurlers from his time period—but there are only two pitchers in the modern era of baseball who have thrown more than 3,000 innings and have an ERA under 3.00 who have not been enshrined in Cooperstown: Red Ames, a right-hander who primarily pitched for the New York Giants in a 17-year major league career that saw him go 183–167, with a 2.63 ERA, and Cooper.

Cooper's qualifications for Cooperstown are perhaps more compelling than Ames's, as he had 33 more victories to go with a .548 winning percentage, compared to Red's .523. The southpaw was a fine control pitcher, with a career mark of 2.206 walks per nine innings. While a baseball historian by the name of Mike Hoban, who wrote the book *Defining Greatness: A Hall of Fame Handbook*, positions Wilbur Cooper as the 25th best pitcher of all-time in his Hall of Fame rating,[3] James puts him at 55th.[4] When looking at the Hall of Fame ratings on Baseball-Reference.com, it appears that the argument about whether to include the leading winner in Pirates history at Cooperstown is not in his favor. In the website's Hall of Fame monitor statistic, which rates players based on their individual stats per season, a rating of 100 seems to put one in serious contention, while 130 apparently makes a player a certainty for enshrinement. Cooper unfortunately has a rating of 76, the 155th-highest mark among pitchers, tied with Bartolo Colon. Using the Baseball-Reference.com rating makes for a less gripping argument for the left-hander, but his career was good enough to put him in the discussion, as Hoban and James seem to think.

Regardless of his all-time rating among the experts, the man who was born in Bearsville, West Virginia, in 1892, is one of the greatest hurlers ever to wear the Pirates uniform. He started his professional career in 1911, with the Marion Diggers of the Ohio State League, a team owned by future president Warren G. Harding, at 19 years of age, where he went 17–11 before pitching one contest for the Mansfield Brownies that season in the Ohio-Pennsylvania League. Cooper would end up with Columbus of the American Association before the season's end. He stayed with the Senators in 1912, finishing with a 16–9 mark, before being dealt to the Bucs at the end of the campaign.

The West Virginia native pitched well for the Bucs the final month of the 1912 season, including an 8–0 shutout over St. Louis in his first major league start on August 7. He was 3–0, with three complete games and two shutouts in four starts with a 1.66 ERA. Cooper followed up his fine debut with a good 1913 campaign, mostly out of the bull pen, before the upstart Federal League made him a generous $5,000 a year contract, hoping to tap into his seemingly unlimited potential. The 21-year-old turned down the offer and decided to stick with the Bucs, and they rewarded him with a spot in the starting rotation.

Wilbur had a phenomenal first season as a starter, with a 16–15 mark and 2.13 ERA for the seventh-place Pirates, before posting a miserable 5–16 mark a year later. Splitting time between the bull pen and the rotation in 1916, he rebounded to finish 12–11; it was the beginning of three-year stretch during which the southpaw would establish himself as the ace of the Pirates staff. Cooper won 19 games twice, going 55–38 with a 2.38 ERA and tossing 13 shutouts. While it was impressive, it paled in comparison to his next three seasons, where he continued to improve, not only as the best pitcher for Pittsburgh, but also in the entire league.

The Bearsville hurler averaged 23 wins a season between 1920 and 1922, with a 69–43 mark, topping the 20-win plateau each time. After winning a career-high 24 in 1920, Cooper had his marquee campaign in 1921. He led the league in wins, with 22, as well as starts, with 38, and innings pitched, coming in at 327. Following a fine 23–14 record in 1922, Wilbur slipped a bit in 1923, with a National League-high 19 losses. He won 20 games a year later, and the 32-year-old was looking forward to being an important piece of the Pirates rotation in 1925, a year that saw them take their second World Series championship.

Instead of putting an exclamation point on a fabulous career with a chance to pitch in his first Fall Classic, Cooper was inexplicably traded to the Chicago Cubs, along with Charlie Grimm and Rabbit Maranville, for Vic Aldridge and George Grantham, two players that would be important in Pittsburgh's world championship run, as well as Al Niehaus. Wilbur was thoroughly disappointed, as his major league career began to go downhill. He was only 14–19 in 1925 and 1926, with the Cubs and Detroit Tigers, exiting the major leagues for good in 1926, when he was sent to the Toledo Mudhens of the International League, never to return to the big leagues.

The all-time Pirates leader in victories spent four seasons in the minors with Oakland, Shreveport, and San Antonio, compiling a 45–48 record that included a 2–11 mark and 6.32 ERA in 1930, his last season in professional baseball, before retiring at 38 years of age.

Following his retirement, Cooper spent three years managing in the Pennsylvania State League, winning the pennant with Jeannette in 1936, and finishing second with Greensburg a year later. Afterward, he spent many years working in real estate in Pittsburgh, moving to South California in 1947.

CHAPTER 15

While he was eventually elected to the Western Pennsylvania Sports Hall of Fame in 1959, and selected by fans as the best pitcher in Pirates franchise history in 1969, he never lived to see his ultimate dream, selection to the Baseball Hall of Fame. Dying of a heart attack in 1973, at the age of 81, Cooper had stated in his later years, "I would die a happy man if they voted me into the Hall of Fame. But if they don't, I will understand."[5] He has never come close to that dream in the years following his death, garnering no more than 4.4 percent of the vote in any year, which came in 1955, his last year of consideration, and never being seriously considered by the Veteran's Committee, a slight that will hopefully be rectified in the near future.

MOST MEMORABLE PERFORMANCE

As the Pittsburgh Pirates were taking on the St. Louis Cardinals in St. Louis on September 6, 1912, they stood in third place, at 75–53, 14½ games behind the New York Giants but only six behind the Chicago Cubs for second place. While a run at the pennant was out of their reach, a shot at the runner-up position was still attainable, which is why it was quizzical that manager Fred Clarke chose to go with a young left-hander he had picked up from Columbus of the American Association the week before the start.

Wilbur Cooper had nominal success with Senators, logging a 16–9 record during the early part of the 1912 campaign, but nothing that suggested he would become one of the greatest pitchers in franchise history.

With the support of Chief Wilson, who had three hits, Bobby Byrne, who chipped in with a triple and two hits, and the great Honus Wagner, who had a hit and made a spectacular play in the field, prompting Cooper to say, "Mr. Wagner, if you field like that behind me, I'll stay up here a long time,"[6] the 20-year-old hurler shut out the Cardinals, 8–0, in his first major league start.

Wilbur scattered nine hits, walked two, and struck out three in his nine innings of work, as St. Louis never threatened to score. Those who had questioned Clarke were quieted, as the manager proudly claimed that the young pitcher had earned his spot on the roster for the rest of the 1912 campaign. According to the *Pittsburgh Press*,

"Wilbur Cooper was the master of the situation at all stages, and while his shutout victory does not mean that he has earned a regular place on the Pittsburg(h) pitching staff, he will be taken east with the Pirates and given a thorough trial."[7]

While they may not have known how good Cooper was going to be at the time, he turned out to be every bit as good as Clarke thought he could be.

NOTABLE ACHIEVEMENTS (YEARLY LEADERS AND AWARDS ARE AS PIRATES ONLY)

One of two pitchers to throw more than 3,000 innings with a career ERA under 3.00 not elected to the Baseball Hall of Fame.

Finished in the top 10 in the National League in wins seven times.

Finished in the top 10 in the National League in ERA six times.

Led the league in wins once (1921).

Led the league in pitcher's wins above replacement once (1922).

Led the league in innings pitched once (1921).

Led the league in saves once (1918)

Led the league in shutouts once (1924).

Led the league in fielding percentage for a pitcher three times (1918, 1920, 1922).

Eclipsed 20 wins in a season four times.

Had an ERA under 3.00 six times.

Had an ERA under 2.00 once.

82nd in most wins in major league history, with 216.

73rd in most innings pitched in major league history, with 3,480.

71st in most shutouts in major league history, with 35.

Only Pirate to win more than 200 games, with 202.

16

FRED CLARKE

The list of Hall of Fame players who also managed is impressive; those who did both at the same time is a legendary compilation as well—Rogers Hornsby, Cap Anson, John McGraw, Leo Durocher, Lou Boudreau, Roger Bresnahan, Frank Chance, Ty Cobb, and Nap Lajoie, just to name a few. While almost all of the men on this list were Hall of Fame talents as either a player or manager, there is one individual who may stand out among the best, with Hall of Fame qualifications as both a player and manager. His name is Fred Clarke.

Looking at the list of the top 20 all-time managers in terms of games won, 18 played in the majors, with Connie Mack, John Mc-Graw, Joe Torre, Bucky Harris, Leo Durocher, Bill McKechnie, and Clarke being the only seven who had been player-managers. Of these, only Torre and McGraw, along with Clarke, had playing careers that could be considered worthy of Hall of Fame discussion.

McGraw had a fine .334 career batting average, but he only played in more than 100 games on six occasions, with 1,309 hits. Torre won the 1971 National League Most Valuable Player Award, leading the league with 230 hits and hitting to a .363 mark, but the rest of his career, while good, was not of Hall of Fame quality. Clarke had 2,678 hits, with a .312 average, hitting over .300 on 10 occasions during the Deadball Era.

As manager, Fred won 1,602 games, the 19th-highest figure in major league history. Only three managers in the top 20 list for wins also appear in the top 20 list for winning percentage: Joe McCarthy, who is the all-time leader, at .615; John McGraw, who is eighth, at .586; and Clarke, who is 16th, with a 1,602–1,181 mark for a .576 percentage.

In the list of the top 20 managers for winning percentage, only Mickey Cochrane, Cap Anson, and Frank Chance, along with Clarke, were Hall of Fame talents as players. Chance was not in Clarke's class as a player, with a .296 average and 1,274 hits. Cochrane had a relatively short career for a hall of famer, hitting .320 in 13 years, while winning two pennants as manager of the Tigers, but he was only at the helm for two full seasons and parts of three other years.

The only person who can really compete with Clarke as the greatest to combine playing and managerial skills is Cap Anson. In looking at the stats, there is little doubt that Anson was a superior player. Hitting .334 as the first player to reach 3,000 hits, Anson finished his 27-year career with 3,435 hits, still the seventh-highest mark of all-time 118 years after his retirement. He was one of the greatest, if not the greatest, players of the 19th century. As a manager, Cap was 1,295–947, with a .578 winning percentage in 22 years, capturing five pennants.

Few men can compete with Clarke when it comes to deciding whether he was the best at his trade, but when it comes to the greatest to both play for and manage the Pirates, it's an argument that begins and ends with him. Danny Murtaugh is the only individual who could challenge Clarke as the top manager in franchise history, but Clarke's superior winning percentage and four pennants puts him over the top. For this book, however, we are only looking at those who played the game, and as far as Fred Clarke goes, few would be better.

Those who saw Clarke as a player could quickly identify his ability on the diamond. As Harold Johnson writes in the book *Who's Who in Major League Baseball*, "Fred was unanimously selected as the greatest left fielder of his time. He was a demon base runner, and he was perhaps the best man ever known to baseball coming in to slide for low line drives."[1]

Fred began his stint in professional baseball through the strangest of circumstances—by putting an ad for his services in the *Sporting News*. "I got the job through an ad I inserted offering my services as a player," Clarke recalled. "The Hastings, Nebraska, club answered my advertisement and offered me $40 a month."[2]

The left fielder worked hard on his game at Hastings and eventually signed with St. Joseph's, Montgomery, and Savannah, where he hit

.316 for two seasons before being inked to a deal with the Louisville Colonels of the National League in 1894. Early on, it looked as if the Winterset, Iowa, native would be a special player, after he had four singles and a triple in his first major league game.

Following his impressive debut, Clarke continued to be a dangerous offensive force with the Colonels, hitting .341 in the five seasons following his rookie campaign, averaging 191 hits per season. Aside from being a talented player, he was also becoming an adept leader, prompting Louisville owner Barney Dreyfuss to make him manager of the team in 1897, when he was only 24 years old.

The new manager brought many impressive attributes to his new position. He always tried to maintain a positive attitude with his team, and while he wanted his players to behave off the field, he taught them to be aggressive on it. Fred had little patience for mental mistakes on the diamond, yet he had no issues making controversial moves that would often work. An example of this would be giving a young Wilbur Cooper his first major league start while battling with the Cubs for second place in 1912, or starting an untested Babe Adams in the first game of the 1909 World Series, which turned out to be a stroke of genius.

When Louisville was about to be contracted from the National League, Clarke was part of a group that included Honus Wagner, Tommy Leach, Deacon Phillippe, Claude Ritchey, Rube Waddell, and Dreyfuss—who purchased a portion of the team and became the Bucs president—and came to Pittsburgh in 1900. A dynasty was born.

Dreyfuss put Clarke in charge of the Pirates, and he led them to four National League crowns, including three in a row between 1901 and 1903, as well as the franchise's first World Series championship in 1909. As impressive as he was on the bench, he was just as good on the field, hitting .312 for the Bucs in the first seven seasons he played in the Steel City, including a fine 1903 campaign, when he hit .351. Fred also had the honor of playing in the first World Series in 1903, hitting .265 in the eight-game upset loss at the hands of the Boston Americans (Red Sox).

In 1907, age began to catch up to the 34-year-old player-manager, as he fell below .300 for four consecutive seasons after being under only three times in his first 13 years. Clarke rebounded with a fine .324

average in 1911, but that would be his last season as a starter in the majors. He only had 17 at bats in his final three seasons before retiring to his ranch in Winfield, Kansas.

The Pirates faltered after Clarke left the bench, and while they rebounded with some success in the 1920s, they kept falling short of winning pennants. Wanting to give the club the edge to put them back at the top, Dreyfuss brought Clarke back in 1925, as a vice president and assistant manager, allowing him to sit on the bench with then-manager Bill McKechnie. The team won that season but voted against giving the Hall of Famer a full World Series share, allotting him only $1,000, the same as the scouts.

Controversy followed Fred the following season, during a situation in which he criticized center fielder Max Carey and tried to talk McKechnie into taking him out of the lineup (see chapter 12 on Max Carey for additional details). The situation prompted Dreyfuss to remove Clarke from the team, and his time in Pittsburgh was over.

Despite the fact he was no longer in the city or organization, Clarke had a wonderful career as a manager, player, and inventor, as he patented such items as flip-down sunglasses and a mechanical system used to make pulling a tarpaulin onto the field easier. He was elected to the Hall of Fame as a player by the Old Timers Committee in 1945 and could easily have been included as a manager as well. It was a perfect combination that perhaps no other man in the history of the game can match.

MOST MEMORABLE PERFORMANCE

In 1901, Fred Clarke was in his second season as manager of the Pittsburgh Pirates, while doubling as their talented left fielder. The team was beginning what would be the first dynasty of the 20th century, and on July 23, 1901, the Bucs would not only show Cincinnati how successful they could be, but Clarke also put his name in the Pirates record book by hitting for the cycle.

In 1887, the Bucs moved into the National League, and on May 2, Fred Carroll became the first Pirate to hit for the cycle. In the 14 years following this feat, no other Pittsburgh player had managed to match Carroll's effort, until 1901, when Clarke became the first Pirate to achieve it in the 20th century.

Fred began his special day in the first inning, with a home run that gave the Bucs an early 1–0 lead. He doubled in the third, before singling and scoring in the seventh frame, extending the Pittsburgh lead to 6–0. As the bottom of the eighth started at Exposition Park, Clarke needed an at bat and a triple, and he promptly got the hit he needed to put the final touches on a 9–2 win.

A year later, he repeated the act, becoming the first Pirates player, and still one of only three (Arky Vaughan and Wally Westlake are the others), to hit for the cycle twice in a Pittsburgh uniform.

NOTABLE ACHIEVEMENTS (YEARLY LEADERS AND AWARDS ARE AS PIRATES ONLY)

Elected to the Baseball Hall of Fame by the Old Timers Committee in 1945.

Part of four National League championship teams (1901, 1902, 1903, 1909).

Part of one World Series championship team (1909).

Finished in the top 10 for the National League batting title seven times.

Led the league in slugging once (1903).

Led the league in on-base plus slugging percentage once (1903).

Led the league in triples once (1906).

Led the league in doubles once (1903)

Led the league in hit by pitch once (1902).

Led the league in putouts for an outfielder once (1909).

Led the league in fielding percentage for an outfielder twice (1907, 1909).

Eclipsed 100 runs in a season twice.

67th in most hits in major league history, with 2,678.

43rd in most singles in major league history, with 2,030.

34th in most steals in major league history, with 509.

7th in most triples in major league history, with 220.

42nd in most runs in major league history, with 1,622.

20th in HBP in major league history, with 154.

22nd in most assists by an outfielder in major league history, with 254.

14th in most putouts by an outfielder in major league history, with 4,795.

19th in most wins by a manager in major league history, with 1,602.

16th in highest winning percentage by a manager in major league history, with .576.

Holds the all-time record for most wins by a Pirates manager, with 1,422.

17

ROY FACE

Roy Face, one of the first successful relievers in the history of the Pirates franchise, arguably remains its best. A little-used starter early in his career, Face saved 186 games in his career, including one during his marquee campaign in 1959, when he was 18–1, with a league-leading .947 winning percentage.
Photo courtesy of the Pittsburgh Pirates.

As much as the game has remained the same throughout the years, there have been moments that have changed the way we look at it. Players like Babe Ruth introduced the home run into our everyday vernacular, and such trailblazers as Maury Wills tried to erase the lumbering, nonexistent running games of the previous two decades. The 1950s also saw a change in another area of the game, one that has continued to evolve to the point that it is a key component of the modern-day game: the relief pitcher.

In the National League in 1940, 44 percent of all pitched games were completed by the starters, while there were only 112 saves among the eight teams. Ten years later, the numbers had changed, but not drastically, as 40.2 percent of games were complete and 133 saved. By the end of the decade, in 1959, the number of complete games had dropped considerably, to 30.2 percent, but this total is still much higher than the 2.3 percent of 2014. Still, this was a dramatic decrease when compared to the use of pitching staffs for most of the 20th century. The era of the reliever had begun, and the Pittsburgh Pirates' Roy Face would be one of its pioneers.

Born on February 20, 1928, in Stephentown, New York, Face was signed as an amateur free agent by the Pirates' cross-state rivals in Philadelphia. He started his professional baseball career in an incredible fashion, going 32–7 for the Bradford Blue Wings of the Pennsylvania-Ontario-New York League, with a 2.88 ERA and an .821 winning percentage in his first two seasons. The next season, Roy was drafted by the Brooklyn Dodgers in the minor league free agent draft and continued his minor league success with perhaps his best season as a pro pitcher up until that time. He went 23–9, with a 2.78 ERA and his lowest walks and hits per innings pitched as a minor leaguer, posting an impressive 1.189 mark while playing for the Pueblo Dodgers in the Western League.

The 24-year-old right-hander continued his impressive run in 1952, at Fort Worth, winning 14 contests and compiling another ERA below 3.00. The general manager who drafted Face in Brooklyn, Hall of Famer Branch Rickey, was now in Pittsburgh, and at the winter meetings in 1952, Rickey took the New York native for the Pirates organization. It may have been Rickey's second-best move as the Bucs' general manager next to drafting Roberto Clemente from the Dodgers in the Rule 5 Draft.

Unfortunately for the hurler, he was immediately thrust into the rotation in 1953. While Face had a hard fastball and curveball, he had no other pitches to complement them. Predictably, he had a subpar rookie campaign, with a 6.58 ERA, and was sent to the team's top minor league club in New Orleans in 1954, to try and develop another pitch for his arsenal.

While playing for his future manager with the Bucs, Danny Murtaugh, Roy developed his famous forkball, a pitch that works in a similar manner to a knuckleball, in which its location is unpredictable before it drops as it enters the strike zone. He perfected it after watching veteran Joe Page in spring training while Page was trying to make a comeback. Even though Face didn't have the success with New Orleans that he had enjoyed in his other minor league seasons, he learned his lessons well, returning to the Bucs in 1955. Unlike his first trip to the Pirates, he remained in the major leagues for the next 15 years.

Face was much more effective in 1955, lowering his ERA to 3.58, before beginning to carve his place in history as a pioneer, becoming a full-time reliever in 1956. Leading the league with 68 games pitched in 1956 (only three starts) and garnering 12 wins, he continued to improve the next year, with 59 games, including his last major league start.

After a decade of losing, the Bucs finally showed they were ready to win with a second-place finish in 1958. The right-hander finished a National League-high 40 games, while leading the circuit with 20 saves. Even though the team faltered a bit in 1959, Face enjoyed a season for the ages that remains one of the most impressive in the history of the game. Starting in May 1958, the diminutive five-foot, eight-inch reliever pitched in 92 games without suffering a loss. He had emerged victorious 22 consecutive times by the time the streak ended, including an 18–1 mark in 1959. His .947 winning percentage remains a major league record for pitchers who have picked up 15 or more wins in a season.

No other reliever has put together such a record, while few starters have matched Roy's success. Rube Marquard (who started the 1912 campaign at 19–0), Don Newcombe (1955), and Max Scherzer (2013) have been the only other pitchers to start the season with equally impressive marks, and none finished the season undefeated or were able to match Face's winning percentage.

In 1960, during the Pirates' world championship year, Roy followed up his impressive campaign with another fine season, with 10 victories and 24 saves, accumulating three more in the World Series against the New York Yankees. Now considered one of the best out of the bull pen in the majors, the reliever went on to a consistent career in a Pirates uniform. Between 1961 and 1967, he led the league in saves twice, garnering 100 and captured the National League Fireman of the Year Award in 1962, when he had a career-high 28 saves. He struggled in 1964, allowing 11 home runs in only 79 $^2/_3$ innings, with a 5.20 ERA, but looked like he was rebounding in 1965, when an injury cut his season short.

The Stephentown native again became a force out of the bull pen in 1966 and 1967, winning 13, while saving 35, with a 2.56 ERA; however, it was the beginning of the end for the 40-year-old pitcher. In 1968, he was enjoying a solid season when the Pirates sold him to the Tigers for $100,000. Knowing that he couldn't be put on the Detroit roster until September 1, Face was one game short of Walter Johnson's major league record of 802 games pitched with one team. Steve Blass started the game and then, after retiring the first batter, went to left field. Face entered the contest for one batter, getting a ground out before exiting the contest with his record in hand, turning it back over to Blass.

When he left, Face held National League records for games pitched (802), games in relief (775), and wins in relief (92). He finished the season pitching in two games with the soon-to-be world champion Detroit Tigers and then pitched one season with the Montreal Expos in 1969, hanging up his spikes up for good after a short eight-game trial with the Hawaii Islanders of the Pacific Coast League in 1970.

Becoming a carpenter following his retirement from the game, Roy left baseball with many records, but most importantly he was one of the pioneers during the relief era and the best to ever come out of the bull pen for the Bucs.

CHAPTER 17

MOST MEMORABLE PERFORMANCE

The 1959 campaign was a memorable one for Pittsburgh Pirates reliever Roy Face, one where he set a major league record with a .947 winning percentage and won 22 decisions in a row, the last of which came in the second game of a doubleheader against the team that had originally drafted him, the Philadelphia Phillies.

Coming into the contest, he was 16–0, having won the final five decisions in 1958, to put his win streak at 21. After the Phils had opened up a 5–0 first-inning advantage, Pittsburgh battled back for five runs in the final three innings at Forbes Field to send the game into extra innings.

Danny Murtaugh brought his undefeated hurler in to pitch in the 10th, and after giving up a leadoff home run to first baseman Ed Bouchee to give Philadelphia a 6–5 advantage, it appeared Roy's streak would end. Fortunately, his teammates did not let him down. Dick Stuart ripped a long double to center field that scored Don Hoak and Bill Virdon to give Pittsburgh the 7–6 win, stretching Face's record to 17–0 and extending his streak to 22 consecutive decisions without a loss.

While he would lose his first game 11 days later, Face won his final decision to end the 1959 campaign with a remarkable 18–1 mark.

NOTABLE ACHIEVEMENTS (YEARLY LEADERS AND AWARDS ARE AS PIRATES ONLY)

Part of one National League championship and world championship team (1960).

Won the 1962 National League Fireman of the Year Award.

Played in six All-Star Games.

Finished in the top 20 voting for the National League Most Valuable Player Award three times.

Led the league in games pitched twice (1956, 1960).

Led the league in games finished four times (1958, 1960, 1961, 1962).

Led the league in winning percentage once (1959).

Saved three games in the 1960 World Series.

Held the major league record for games pitched with one team upon his retirement, with 802.

Held the National League record for games pitched upon his retirement, with 802.

Held the National League record for relief games pitched upon his retirement, with 775.

Held the National League record for relief wins upon his retirement, with 92.

Holds the major league record for winning percentage in a season, at .947.

Holds the major league record for most wins in relief, with 18.

37th in most games pitched in major league history, with 848.

21st in most games finished in major league history, with 574.

51st in most saves in major league history, with 191.

18

SAM LEEVER

In 2005, ESPN.com generated an article proclaiming the greatest starting rotations in the history of the game. True to form, the list mostly included rotations from the last half of the 20th century. The top five went as follows:

1. 1998 Braves: Maddux, Glavine, Neagle, Millwood, and Smoltz
2. 1971 Orioles: Cuellar, Dobson, Palmer, and McNally
3. 1986 Mets: Darling, Gooden, Fernandez, Ojeda, and Aguilera
4. 1993 Braves: Maddux, Glavine, Avery, and Smoltz
5. 1966 Dodgers: Koufax, Drysdale, Osteen, and Sutton

While these were all great rotations, there was one in the second year of the 20th century that was comparable and should have been seriously considered when putting together this vaunted listing—that of the 1901 National League champion Pittsburgh Pirates. The group included Deacon Phillippe (22–12/2.22), Jack Chesbro (21–10/2.38), Jesse Tannehill (18–10/2.18), and a school teacher from Goshen, Ohio, nicknamed the "Goshen Schoolmaster" by the name of Sam Leever (14–5/2.86).

In his book *Whatever Happened to the Hall of Fame?* Bill James recognizes this group when looking into why certain players are in Cooperstown and some are not (his premise is that the player who had the big season seemingly always got the nod). Writes James,

The four pitchers who were the Pirates' rotation when they won the National League in 1901 ([Jack] Chesbro, [Jesse] Tannehill, Sam Leever, and Deacon Phillippe) all had extremely similar career records. Chesbro had probably the poorest career record of the four, Sam Leever the best, yet Chesbro is the only one who is in the Hall of Fame. Why? You all know the answer. He had the big year.[1]

Chesbro did have two big years, going 28–6 for Pittsburgh in 1902, still the Pirates record for wins in a season, and 41–12 with the New York Highlanders (Yankees) in 1904, a modern-day major league record for wins in a season. But Leever had the better career, with a 194–100 record and a 2.47 ERA, compared to Chesbro's 198–132/2.68 marks.

This is not to suggest that Sam Leever, who had a masterful curveball, should be inducted into the Hall of Fame, but he does deserve a closer look. While his record and stats are impressive, his rankings on Baseball-Reference.com's Hall of Fame index, meant to detail whether a player belongs in Cooperstown, puts Leever close to the ranking of a likely Hall of Fame player. In the Hall of Fame monitor, he has a rating of 97, with the likely Hall of Famer ranking being 100, and his Hall of Fame standard rating is 46, where the average Hall of Famer's rating is 50. Unfortunately, Sam was little more than an afterthought to the voters, garnering only 0.5 percent of the vote in 1937, his only year on the ballot.

Two things cost the right-hander more impressive stats that would have enhanced his Hall of Fame résumé: the fact that he didn't pitch in his first major league game until 1898, when he was 26 years old, and several arm injuries during the course of his 13-year career. Nonetheless, the Ohio native was an important part of the first great Pirate dynasty of the 20th century.

There is the story that the Bucs discovered Leever while playing a throwing game at his farm, one where two people play catch while throwing the ball over the roof of the barn. It was said that the schoolmaster curved his ball around the barn to his friend instead of throwing it over the top. Whether the story is fact or fiction, the Pirates signed the hurler, sending him to the minors, where he was 21–18, with a miniscule 1.05 ERA, for the Richmond Giants of the Atlantic League in 1897.

Leever played with Pittsburgh for a short time in 1898, winning his only decision in five games before heading back to Richmond, where he helped the Giants to a league championship. He returned to the big leagues a year later and won 21 games in his official rookie campaign in 1899, while leading the Senior Circuit in games pitched, with 51, and innings pitched, with 379, becoming a staple in the Pirates rotation.

The Bucs were a young, exciting team in the first decade of the 20th century, capturing the franchise's first pennant in 1901, a year where Sam led the circuit with a .737 winning percentage. By 1903, *Sporting News* was calling him one of the top pitchers in baseball, as he won what would be a career-high 25 contests, while again finishing at the top of the Senior Circuit in winning percentage, at .781, and adding his only ERA crown, ending with a 2.06 mark.

Things were going well for the team and their ace, with the Bucs winning their third-consecutive National League championship that season and earning a spot in the new postseason series that would become one of the greatest championships on the American sports calendar, the World Series.

The Pirates went into the initial Fall Classic as the prohibitive favorites against the upstart Boston Americans of the American League. After taking a 3–1 lead, the team fell apart, mainly because of injuries, one being a sore shoulder suffered by Leever in a trap-shooting contest in Charleroi before the series began. He was far from his normal self, giving up two runs, a homer, and three hits in his Game Two loss, and in Game Six, he surrendered six runs, four earned, to lose his second game in as many starts. The hurler complained about his shoulder after the contest, but according to author Frederick G. Lieb, "He gave a fair performance."[2]

Leever was accused by some of not giving his full effort in the series. Ralph Davis of *Sporting News* defended his honor, claiming the criticism was unfounded and that "there is not a more honest man in the game."[3] But it didn't matter who tried to protect his honor. The subpar series would go down as the low point of an otherwise fine career in the majors.

Sam managed to rebound, going 89–39, with a 2.20 ERA, in the five seasons following the World Series debacle. Possessing a dour personality at times, he offered to give away his potential World Series share for 10 cents in 1908, as he was distraught about the probability that the Bucs would not win the pennant (which they came close to securing, losing a chance to tie on the final day of the season).

Leever spent two more seasons in the majors, pitching mostly out of the bull pen, as he started only 12 of the 45 games he pitched. He went 14–6 but was not as effective, allowing 178 hits in 181 innings, more than the 8.2 hits per nine innings pitched that he allowed in the first 11 seasons of his career. While he was on the team in 1909, he did not get the opportunity for World Series redemption, failing to get a start in the Fall Classic.

After 39-year-old right-hander claimed he was insulted by the contract the Bucs sent him in 1911, Pirates president Barney Dreyfuss gave him his unconditional release. Sam pitched for the Minneapolis Millers of the American Association that season, going 7–4, before quitting the game for good. He retired, went back to teaching, and purchased a farm. He also remained a champion trap shooter, the sport that had caused the injury that perhaps cost the Pirates a world championship in 1903. Leever remained in Goshen until his death in 1953, at the age of 81, rarely talking about his career, a career that should have been more respected by those who decide who enters the Hall of Fame.

MOST MEMORABLE PERFORMANCE

After capturing two consecutive National League crowns in 1901 and 1902, the Pittsburgh Pirates came into the 1903 campaign looking to make it three. The effective starting rotation of Jesse Tannehill, Jack Chesbro, Deacon Phillippe, and Sam Leever had been cut in half, with Tannehill and Chesbro moving to the rival American League, but they were still good, with Ed Doheny turning out to be an ample replacement.

The staff set out to show that they were still successful when they reeled off six consecutive shutouts between June 2 and June 8. Leever, who would have the marquee season of his career in 1903, shut out the Giants in the second game of the streak, 5–0, and his impressive curveball was just about perfect for the sixth and final consecutive shutout, walking one and scattering eight hits in the 2–0 victory.

While Sam pitched well, the streak almost ended in the ninth inning, when Shad Barry and Kid Gleason singled, and both ended up in scoring position, with Barry being the first man to reach third on the hurler. With two out, Tully Sparks came up and hit a line drive that looked like it would drop in shallow left field for the hit that would tie the game. Honus Wagner was playing deep at short and leapt high in the air to snag the liner and win the game for the Bucs.

The gem proved to be one of a league-leading seven shutouts for Leever and was perhaps the most clutch performance of his banner season. For the team, the six consecutive shutouts and 56 consecutive innings without giving up a run remain major league records.

NOTABLE ACHIEVEMENTS (YEARLY LEADERS AND AWARDS ARE AS PIRATES ONLY)

Part of four National League championship teams (1901, 1902, 1903, 1909).

Part of one world championship team (1909).

Led the league in games pitched once (1899).

Led the league in games finished once (1899).

Led the league in winning percentage three times (1901, 1903, 1905).

Led the league in ERA once (1903).

Led the league in innings pitched once (1899).

Led the league in shutouts once (1903).

39th in lowest ERA in major league history, at 2.47.

17th in highest winning percentage in major league history, at .660.

51st in walks and hits per innings pitched in major league history, at 1.141.

51st in most shutouts in major league history, with 51.

31st in home runs per nine innings pitched, at .098.

Won 20 games on four occasions.

19

DEACON PHILLIPPE

There have been many World Series heroes in the history of the Pittsburgh Pirates—Babe Adams, Kiki Cuyler, Pie Traynor, Bill Mazeroski, Roberto Clemente, Steve Blass, and Willie Stargell, just to name a few. But prior to these six legendary figures achieving Fall Classic success there was a hurler who had such an impressive performance in the sport's first World Series in 1903, that no pitcher has ever bettered his feat. His name is Charles "Deacon" Phillippe.

Nicknamed Deacon in honor of the trouble-free life he led, Phillippe was the lone shining star in the Pirates' best-of-nine upset loss to the upstart Boston Americans. The Bucs lost the series in eight games after taking a commanding three-games-to-one lead, but it was Phillippe who led a tiring, injured staff, which included himself with a sore arm. The Deacon won Game One, Game Three, and Game Four, becoming the first pitcher to emerge victorious three times in a single Fall Classic.

In the 112 years that have passed since then, only Bill Dineen (who also won three games in 1903), Christy Mathewson, Babe Adams, Jack Coombs, Joe Wood, Red Faber, Stan Coveleski, Harry Brecheen, Lew Burdette, Bob Gibson, Mickey Lolich, and Randy Johnson have matched his totals—none have bettered him (Madison Bumgarner almost joined the 13 hurlers in 2014, after a heroic Game Seven performance in relief, for which he was originally given the win but later credited with a save).

Phillippe's feat is often forgotten when the story of the franchise is told, not only because the series took place more than a century ago, but also because the team lost. Remarkably, the hurler had two opportunities to set a record that could never be surpassed, with the chance for a fourth victory. Unfortunately, by the time the series was coming to an end in 1903, Phillippe was tiring from his incredible workload, and the arm that had been injured at the beginning of the series was getting worse. He lost the final two contests, 7–3 and 3–0.

While Deacon was a hero in the 1903 World Series especially when compared to teammate Sam Leever and his goat-like performance, he ironically had a career similar to Leever's. They both lived a fine and relatively trouble-free life, with major league careers that started later than most, lasting 13 years.

Born in 1872, in Rural Retreat, Virginia, where his family had lived for generations and had a spring named after them, Phillippe Springs, the right-hander began his professional baseball career in Mankato, Minnesota, before signing with the Fargo Divorcees of the Red River Valley League in 1897. He hooked on with the Minneapolis Milers in the Western League later that season, where he was an unspectacular 7–12.

Phillippe improved to 22–18 in 1898, before being taken by the Louisville Colonels of the National League in the 1898 Rule 5 Draft. He was impressive in his major league rookie campaign, winning 21 games, while tossing a no-hitter in his seventh big league contest against the New York Giants. In the off-season, the Senior Circuit decided to contract four teams, including Louisville, which prompted a trade of several future stars, including Honus Wagner, Fred Clarke, Tommy Leach, and Phillippe to the Pirates, where Colonels owner Barney Dreyfuss was now president.

The 28-year-old second-year hurler became the top pitcher for a strong and talented starting rotation in 1900. The infusion of talent from the Colonels took the Bucs from a below-average major league franchise to one of the most powerful in the league. The team finished in second place in 1900, for only the second time in franchise history, and found themselves playing the regular-season champion Brooklyn Superbas in a postseason series known as the Chronicle-Telegraph Cup. Despite the fact that Brooklyn defeated the Pirates in the best-of-five series, Phillippe won the first postseason contest in the history of the franchise, shutting out the Superbas, 10–0, in the third game.

The Virginia native was a model of consistency for Pittsburgh in his first four campaigns. His attention to detail, making sure he knew the tendencies of the batters he was facing, as well as his legendary control, which saw him finish his career with the 16th-lowest walks per nine innings rate in the history of the game (the best mark of any pitcher after the 20th century), were the keys to his success. He won more than 20 games in each season, including a career-high 25 in 1903, helping lead Pittsburgh to three straight National League pennants. The 1903 season was also a pivotal year in the history of the game, as the National and American leagues agreed to play in a postseason series that would be called the World Series. That was when Phillippe became a Pirates icon.

Playing at the Huntingdon Avenue Baseball Grounds in Boston, the Pirates and the Boston Americans met in the first contest in World Series history. With the Deacon on the hill, Pittsburgh broke out to a 7–0 lead after six innings, before winning the game, 7–3. The Americans won the second game, but manager Fred Clarke called on his ace in the third and fourth contests, and Deacon won both. In Game Four, Phillippe dazzled the American hitters, as the Bucs led 5–1 going into the last frame. Pitching three times in four games, the right-hander began to tire, allowing three runs in the ninth to make it close, but the team emerged victorious and the nation began to take notice of Phillippe's achievements. The *Pittsburgh Dispatch* proclaimed, "If any small boy from Maine to California were asked this morning to name the greatest pitcher in the world, he would most likely say Phillippe, though he could not spell the name."[1]

Of course, as stated earlier in the chapter, injuries caught up to the Bucs, and they dropped the final four games of the Fall Classic, including two by Deacon, who was exhausted and sore by that point. Despite the losses, Phillippe was still considered a hero. Following his legendary performance, he was playing on Honus Wagner's basketball team in the off-season and contracted an illness that spread to his eyes, putting him in the hospital. It limited Deacon to only 21 games in 1904, when he slumped to 10–10.

Rebounding in 1905, when he was a 20-game winner for the fifth and final time, Phillippe was 29–21 in the next two seasons, when a sore shoulder derailed the 36-year-old hurler's career. He pitched in a scant 27 contests in 1908 and 1909, including only 12 innings in 1908, when a broken finger also kept him off the mound.

Pitching in six scoreless innings in the 1909 World Series, Phillippe would have a short renaissance in 1910, with a 14–2 mark, mostly out of the pen, leading the Senior Circuit with an .875 winning percentage. He pitched in three ineffective games in 1911, retiring from the majors at that point.

Coming back for a short time in 1913, as a player-manager with Pittsburgh's entry in the Federal League, called the Filipinos by the press in honor of him, Deacon ended his career for good after the initial version of the league folded, with Pittsburgh sporting a 16–8 mark. He worked in various jobs in the Pittsburgh area following his retirement, passing away in Avalon at the age of 79.

MOST MEMORABLE PERFORMANCE

The most memorable moment for Deacon Phillippe is a memorable moment for the game in general. On October 1, 1903, in Boston, Phillippe was on the mound starting the first game in World Series history. Coming into the contest, he had won a career-high 25 games in leading the heavily favored Pittsburgh Pirates to their third consecutive National League championship. While he was tired and his arm sore, manager Fred Clarke called on his ace to start the historic contest.

Jimmy Sebring knocked in four runs and Tommy Leach had four hits as Pittsburgh raced to a decisive 7–0 lead after six innings of play. Phillippe was dominant, striking out 10, scattering six hits, and walking none in the complete game. Boston chipped away for three runs in the final three innings to at least make the final less embarrassing for the American League champs, but the late surge was not enough to deny Deacon his place in history as the first winning pitcher in the World Series.

NOTABLE ACHIEVEMENTS (YEARLY LEADERS AND AWARDS ARE AS PIRATES ONLY)

Part of four National League championship teams (1901, 1902, 1903, 1909).

Part of one world championship team (1909).

Led the league in winning percentage once (1910).

Led the league in walks and hits per innings pitched once (1903).

Led the league in walks per nine innings pitched five times (1902, 1903, 1905, 1906, 1907).

Led the league in strikeouts per walks four times (1902, 1903, 1904, 1906).

53rd in ERA in major league history, at 2.59.

44th in highest winning percentage in major league history, at .634.

23rd in WHIP in major league history, at 1.105.

16th in walks per nine innings pitched, at 1.253.

88th in home runs per nine innings in major league history, at .142.

143rd in most wins in major league history, with 189.

Allowed no home runs in 1905.

One of 13 pitchers to win three games in a single World Series.

Won the first World Series game in history, 7–3, over Boston in the first game of the 1903 World Series.

Won 20 games on five occasions.

20

HAZEN CUYLER

If not for Bill Mazeroski's historic blast in 1960, the greatest hit in franchise history would have come off the bat of Hazen "Kiki" Cuyler. With the Bucs battling back against the great Walter Johnson, Cuyler hit a controversial ground rule double in the eighth inning of Game Seven in the 1925 World Series to give the Pirates a 9–7 victory and the franchise's second world championship.
Photo courtesy of the Pittsburgh Pirates.

Three years in the majors is generally not long enough to put a player on a list of the top 50 players in the history of an esteemed team like the Pittsburgh Pirates, but in the case of Barry Bonds, Andrew Mc-Cutchen, and a right fielder from Harrisville, Michigan, by the name of Hazen (Kiki) Cuyler, who burst onto the major league scene in 1924, it was more than enough time to push these special players into the top 20.

While McCutchen and Bonds had spectacular three-year stretches, both were regulars for a few seasons before they hit their peak. Cuyler's peak was immediate and devastating to opponents of the Bucs. The other difference between the trio is that while Bonds and Mc-Cutchen helped lead their teams from the basement to playoff spots, neither really established themselves in the postseason; Cuyler not only helped Pittsburgh win a world championship, but also had what can be considered the second-greatest hit in franchise history. In short, despite the fact that he did not win a Most Valuable Player Award, he had arguably the best three-year span in the franchise history.

Table 20.1 is a comparison of the three-year peaks. Table 20.2 shows where the three ranked in the National League during the time period, including a score based on 10 points for first place down to one point for 10th when ranked versus one another.

Their rankings in the league during their peaks show that Cuyler was very competitive when talking about the greatest three-year run in team history. Unfortunately for Pirates fans in the 1920s, while they appeared to have one of the best players in the game, their manager, Donie Bush, made sure that they would only get to see him play in a Pirates uniform for a brief time.

Before his controversial exit, Cuyler was what in modern times would be called a five-tool prospect. The nickname Kiki has two possible origins: a charming story he told or a rather cruel taunt from

Table 20.1. The three-year peaks of Andrew McCutchen, Barry Bonds, and Kiki Cuyler.

Player	HR	RBI	AVE	2B	3B	SB	OPS
McCutchen (2012–2014)	77	263	.320	105	17	65	.939
Bonds (1990–1992)	92	333	.301	96	13	134	.990
Cuyler (1924–1926)	35	279	.343	101	57	108	.933

Table 20.2. **Table 20.2.** National League standings of Andrew McCutchen, Barry Bonds, and Kiki Cuyler during their respective time periods.

Player	HR	RBI	AVE	2B	3B	SB	OPS	Total Pts.
McCutchen (2012–2014)	5th	7th	1st	4th	9th	11th	3rd	37
Bonds (1990–1992)	1st	1st	9th	4th	18th	5th	1st	44
Cuyler (1924–1926)	9th	7th	4th	4th	1st	1st	4th	47

his teammates. To hear Cuyler tell the tale it was a shortened version of Cuy, Cuy, which is what the shortstop and second baseman would scream when he went after a fly ball. The other, not so nice version is that it was to mock him when he said his name, since Cuyler had a bad speech impediment.

No matter what the reasoning for his legendary nickname, Kiki was one of the most complete ballplayers of his time. Fast on the bases, as well as chasing balls in the outfield. He mixed a cannon arm with impressive hitting skills, making him one of the best on the diamond in the mid-1920s and 1930s.

The 1926 *Reach Guide* states,

> Outfielder Hazen Cuyler is another two-year man, but already one of the greatest players of the day. Cuyler can do everything—hit, throw, cover the ground, and run bases. He is the best batter among the Pirates, near the top of the National League hitting list, leads the league in runs scored, and is right among the leaders in stolen bases.[1]

Kiki signed with the Bay City Wolves in the Michigan-Ontario League in 1920, and had a subpar season his first year before hitting .317 in 1921. Ty Cobb, who was a player-manager with the Tigers that year, was interested in signing him, but there was a scouting report that said Cuyler had trouble hitting curveballs, so Cobb was told not to go after him. In came the Pirates, who inked him for $2,500.

The outfielder improved with Charleston and Nashville but was unimpressive in short trials with the Bucs between 1921 and 1923, hitting .233 in only 43 at bats. After a .340 performance with the

Nashville Volunteers in 1923, Cuyler spent most of the 1924 campaign as the starting left fielder for Pittsburgh. His official rookie campaign was spectacular, with a .354 average, good enough for fourth in the league, while he knocked in 85 runs in only 117 games, arguably the best rookie season in Pirates history.

In 1925, his play continued to improve, while helping lead the team to their fifth National League pennant. He led the circuit with 144 runs and 26 doubles. Kiki was fourth in the National League with a career-high .357 average, while knocking in 100 runs for the first time, with 102. He finished second in the MVP race to Rogers Hornsby.

Hitting only .269 in his first trip to the World Series, Cuyler saved his best for last with a hit that stands as one of the greatest in franchise history, next to Bill Mazeroski's home run in 1960. With the score tied at seven in the bottom of the eighth of the seventh game versus Washington, the bases were loaded as Kiki came to the plate against the legendary Walter Johnson. In the driving rain, Cuyler belted a hard line-drive foul, before ripping a Johnson offering down the right-field line in a darkening Forbes Field. Not seeing where it went, the Bucs thought it was a grand slam, but the umpires ruled that it was stuck in the Washington bull pen and instead called it a ground rule double, plating only two runs. Regardless, it was enough to give Pittsburgh a 9–7 win and a world championship; Cuyler was a hero.

He held out for more money following his remarkable campaign, angering Pirates owner Barney Dreyfuss. Kiki eventually signed and had another phenomenal year in 1926, leading the National League in runs and stolen bases, while hitting .321. Unfortunately for the star player the Pirates hired Donie Bush to run the club in 1927. Bush was a tough disciplined leader and did not get along with Cuyler. The Michigan native tore ligaments in his ankle while sliding into third, and when he returned to the lineup, he was moved from center to right field and shifted from third to fifth and second in the batting order. After failing to slide into second on a force play against the Giants on August 6, he was fined before eventually being benched. Dreyfuss, perhaps remembering Cuyler's holdout, was in favor of the benching, and, to the fans' dismay, he traded Kiki to the Cubs after the season for Sparky Adams and Pete Scott, one of the worst deals in franchise history.

CHAPTER 20

Cuyler went on to greatness with the Cubs, playing in two more World Series, while Adams and Scott had nondescript Pittsburgh careers. Sadly, Kiki died of a heart attack in 1950, at just 51 years of age, but 18 years later was given baseball's ultimate honor, as he was elected into the Baseball Hall of Fame by the Veteran's Committee. It was a much-deserved honor that came in part because of his phenomenal three-year run with the Pirates.

MOST MEMORABLE PERFORMANCE

Kiki Cuyler's greatest moment in a Pirates uniform came on the biggest stage in the game—a seventh and deciding contest in the 1925 World Series. After capturing their sixth National League crown, the Pirates fell behind Washington three games to one. They battled back, capturing Game Five and Game Six, and forcing a seventh and deciding game at Forbes Field against one of the greatest pitchers the game has ever known in Walter Johnson.

In the driving rain and darkening skies in Pittsburgh, the Bucs came back twice from 4–0 and 6–3 deficits to tie the score at seven in the bottom of the eighth. With two out and the bases loaded, Cuyler came up to bat, looking to etch his name in Pirates history. He had already doubled once in the contest, knocking in Max Carey to cut the three-run Washington lead to two in the fifth. He again battled Johnson, fouling off several pitches with hard liners. Kiki finally caught one, ripping it into fair ground down the right-field line. While it was eventually ruled a ground rule double, in spite of the Pirates bench arguing that it should have been a grand slam (although Washington Hall of Famer Goose Goslin always claimed it was foul by two feet), the Bucs scored two runs, winning the title with a dramatic 9–7 victory.

NOTABLE ACHIEVEMENTS (YEARLY LEADERS AND AWARDS ARE AS PIRATES ONLY)

Elected to the Baseball Hall of Fame by the Veteran's Committee in 1968.
Part of two world championship team (1925)

Finished in the top 10 voting for the National League MVP twice.

Finished in the top 10 for the National League batting title twice.

Led the league in runs scored twice (1925, 1926).

Led the league in triples once (1926).

Led the league in stolen bases once (1926).

Led the league in hit by pitch once (1925).

Led the league in putouts for a right fielder once (1925).

Eclipsed 200 hits in a season once.

Eclipsed 100 RBIs in a season once.

47th in highest batting average in major league history, with .321.

45th in most triples in major league history, with 157.

21st in most double plays by a right fielder in major league history, with 31.

49th in most double plays by an outfielder in major league history, with 44.

67th in most putouts by an outfielder in major league history, with 4,034.

61st in most assists by an outfielder in major league history, with 191.

21

RAY KREMER

Ray Kremer's dream of a major league career would be delayed, but after making his debut at age 31 for the Pirates, he made the most of it, winning 143 games in 10 seasons in Pittsburgh and becoming a 20-game winner on two occasions.

Photo courtesy of the Pittsburgh Pirates.

For most major league stars, the journey to baseball greatness begins at a young age, their early to mid-20s. The longer they stay in the minors, the less likely they are to find success in the big leagues. For Pittsburgh Pirates pitcher Ray "Remy" Kremer, as he toiled in the Pacific Coast League into his 30s, it was becoming apparent that his baseball dreams were not going to come to fruition—that is, until Pirates president Barney Dreyfuss took a gamble on the 31-year-old hurler—and the results were amazing, as he helped lead the franchise to their second world championship.

There have been several men in the history of the sport who may have started later than Kremer, including such Negro League veterans as Satchel Paige, Quincy Trouppe, Pat Scantlebury, Bob Thurman, and Buzz Clarkson, all of whom got a late entry due to the fact that African Americans were not permitted in the majors until Jackie Robinson broke the color barrier in 1947. There was also Jim Morris, whose tale of making the majors at an advanced age is celebrated in the Disney movie *The Rookie*, as well as Les "Wimpy" Willis, Leon Riley, Billy Williams (not the more famed one with the Cubs), Otho Nitcholas, the Pirates' Diomedes Olivo, and Chuck Hostetler, who was 38 when he took his first major league at bat. All had interesting stories, but none had the impact that Kremer had during his time with the Bucs.

Born in Oakland, California, in 1893, Remy started his professional baseball career at an early age, 21, when he signed with the Sacramento/Mission Wolves of the PCL in 1914. He was no match for the more experienced hitters, with a 2–8 mark and 5.20 ERA. When the Wolves disbanded, he ended up in Vancouver, playing for the Beavers of the Northwestern League, where he showed enough improvement that the New York Giants signed him to a contract before the 1916 campaign.

A case of rheumatism caused Kremer severe joint paint, derailing his major league quest, but he soon recovered and began to pitch well again with Rochester in the International League, until the symptoms returned and he was released by the Giants. Depressed, the hurler was traveling back to his hometown when he was hospitalized in Altoona for what was described as a nervous breakdown.

CHAPTER 21

Once Remy returned home, he resurrected his career with the Oakland Oaks in the circuit where he began, the PCL. In Oakland, the 24-year-old right-hander began to pitch successfully for the Oaks, despite the fact that they were one of the worst teams in the league. He was 42–74 between 1917 and 1920 but pitched much better than his record indicated. In 1919, he was the ace of the pitching staff, having perhaps his finest season in the minors. Winning double digits for the first time, Kremer emerged victorious 15 times, allowing only 233 hits in 298 innings, while walking 88, for an impressive 1.077 walks and hits per innings pitched.

Kremer had an effective fastball, which he combined with a curve and screwball to fluster hitters in the PCL. He continued to be effective in 1921, when the hometown hero had his first winning mark since his second season in Vancouver during the 1915 campaign. It was the beginning of a three-year run that saw him go from a career minor leaguer to a serious major league prospect once again. Winning more than 20 games in each of the next two seasons as he was entering his 30s, his long-awaited dream seemed to finally become a reality when the Pirates signed him in December 1923.

While he was about to achieve his goal, the moundsman balked at the transaction, thinking he should have received a percentage of the fee the Bucs paid to Oakland for his services. Once Dreyfuss negotiated a compromise, he had his 31-year-old pitcher. It was a controversial move, as Dreyfuss and manager Bill McKechnie were being criticizing for adding the older minor league vet to the rotation. Fans didn't grasp how successful Kremer would be, but those who knew were confident the Bucs were getting an ace. In his book on the Pirates, famed writer Frederick G. Lieb states, "It's still a mystery how scouts overlooked Kremer so long."[1]

Those who had overlooked him would soon take notice. His rookie campaign in 1924 was amazing. He led the circuit with 41 games pitched and four shutouts, while going 18–10, the best record in his professional career to that point. It was the beginning of Kremer's ascension as one of the premier pitchers in the National League.

A year later, Remy struggled a bit but was still effective, winning 17 contests during the Bucs' 1925 world championship season. It was in the World Series that he really proved to be the ace of the Pirates staff.

After losing to Washington in the third game, 4–3, Kremer allowed two runs in the first two innings of Game Six with the season on the line. He threw a shutout against the Senators the rest of the game, as the Bucs battled back for a 3–2 victory.

Two days later, the two teams squared off at Forbes Field for the seventh and deciding contest. As a heavy rain fell in Pittsburgh, the Pirates were behind Washington, 6–3, and the game was entering the fifth inning. Manager Bill McKechnie called on Kremer to see if he could stem the tide; the hurler did that and more, limiting the powerful Senator lineup to only one more run, as Pittsburgh battled back for an exciting 9–7 victory.

A major league career that only two seasons prior had seemed unattainable was now more successful than Remy ever could have imagined. During the next five seasons, he was among the best pitchers in the game, with a spectacular 92–49 record, leading the National League twice in victories and ERA.

While he won 20 games in 1930, Kremer's ERA ballooned to 5.02; it would be the beginning of the decline in his career in the majors. Poor run support limited him to only 11 victories in 1931, and by 1932, at 39 years of age, the right-hander had only started in 10 games. A year later, he was ineffective in seven contests in relief, with a 10.35 ERA and 2.250 WHIP, and released by Pittsburgh.

Not ready to give up as a professional ballplayer, the 40-year-old pitcher returned to the Oakland Oaks, where it quickly became apparent that he was done, posting a combined 1–6 record and 7.26 ERA in 1933 and 1934, and finally retiring from professional baseball for good. Following his retirement, Kremer stayed in the Bay Area and became a postal carrier, passing away in 1965, at 71 years of age. Winner of 258 contests in his 21-year career in the minor and major leagues, he was a great example of what one can accomplish by staying focused on your dreams.

MOST MEMORABLE PERFORMANCE

Down three games to two in the 1925 World Series against the Washington Senators, the season was on the line as Pittsburgh took the field for Game Six at Forbes Field. Manager Bill McKechnie was looking to 32-year-old hurler Ray Kremer to keep the season going.

Kremer had lost the third contest, 4–3, and things looked dire early in the matchup after he allowed a first-inning home run to Goose Goslin and another run an inning later, when Roger Peckinpaugh doubled, scoring Oscar Bluege to give Washington a 2–0 advantage.

The right-hander was invincible following the second inning, limiting the Senators to only three hits and a walk in the final seven frames. The offense finally came around in the third, tying the game on a fielder's choice by Clyde Barnhart and a single off the bat of Pie Traynor. The Bucs went ahead two innings later on Eddie Moore's leadoff homer. With Kremer dominating, the 3–2 score held, forcing a seventh game.

The Oakland native also played an important role in the next contest, with his team down by three, coming on in relief in the fifth and once again silencing Washington, picking up his second win in three days as Pittsburgh captured the world championship.

NOTABLE ACHIEVEMENTS (YEARLY LEADERS AND AWARDS ARE AS PIRATES ONLY)

Part of two National League championship teams (1925, 1927).
Part of one world championship team (1925).
Finished in the top 10 voting for the National League Most Valuable Player Award twice.
Led the league in ERA twice (1926, 1927).
Led the league in wins twice (1926, 1930).
Led the league in winning percentage once (1926).
Led the league in games pitched once (1924).
Led the league in shutouts once (1924).
Led the league in fielding percentage for a pitcher twice (1925, 1929).
Eclipsed 20 wins twice.
Won Game Six and Game Seven in the 1925 World Series.
58th in highest winning percentage in major league history, at .627.

22

VERN LAW

Dick Groat may have been named the MVP in 1960, but make no mistake, there may have been no more important player to the 1960 world champions than Vern Law. A deacon in the Mormon Church, Law, who won 162 games in his Pirates career, was 20–9 that season, becoming the first player in franchise history to win the Cy Young Award.

Photo courtesy of the Pittsburgh Pirates.

To raise a world championship trophy at the end of a campaign it takes every member of a 25-man roster and then some. While it is impossible to go through the entire season without team-wide contributions, there is usually one player who, more so than the rest, is the key factor in keeping the club on its path to greatness. In 1960, Dick Groat won the Most Valuable Player Award, third baseman Don Hoak came in second in the voting, and Roberto Clemente was eighth. As good as each of these players were, there was one other man who had arguably the greatest season of any Pirates pitcher since the 1920s: Vern Law.

Law won 20 games, with a 3.08 ERA and a league-leading 18 complete games, to capture the Cy Young Award, but it was his performance when the team needed him most—to end a losing streak—that is the most memorable moment of his magnificent campaign. Twelve of Law's 29 decisions came after losses, and he was spectacular in those games. The results of those contests appear in table 22.1.

After the team suffered a loss, Vern won 9, lost 3, allowed 23 earned runs, pitched 94 $^2/_3$ innings, threw 8 complete games, and compiled a 2.19 ERA. For the remaining games, he won 11, lost 6, allowed

Table 22.1. Game data, April 14 through September 18.

Game	IP	ER	Score	Opp.	Result	Notes
April 14	9	0	13–0	CIN	W	
April 20	9	1	4–2	PHI	W	
May 10	9	2	3–2	LAD	W	Team lost six of previous seven
June 7	1 $^2/_3$	1	2–13	CHC	L	Gave up five unearned runs
June 12	9	3	15–3	STL	W	Team lost five of previous seven
June 21	8	2	3–2	STL	W	
June 26	8	4	5–7	CHC	L	
July 21	9	1	4–1	LAD	W	Team lost five of previous seven
August 2	9	0	3–0	LAD	W	
August 29	9	2	10–2	LAD	W	Team previously lost four in a row
September 14	5	4	2–5	LAD	L	
September 18	9	3	5–3	CIN	W	

70 earned runs, pitched 177 innings, threw 10 complete games, and compiled a 3.56 ERA.

These statistics clearly show Law's net worth to the Bucs in their championship run. When the team was down and needed a clutch start to help them, Vern was the guy they counted on, showing that despite the great performances by some of the other players, he was arguably the most important man on the team.

But before he made it to that point, Law was a young hurler out of Meridian High School in Meridian, Idaho. The advantage of having a Hollywood superstar as a part-owner came into play when the Pirates were attempting to sign the pitcher. Future Idaho senator Herman Welker had gone to the Law household to try to convince Vernon, who was nicknamed Deacon due to the fact he had become a deacon and an elder in the Mormon Church by the time he was 19, to sign a deal with Pittsburgh. Not long after he got to the house, his classmate at Gonzaga University, Bing Crosby, called Law's mother, which sealed the deal.

Beginning his professional baseball career with the Santa Rosa Pirates in the Far West League in 1948, Deacon didn't have the greatest record in the three seasons he spent in the Bucs' farm system, with a combined 19–20 mark, but his ERA was spectacular the final two years, at 2.84. He struggled with his control, walking 211, but the Bucs, desperate for starting pitching, called him up in 1950. He made his debut against Philadelphia on June 11, surrendering five runs in a complete-game loss and had a decent rookie campaign, with a 7–9 record for the moribund Pirates.

New Pirates general manager Branch Rickey felt Law could be a fine major leaguer; he just wasn't sure where he would play. Said Rickey, "Law . . . has a chance for the outfield. He is highly intelligent, a good athlete, a good runner, and very adventurous. Could easily be the best base runner in the Pittsburgh organization. He has never had an opportunity of hitting very much, for he has always been a pitcher."[1] Luckily for Pittsburgh baseball fans, Rickey's normally astute judge of talent was incorrect.

Winning six more the next season, Law enlisted in the U.S. Army in 1951, where he played ball during the Korean War for the base in Fort Eustis, Virginia. He was out of the majors for two seasons, returning in 1954, when he once again struggled. Deacon finally gained some confidence a year later and became a quality starter for the Bucs, with a 42–46 record during the four-year period between 1955 and 1958, with a much improved 3.77 ERA.

In his seven-year major league career to that point, Vern was a promising pitcher who looked like he could be an effective starter in the middle of the rotation. In 1959, he was one of the few bright points in an otherwise disappointing season, winning 18 contests in an 18–9 campaign.

During the off-season, Law trained hard, running as many as six miles a day, and it paid off with his lone 20-win campaign. With magnificent pitching in the clutch, he was not only selected to pitch in his only All-Star Game, but also became the first Pirate to win the Cy Young Award, while finishing sixth in the MVP race, behind teammates Dick Groat and Don Hoak.

It was an amazing year, as the Bucs captured their seventh National League pennant. During the celebration, Law hurt his ankle when his shoe was aggressively pulled off to be used as a champagne glass. While his foot needed rest, he nonetheless played in the World Series, pitching effectively and winning two contests, while leaving the seventh and final game with a 4–2 lead in the top of the sixth.

Deacon was angry Murtaugh took him out, commenting in an interview,

> The toughest moment was being taken out of the seventh game of the World Series, as I had a 4–2 lead going into the sixth and was in pretty good control of the game. I had pitched on a bad ankle (in the series), and I guess Murtaugh had enough faith in our bull pen. We managed to win through some great hitting, and I guess if Murtaugh hadn't taken me out of the game, we wouldn't have had that dramatic finish and just maybe Maz wouldn't have had the chance to hit in the ninth . . . and might not have made the Hall of Fame, as that home run really jumpstarted his election.[2]

Aside from helping Bill Mazeroski, Law's ankle was hurting, and it was probably best that he was taken out of the contest. Unfortunately, pitching on the ankle caused him to alter his delivery, which led to torn muscles in his shoulder, minimizing his contributions throughout the next three seasons. It looked as if his career was all but over in 1963.

Surprisingly, instead of retiring, the injury healed in 1964, and Vern was practically his old self, winning 12 games. A year later, he lost his first five decisions, before winning 17 of his final 21. The Idaho native had perhaps his best campaign statistically, with a career-low 2.15 ERA, capturing the National League's Comeback Player of the Year Award. He pitched well again in 1966, with a 12–8 mark, but a year later the 37-year-old right-hander hurt his groin and was ineffective, winning only twice in eight decisions. At that point, Law retired for good, with 162 career wins, while being remembered for being a crucial part of a memorable world championship win.

MOST MEMORABLE PERFORMANCE

As great as Vern Law performed in 1959 and 1960, the injured ankle he suffered celebrating in 1960, which in turn led to his arm injury, left the right-hander seemingly at the end of his career. But he believed he could come back, and in 1965, his optimism paid off, when he once again found his form, turning out a spectacular 17–9 campaign and a 2.15 ERA.

In that remarkable comeback season, Deacon produced perhaps the most spectacular start of his 16-year major league career on June 5, tossing a two-hit shutout against the New York Mets. Catcher Jim Pagliaroni and Willie Stargell gave him all the offense he needed, as Stargell had four hits and four runs batted in and Pagliaroni chipped in with a three-run homer in the 9–0 onslaught. Vern was unhittable, surrendering only a single to Bobby Klaus to lead off the game and one to Ed Kranepool in the fourth. He walked only one, Joe Christopher, who got a free pass before Kranepool's hit for the Mets' only true threat of the day. Retiring the last 15 Mets in order, the hurler put an exclamation point on a superb season.

NOTABLE ACHIEVEMENTS (YEARLY LEADERS AND AWARDS ARE AS PIRATES ONLY)

Part of one National League championship and world championship team (1960).

Won the 1960 Cy Young Award.

Won the 1965 Lou Gehrig Award.

Played in two All-Star Games.

Finished in the top 20 voting for the National League MVP on three occasions.

Led the league in complete games once (1960).

Led the league in putouts as a pitcher once (1965).

Led the league in fielding percentage for a pitcher three times (1956, 1958, 1966).

Eclipsed 20 wins once.

Won two games in the 1960 World Series.

97th in walks per nine innings in major league history, at 2.011.

87th in most putouts by a pitcher in major league history, with 212.

23

BOB FRIEND

Bob Friend demonstrated why a win–loss record is not the best way to show the effectiveness of a pitcher. While he won 197 games in his career, he had a losing record, with 230 losses; however, this in no way detracts from the fact that he is one of the greatest Pirates pitchers of all-time. He won 22 games in 1958 and captured the league's ERA title in 1955, while pitching for a last-place team.

Photo courtesy of the Pittsburgh Pirates.

Wins and losses. It used to be the mark on which all pitchers were judged. In today's game it is considered by most experts to be one of the last statistics to look at when rating a pitcher. One need only look at former Phillies and Pirates pitcher Hugh Mulcahy to see a prime example of this. Mulcahy had the misfortunate of pitching on some of the worst teams in baseball history in Philadelphia, and because of this he would often come up on the wrong end of win–loss ledger, to the tune of a 45–89 mark, the worst losing percentage of any pitcher with at least 100 decisions. He lost so much that writers dubbed him LP, for losing pitcher, since it appeared next to his name so many times in the box score. It was a misnomer, however, as Mulcahy was a good pitcher, a fact that the experts fully recognized, as evidenced by an All-Star berth and votes for National League Most Valuable Player Award on two occasions, with both coming in seasons where he lost more than 20 games.

The Pittsburgh Pirates had such a pitcher, one who proved just how unreliable a win–loss record is in judging the worth of a moundsman, the only pitcher to lose 200 games and not win at least 200. Yet, despite the fact he did not have a stellar career record, he is celebrated as one of the best pitchers in franchise history, and rightfully so. His name is Bob Friend.

A fine website called On Deck Circle rates the all-time best pitchers with losing records. To be included on this list, pitchers must have at least 100 wins, 1,500 innings pitched, 200 career starts, and an ERA under 4.00. With these restrictions in place, the listing includes such impressive pitchers as Pat Dobson (an important part of the memorable 1971 Baltimore Orioles starting rotation), Mark Gubicza, Bill Singer, Jon Matlack (who gave up Roberto Clemente's 3,000 hit), Randy Jones (winner of a Cy Young Award), Zane Smith, Woody Fryman, Jim Barr, and Jim Rooker, just to name a few.

Looking at the parameters, for example, wins above replacement and such Baseball-Reference.com ratings as the black ink test, the site chose the best three losing pitchers of all-time. Mark Gubicza and Tom Candiotti tied for third place, Jon Matlack came in second, and Bob Friend placed first.

In looking at the analysis, it seems as if Friend is far and away the best hurler in baseball history with a losing record. He was a great

150   **CHAPTER 23**

pitcher who just happened to have the hard luck of playing with teams who were awful, which is exactly what he did for the first seven years of his major league career.

Born in Lafayette, Indiana, where he was a star halfback on the West Lafayette High School football team, as well as a star pitcher for their baseball squad, Friend was dubbed "Warrior," a nickname he garnered because of his toughness on the gridiron and a moniker that would stick with him throughout the years. While he had a dream of playing both sports at Purdue University, a shoulder injury ended his football career. There was one more factor that rendered his two-sport dream secondary: He signed a contract with the Pittsburgh Pirates in 1949.

In the 1950s, the Pirates were in the middle of one of their worst decades in the history of the franchise, and after a short stint in the minors with the Waco Pirates and Indianapolis Indians, where he went a combined 14–13 in 1950, with a 3.62 ERA, the Warrior was thrust into the melee, beginning his major league career in 1951.

When Friend made the club in 1951, he was only 20 years old, and the combination of youth and playing for a poor team made for a predictable outcome. In his first four seasons, he was 28–50, with a 4.61 ERA, respectable for the time period. The Pirates teams he played on were a combined 209–407/.339. Thus, his personal .359 winning percentage was at least above the team average. While the Bucs continued to lose in 1955, the days where the Indiana native's winning percentage would be similar to that of the team were over.

Pittsburgh finished in last place that year, but Bob had a breakout campaign, with a 14–9 record on a team that was 60–94 (46–85 without him), becoming the first player in major league history to capture the ERA crown while pitching for a last-place team. The Warrior's arsenal was led by an incredible sinker, to go along with his effective curve and off-speed pitch, but it was the work the coaching staff did with him in the off-season that really helped him succeed during the campaign. Said Friend,

At the end of the 1954 season, Fred Haney, Bill Posedel, and other coaches got together with me and altered my pitching windup so I could hide the ball a little better. That gave me a real good breaking ball. The batters had a tough time picking up the pitches from me because of the new windup.[1]

His newfound windup brought him consistent success as one of the best hurlers in the league, leading the circuit in games pitched for three consecutive seasons between 1956 and 1958, and innings pitched in 1956 and 1957. In the 1958 campaign, Friend did something that he had never done before and would never accomplish again: win 20 games in a season. He was the National League leader that year, with 22, as the Bucs finally turned things around with a surprising second-place finish. Bob finished third in the Cy Young race, behind Bob Turley and Warren Spahn, and sixth in the MVP vote.

The Bucs slumped a bit in 1959, as Friend faltered considerably, having arguably the worst season in his professional career. He won only eight games, while losing a career-high 19. Reflecting on his performance, the Warrior said, "I came to camp in lousy shape. I tried to take off too much weight. I was weak and my legs were weak. It was my fault. I felt bad about it, and I suffered for it. I was fortunate that Murtaugh stayed with me."[2]

Luckily for the team, Murtaugh did. The Indiana native rebounded nicely in 1960, forming a devastating one-two punch with Vern Law, as he had 18 wins and captured United Press International's Comeback Player of the Year Award. After 10 seasons with the team, Friend finally got to play in a World Series that season. While Law pitched effectively despite an ankle injury, the Warrior had a Fall Classic to forget, losing twice while registering an astronomical 13.50 ERA. Despite his poor outings, the team still won, and Friend was able to raise a World Series trophy for the only time in his career.

The right-hander went on to be a dependable starter for the club in the next four seasons, with a 3.12 ERA, but his record again dropped to below .500 during the time period (62–67), due in part to the team becoming surprisingly mediocre after their World Series victory.

In 1965, Friend stumbled, with an 8–12 mark, and while he didn't pitch poorly, he knew that his career was coming to an end. He said, "I didn't have the strikeouts, and my overall stuff was down. My control was pretty good and my ERA was good that year, but I wasn't effective. . . . Maybe the toll of pitching all those innings caught up, but I did not have any arm trouble."[3]

CHAPTER 23

Bob never had arm trouble during his career, never spending time on the disabled list in the majors, but his time with the Bucs had come to an end. He was traded to the Yankees in the off-season for Pete Mikklesen, before being sold to the Mets in the middle of the 1966 campaign, where he retired after the season ended. Friend lived in Pittsburgh following his retirement, where he remains today.

His final record was 197–230, with a fine 3.58 ERA. While losing records do not equal Hall of Fame consideration, as only four pitchers in Cooperstown have losing records (Rollie Fingers and Bruce Sutter [who, as relievers, are in for their impressive save totals more so than their win–loss records], Satchel Paige [who had an abbreviated major league career and is enshrined for his spectacular career in the Negro Leagues], and Hank O'Day [who, while he was a pitcher in the majors, is included in the Hall as an umpire]), they should not define the worth of a pitcher's career. In the case of Robert Friend, other than the fact it's an answer to a trivia question, his record certainly did not.

MOST MEMORABLE PERFORMANCE

The 1955 campaign was a special one for 24-year-old right-hander Bob Friend. It was his breakout year, during which time he was 14–9, becoming the first player with a last-place team to win the ERA title. It was during that season that he pitched what could be considered his greatest game, on September 7, against the Chicago Cubs.

Only 3,076 fans showed up at Wrigley Field for the late-season game between the two second division clubs. Helping himself with a RBI single, Friend only received two runs in support of his effort, but it didn't matter, as he struck out eight, allowing no walks and a lone fourth-inning single by left fielder Frank Baumholtz, keeping him from a perfect game and a date with history. It was an incredible performance that showed the league that he was going to be one of the best in the Senior Circuit.

NOTABLE ACHIEVEMENTS (YEARLY LEADERS AND AWARDS ARE AS PIRATES ONLY)

Part of one National League championship and world championship team (1960).

Won the 1960 UPI Comeback Player of the Year Award.

Played in four All-Star Games.

Finished in the top 20 voting for the National League MVP on three occasions.

Finished third in the 1958 Cy Young Award voting.

Led the league in ERA once (1955).

Led the league in wins once (1958).

Led the league in walks per nine innings once (1963).

Led the league in innings pitched twice (1956, 1957).

Led the league in games started three times (1956, 1957, 1958).

Led the league in shutouts once (1962).

Eclipsed 20 wins once.

61st in walks per nine innings in major league history, at 2.011.

64th in most putouts in major league history, with 228.

63rd in most shutouts in major league history, with 36.

47th in most games started in major league history, with 497.

24

ANDY VAN SLYKE

According to History.com, April Fools' Day, which was popularized in 1700, may date back to as early as 1582. Since then there have been many classic April Fools' hoaxes, for instance, the BBC broadcasting the Swiss harvesting spaghetti from a tree in 1957 or the Swedish national channel's 1962 broadcast that if you put nylons in front of a black-and-white television you could turn it into a color TV. In Pirates history, on April 1, 1987, many Bucs fans thought their local news was playing the ultimate April Fools' joke on them when they announced that general manager Syd Thrift had traded the extremely popular catcher Tony Pena to St. Louis for a group of players that included Mike Dunne, Mike LaValliere, and a center fielder by the name of Andy Van Slyke.

Unfortunately at that point, but fortunately in the long run, it was no April Fools' joke. The move angered much of Pirates nation; after all, it was a group of players that wasn't on the same level as Pena, who was not only the best player on the Pittsburgh roster, but also one of the top catchers in the game. As it turned out, the rest of the National League Eastern Division had wished it was a joke, with Thrift adding two important pieces for the soon-to-be three-time division champions, the most essential being Van Slyke, who was arguably the greatest defensive center fielder in franchise history.

While the Gold Glove Award had only been given for the first time in 1957, it would be tough for any of the previous Pirates center fielders to lay claim to the honors given to the former Cardinal. Van Slyke spent eight seasons in a Pittsburgh uniform, the last two being stifled by injuries, and was given the award as the National League's best defensive center fielder on five consecutive occasions between 1988 and 1992. Thrift said Van Slyke "was able to read the ball on a dead run and make some great plays on shots hit to the alleys. He's always had an outstanding arm."[1]

To show even further how impressive he was, only two other Pirates won more Gold Gloves than Van Slyke: Roberto Clemente with 12 and the man who is widely considered the greatest defensive second baseman in the history of the game, Bill Mazeroski, with nine. His five are more than such defensive luminaries as Barry Bonds, Dave Parker, and Pena, the man he was traded for, all of whom won three apiece.

What made the Utica, New York, native even more impressive was that he wasn't just a defensive player, he was also an offensive threat. He could hit for power, as well as average, and was a threat on the base paths; the all-around player St. Louis had hoped he would be when they drafted him with the sixth overall pick in the 1979 Amateur Draft.

The center fielder struggled his first two seasons in the Cardinal organization, before showing the talent they had envisioned in his last two, including a .368 average at Louisville in 54 games in 1983, before being called up to St. Louis, where he debuted on June 17. Van Slyke showed glimpses of potential with the Cards, hitting .259 in four seasons with 41 homers, but the opportunity to land Pena instead of hoping the 25-year-old would somehow live up to his potential was too tempting.

After several years of subpar baseball, Pittsburgh was rebuilding, with a new regime that included a minor league manager by the name of Jim Leyland and Thrift, and the trade with the Cardinals brought them players who immediately improved the club. Van Slyke had his best season of his young career his first year with the Bucs, hitting .293, with 21 homers and 34 stolen bases.

A year later, in 1988, the Utica native showed St. Louis, as well as the entire baseball world, that 1987 had been no fluke, not only becoming one of the best players on the Pirates, but also the majors. Andy eclipsed just about every career high in his short major league career to that point with 25 home runs; 100 RBIs, including at least one in 11 consecutive games, one short of Paul Waner's team record; and a league-leading 15 triples, the most for the Bucs since 1944, when

Johnny Barrett had 19 and Bob Elliott had 16. He was awarded the Silver Slugger Award and his first Gold Glove, and named the *Sporting News* Player of the Year for the National League.

Van Slyke slipped in 1989, being sidelined for part of the season with a strained muscle in his rib cage, but he rebounded the next two seasons with a combined .274 average, helping lead Pittsburgh to their first division titles since they had won the World Series in 1979. While he had regular-season success, Andy was the polar opposite during the postseason. After hitting .091 in his first venture with St. Louis in 1985, he would do no better in 1990 and 1991, with a subpar .184 average.

He had his chance to be a hero in the ninth inning of the sixth game of the 1991 National League Championship Series. With the Pirates needing a win to go to the World Series, they were down 1–0, with two out and Gary Varsho on third. Van Slyke ripped an Alejandro Pena offering down the right-field line that looked like it had a chance for a home run, but it curved foul. He then struck out, ending the game and what would turn out to be the Pirates' best chance at the pennant.Van Slyke had an incredible year in 1992, with a career-high .324 average, leading the National League in hits, with 199, and doubles, with 45. Management controversially decided to sign their star center fielder instead of investing money in two-time Most Valuable Player Barry Bonds, prompting critics to claim that they had done so because of race. This is not to say that Bonds would have signed with the team, but had they been able to ink him instead of their center fielder, they may not have endured 20 consecutive losing seasons, which began in 1993.

Van Slyke had a fine start in 1993, hitting .322 by June 14, when his career took a jolt when he ran into the center-field fence in Busch Stadium and broke his collarbone, limiting him to only 83 games that season. Hitting only .246 in 1994, he left the team following the 1994 campaign, signing a contract with the Orioles, where he hit .159 before being traded to the Phillies at midseason. He fared no better in Philadelphia and was out of the game following the campaign.

Since then, Andy has coached for the Detroit Tigers under Leyland and is currently with the Seattle Mariners as a first-base coach for former teammate Lloyd McClendon. While his career in Pittsburgh came to a disappointing end, he was a huge part of a winning era, making Pirates fans happy he wasn't just the butt of an April Fools' joke gone bad in 1987.

MOST MEMORABLE PERFORMANCE

In 1987, the Pirates were trying to piece together a team that would hopefully end the string of losing seasons they had suffered in the mid-1980s. They made several trades to try to accelerate the process, including acquiring center fielder Andy Van Slyke, who would prove to be an important piece of the puzzle.

After rallying from 18 games under .500 on August 23, 1987, to win 80 games, the young team continued to improve in 1988, challenging for the National League title until late in the season. With no hope of catching the New York Mets, the team looked to secure a second-place finish with a win over the St. Louis Cardinals on September 27.

The two teams battled throughout the contest, with Pittsburgh taking a 3–0 lead on the strength of two RBIs from Bobby Bonilla before the Cards came back to cut the score to 3–2 with two runs in the fourth. Both offenses had been held scoreless going into the bottom of the ninth, as a sparse crowd of 8,994 at Three Rivers Stadium was cheering for their team to hold on and clinch second. With men on first and third, and one out, second baseman Luis Alicea came to the plate against Pirates closer Jim Gott and promptly hit a fly ball to Van Slyke in center for the second out. Jose Oquendo, who was the runner on third, tagged and attempted to score the tying run. As good as an overall player Van Slyke was, his spectacular defense and rifle arm in center were truly his strength. He launched a perfect strike to LaValliere, who tagged Oquendo out to end the game and clinch second place for the Bucs. It would be the last time a game would end with a double play on a throw from the center fielder to home until 2011.

NOTABLE ACHIEVEMENTS (YEARLY LEADERS AND AWARDS ARE AS PIRATES ONLY)

Part of three National League championship teams (1990, 1991, 1992).

Won the 1988 *Sporting News* Player of the Year Award.

CHAPTER 24

Won five Gold Glove Awards (1988, 1989, 1990, 1991, 1992).

Won two Silver Slugger Awards (1988, 1992).

Played in three All-Star Games.

Finished fourth in voting for the National League MVP twice.

Led the league in hits once (1992).

Led the league in doubles once (1992).

Led the league in triples once (1988).

Led the league in putouts for a center fielder and outfielder once (1988).

Led the league in assists for a center fielder twice (1988, 1994).

Led the league in doubles turned as a center fielder once (1988).

Led the league in doubles turned as an outfielder twice (1987, 1989).

Led the league in fielding percentage as a center fielder once (1987).

Eclipsed 100 RBIs twice.

49th in highest fielding percentage for a center fielder in major league history, at .989.

69th in most assists by a center fielder in major league history, with 75.

72nd in most putouts by a center fielder in major league history, with 2,762.

72nd in most double plays by a center fielder in major league history, with 18.

25

DICK GROAT

Like the franchise's greatest player, Honus Wagner, shortstop Dick Groat
was a proud son of the city of Pittsburgh who also led his hometown team
to a World Series title. Groat was not only one of the first two-sport stars,
averaging 11.9 points per game for the NBA's Fort Wayne Pistons, but also a
National League MVP, capturing the award in 1960, despite missing a month
with a broken wrist.
Photo courtesy of the Pittsburgh Pirates.

While there were a couple attempts by Major League Baseball to honor the greatest player in the league with an award during a particular campaign—the Chalmers Award (1911–1914) and the League Award (1922–1929)—the official Most Valuable Player Award, given by the Baseball Writers' Association of America, wasn't handed out in 1931. It took 29 years after the inception of the honor for a member of the Pittsburgh Pirates to win it; his name was Dick Groat.

Starting shortstop for the 1960 world champion Pittsburgh Pirates, Groat captured the trophy despite missing the final month of the season with a broken left wrist. The 1960 MVP vote was also controversial, as his teammate, Roberto Clemente, finished eighth, something Clemente remained bitter about throughout his career, choosing to wear the ring he was given for his All-Star Game appearance instead.

Table 25.1 is a look at the top offensive candidates for the award (the top eight vote-getters, minus Lindy McDaniel and Vern Law, who were both pitchers), using a point system based on their finish in the National League offensive categories (first place is worth 10 points, while 10th place is worth 1) to identify the most worthy candidate.

While the list quantifies the best statistical player in the league, the MVP must take into account intangibles that can't be quantified. The MVP is often a player who was most important in leading his team to the pennant or keeping them in contention. Mays played on a team that finished fifth, Banks on one that ended up seventh, and Boyer on a third-place club that was nine games behind Pittsburgh. As shown in table 25.1, there were better hitters, but Groat looked to be the most valuable to the team that won the pennant. Even though statistically Clemente appears to have been slighted in the balloting, it wasn't as

Figure 25.1. Top offensive candidates for the 1960 MVP Award.

Player	HR	RBI	AVE	OPS	WAR	D WAR	Pts.
Groat	2(NR)	50(NR)	.325(10)	.766(NR)	6.2(2)	2.6(10)	22
Hoak	16(NR)	79(NR)	.282(NR)	.810(NR)	5.4(NR)	1.1(1)	1
Mays	29(5)	103(7)	.319(8)	.936(8)	9.5(10)	1.4(7)	45
Banks	41(10)	117(8)	.271(NR)	.904(5)	7.8(8)	2.0(8)	39
Boyer	32(7)	97(6)	.304(6)	.932(7)	6.8(4)	1.0(NR)	30
Clemente	16(NR)	94(4)	.314(7)	.815(1)	3.9(NR)	0.4(NR)	12

bad as he thought, with Hoak being perhaps the only player he should have been ahead of. Groat was nonetheless the MVP of the pennant-winning Bucs.

A hometown boy from nearby Wilkinsburg, Dick first became a national star as a basketball player at Duke University. He was a consensus All-American and College Basketball Player of the Year in 1952, and became the first basketball player to have his number retired at the prestigious school.

The Wilkinsburg native chose baseball over basketball between his junior and senior seasons, even though he loved to play the latter more, but he didn't want to leave Duke until he graduated. He once commented, "Baseball was always like work for me. Basketball was the sport I loved, but it was baseball where I knew I would make a living."[1] He went on to say that Branch Rickey told him, "Young man if you will sign a contract tonight, I'm going to start you against the Cincinnati Reds tomorrow night."[2]

Groat told Rickey if he made him the same offer after his senior year he would sign, which he did. He kept his promise to Rickey by signing a contract with the Bucs for twice what the Pirates general manager had originally offered. Rickey kept his promise, too, never sending his young shortstop to the minors, as he hit .284 his rookie season, finishing third in the Rookie of the Year voting, behind Joe Black and Hoyt Wilhelm.

After his rookie campaign, Dick returned to Duke to finish his degree, while also signing a contract with the Fort Wayne Pistons of the National Basketball Association, who selected him third in the first round of the 1952 NBA Draft. He averaged 11.9 points per game in his lone NBA campaign, which lasted only 26 games, as he was drafted into the U.S. Army, where he served for two years before returning to the Bucs in 1955.

Pittsburgh was going through one of its worst eras in franchise history in the 1950s but was forming a young foundation with Groat, Roberto Clemente, Bill Mazeroski, Vern Law, and Bob Friend that would eventually see them compete for the National League pennant. Between 1955 and 1957, the shortstop hit a consistent .285, before rising to .300 in 1958, with 66 RBIs, his best total in a Pirates uniform, in helping to lead the team to a surprising second-place finish.

Groat was selected to play in the All-Star Game for the first time the next season, leading to his marquee campaign in 1960, when he carved out a spot for himself in Pirates history. He was spectacular that season, leading the league in hitting, with a .325 average, and defensive wins above replacement, also showing his defensive abilities. He had six hits in a game on May 13, against the Braves, and was having the greatest campaign of his career when it almost came to a sudden end.

Milwaukee's Lew Burdette, who had outdueled Harvey Haddix in his near-perfect 13-inning game the season before, was once again a thorn in the Bucs' side, hitting Groat's wrist with a pitch and breaking it, taking him out for the majority of the rest of the season. He returned in late September and hit a disappointing .214 in the World Series.

Dick continued to hit well for the Pirates during the next two seasons, but at 31 years of age his fielding was slipping, with 70 errors in 1961 and 1962. Rumors swirled following the 1962 campaign that he would be traded, and the speculation became reality when he was dealt to the Cardinals with Diomedes Olivo for Don Cardwell and Julio Gotay.

But the Bucs got the short end of the deal, as Groat enjoyed a fabulous 1963 season that saw him finish behind only Sandy Koufax for the MVP Award. A year later he returned to the World Series with the Cards, winning a second world championship, although he once again had a poor Fall Classic, with a .192 average. Three years later he retired, after spending time with the Phillies and Giants, eventually becoming the legendary color man on broadcasts for the University of Pittsburgh basketball team, as his life has come full circle, working in the sport he loved and not in the one he made a living playing.

MOST MEMORABLE PERFORMANCE

In a season where everything seemed to be working out for the hometown product of the Pittsburgh Pirates, shortstop Dick Groat had the game of a lifetime on May 13, 1960, against the Milwaukee Brewers at County Stadium, during which he had six hits in an 8–2 Pirates victory.

Groat started his perfect day in the top of the first with a double, one of three he had in the contest, but was doubled off second after

Bob Skinner flied out to left. He again doubled in the third and then singled in the fifth, but his hits were for naught, as they trailed Milwaukee, 2–0, after six.

The rest of the Pirates offense woke up in the seventh, with Groat leading off with a single before being plated with a Dick Stuart home run to tie the game at two. Pittsburgh continued the onslaught with eight runs in the seventh, one of which came after the shortstop smacked his third double and fifth hit of the day and came home on a two-run single off the bat of Skinner.

With the game out of hand, Groat came up once more in the ninth to complete his perfect day with his sixth hit, a single to right, tying a team record that would hold for 15 years, until being broken by Rennie Stennett with his amazing seven-hit performance against the Cubs.

NOTABLE ACHIEVEMENTS (YEARLY LEADERS AND AWARDS ARE AS PIRATES ONLY)

Part of one National League championship and world championship team (1960).

Played in six All-Star Games.

Won the 1960 Most Valuable Player Award.

Won the 1960 Lou Gehrig Award.

Finished in the top 20 voting for the National League MVP three times.

Won the 1960 batting title.

Led the league in singles once (1960).

Led the league in assists overall and at shortstop once (1962).

Led the league in putouts by a shortstop four times (1955, 1958, 1959, 1962).

Led the league in double plays by a shortstop four times (1958, 1959, 1961, 1962).

28th in most defensive games at shortstop in major league history, at 1,877.

13th in most double plays turned by a shortstop in major league history, with 1,237.

50th in most assists in major league history, with 5,864.

26th in most putouts by a shortstop in major league history, with 3,505.

30th in most assists by a shortstop in major league history, with 5,811.

26

CLARENCE BEAUMONT

While sluggers and 100-mile-per-hour pitchers make most of the headlines in baseball, it's the leadoff hitters that can be the most important part of a baseball team. In the first decade of the 20th century, the Pittsburgh Pirates had a championship squad with a prolific offense that included such Hall of Fame talents as Honus Wagner and Fred Clarke. In addition to Wagner and Clarke giving the offense its effectiveness, the team had a player many experts consider the best leadoff hitter in the Deadball Era: Clarence Howeth "Ginger" Beaumont.

Nicknamed Ginger by Bucs president Barney Dreyfuss for his red hair, Beaumont was a speedy contact hitter who was the second Pirate to lead the league in hitting, with a .357 average in 1902. Famed Pittsburgh sportswriter John Gruber once said of the center fielder,

> He was an excellent base runner, being very fast on his feet, but nobody who saw him for the first time ambling his way to the batter's box would admit this. A lazier or more indifferent-appearing player, emphasized by a burly body, could not be conceived. But when he hit the ball he was off like a streak, which astonished the uninitiated and made him one of the wonders of the century.[1]

Other than the fact that he won a batting title, Ginger etched his name in baseball history for two separate things: He was the first player in major league history to go 6-for-6 with six runs, a feat he achieved on July 22, 1899, against Philadelphia, and the first player to come to bat in a World Series, facing the great Cy Young in the first game of the 1903 Fall Classic and flying out to center fielder Chick Stahl of the Boston Americans.

Born in Rochester, Wisconsin, Beaumont attended nearby Beloit College before signing with the Milwaukee Brewers of the Western League in 1898, as a catcher. After suffering several injuries he was moved to center field and became a star, hitting .354. Ginger attracted much interest in the National League, but Milwaukee's manager, Hall of Famer Connie Mack, arranged a sale of his slugger to Louisville in an attempt to avoid losing him in the minor league draft. Colonel owner Barney Dreyfuss agreed to return Beaumont to the Brewers, and Mack was then able to trade him to the Pirates for Bill Gray and Bill Hart. It was a fortuitous trade for not only the Bucs, but also Dreyfuss, who would eventually become president of Pittsburgh when Louisville was contracted by the National League following the 1899 campaign.

The Wisconsin native enjoyed a phenomenal rookie season once Patsy Donovan took over as manager for William Watkins, who was only using the young redhead in a reserve role. Much to the chagrin of Tom McCreery, who was the starting center fielder at the beginning of the season, Donovan inserted Beaumont into the spot, and he rewarded the new manager with a .352 average, finishing sixth in the Senior Circuit. His initial season included the aforementioned rare feat on July 22, when he had a perfect 6-for-6 game, scoring six times. The six runs are not only a major league record shared with 14 other players, but they also remain the franchise mark for the Bucs. Ginger's achievement when including his six hits in six at bats is one that took 103 years to be replicated, when Shawn Green of the Dodgers matched it in 2002.

A year later, after Louisville's best players had become members of the Pittsburgh Pirates, the speedy outfielder was part of one of the most intimating lineups in the game, featuring Wagner, Clarke, Tommy Leach, and Jimmy Williams. Despite the protection from the lineup, Beaumont's stats suffered in his sophomore season, dipping to .279. Luckily for the Bucs it would only be a one-year drop, as the team's leadoff hitter found his stroke again in 1901.

The 1901 campaign not only proved to be successful for Ginger, but also for his team, as they captured their first National League pennant. Wagner won the first batting title in Pirates history, with a .381 mark, but Beaumont was not far behind, finishing 10th in the circuit, at .332.

In 1902, the Beloit College alum began a three-year stretch that would place him among the elite ballplayers in the game. The squad had what would become the best season for the Pirates team that year, with Beaumont succeeding Wagner as the best hitter in the Senior Circuit with a league-leading .357 average and 193 hits. A year later, while not retaining his batting title, Ginger finished sixth, at .341, and at the top of the National League standings in games played (141), at bats (613), plate appearances (675), runs (137), and hits (.209).

As well as Beaumont played in 1903, helping to lead the Bucs to their third-straight pennant and a spot in the first World Series against the Boston Americans, it was his position in the batting order on October 1 that permanently put the center fielder in the record books. The game took place at the Huntingdon Avenue Baseball Grounds in Boston in front of 16,242 rabid fans. As the visitors in the game, the Pirates batted first. Since Beaumont was the leadoff hitter, he had the honor of being the first batter in World Series history. Even though he flied out and was hitless in five at bats, he will be forever the answer to the trivia question, Who was the first batter in World Series history?

While he only hit .265 for the series, the redhead enjoyed two more successful campaigns in a Pirates uniform, during which time he compiled a .311 average and, in 1904, led the league for a third consecutive time in hits, with 185. Ginger developed knee issues in 1905, and they worsened the following year, as he hit a low with the Bucs of .265, while only playing in 80 games.

Following the 1906 campaign, the injury prompted Dreyfuss to trade his leadoff hitter to the Boston Braves, along with Patsy Flaherty and Claude Ritchey, for Ed Abbaticchio. Beaumont's knee began to heal, and he made Dreyfuss appear foolish for the transaction, rebounding with a .322 mark, while once again finding himself on top of the Senior Circuit in hits, with 187.

But it was a temporary resurgence, as the knee issues returned and Ginger's game suffered. By 1910, he was with the Cubs, and while he once again found himself in the World Series, he was hitless in two at bats during Chicago's loss to the Philadelphia A's. It turned out to be the end for Beaumont in the majors, as 1910 was his last season. He played with the St. Paul Saints of the American Association in 1911, hitting only .249, and then retired to his farm in Honey Creek, Wisconsin, where he lived until his death in 1956, at the age of 79.

MOST MEMORABLE PERFORMANCE

There have been many amazing feats in the history of the game, including several by men in Pittsburgh Pirates uniforms, but perhaps none as impressive or unique as Ginger Beaumont's offensive performance on July 22, 1899, against Philadelphia.

Beaumont was in his rookie season and having a phenomenal year, one that would see him hit .352. On that warm July day, he became the first player to go 6-for-6 in a game, while scoring what is still a major league record six runs, a feat that took 103 years to equal. While brilliant, the accomplishment wasn't even the most unique part of the day; the most unique aspect of the game is that he pulled off his perfection at the plate without ever getting the ball out of the infield.

A phenomenal bunter, Beaumont got on board each time via the bunt. Going back and forth with whether he was going to bunt or try to hit the ball over the Philadelphia infielders when they were expecting the bunt, they never knew how to position themselves.

Ginger made it to first base in the first inning by beating a throw by Chick Fraser by a couple of steps. With two out in the second, he then tapped the ball down the first-base line, starting a four-run rally that increased the lead to 7–0. In the fourth frame, he chopped the ball off the plate and beat the throw to first, before bunting the ball toward shortstop Monte Cross in the fifth. Cross couldn't come up with it to make the throw to first.

By the seventh, Pittsburgh had built a 13–4 advantage, but Beaumont wasn't done, bunting the ball toward second baseman Pearce Chiles and beating the throw to first for his fifth bunt single of the day. The rookie's perfect day was almost squashed in the eighth, when he had two strikes called on him and pulled out of the bunt, swinging hard but fouling the ball off. With the Philadelphia defense playing back, not expecting him to bunt with two strikes, Ginger did just that and once again beat the throw to first. He eventually scored his sixth run in the eighth, when Jack McCarthy singled and both Elmer Flick and Duff Cooley fumbled the ball, allowing both men to score and handing the Bucs an easy 18–4 victory.

NOTABLE ACHIEVEMENTS (YEARLY LEADERS AND AWARDS ARE AS PIRATES ONLY)

Part of three National League championship teams (1901, 1902, 1903).

Won the 1902 batting title.

Finished in the top 10 for the National League batting title six times.

Led the league in hits three times (1902, 1903, 1904).

Led the league in runs once (1903).

Led the league in total bases once (1903).

Led the league in singles three times (1902, 1903, 1904).

Led the league in double plays by an outfielder once (1902).

100th in highest batting average in major league history, at .311.

28th in most double plays by an outfielder in major league history, with 52.

91st in most assists for an outfielder in major league history, with 167.

First batter in World Series history in 1903.

Scored major league record six runs on July 22, 1899.

One of two players in major league history to go 6-for-6, with six runs.

27

TOMMY LEACH

Think of the championship Pittsburgh Pirates teams in the first decade of the 20th century and the names Honus Wagner, Fred Clarke, Sam Leever, and Deacon Phillippe are usually the first that come to mind. But there is another important member, one who was there for all four National League championships, including their first World Series title in 1909: Tommy Leach.

Leach is truly a forgotten name among the early Pirates greats, but make no mistake, during his time he was one of the best players in the game. In looking at the first 15 years of the 20th century, Leach rates high in several offensive categories. Only four players had 2,000 hits during that time period. Sam Crawford had 2,812, Honus Wagner 2,782, Nap Lajoie 2,568, and Leach 2,011.

While only five feet, six inches and 150 pounds, the third baseman was on the top 10 home run list during the time period, coming in ninth, with 57. Of his career total 63 long balls, 49 of them came via the inside-the-park method, as he made use of his incredible speed after placing the ball in a gap of the immense outfields of the day. Leach recalled, "I wasn't a home run hitter like you see today. The fields were big then, and if you hit a ball between the outfielders and were fast enough, you had a home run. None of those I hit went over the fence."[1] Fourteen of them actually did.

The remaining categories that Tommy rated highly in were triples, where he was third, with 163; RBIs, where he was ninth, with 748; runs, where he was third, with 1,266; and stolen bases, where he was tenth, with 340. In each category, he rates higher than his manager and the starting left fielder for the Bucs at the time, Fred Clarke, who was elected to the Hall of Fame, yet Leach remains on the outside of Cooperstown looking in and is remembered by few in Pirates nation.

Born in West Creek, New York, Leach began his professional baseball career with Petersburg and Hampton in the Virginia League in 1896, before moving to the Hanover Tigers in the Cumberland Valley League and then the Youngstown Puddlers in 1897. After hitting .325 with Auburn in the New York State League a year later, Tommy was given a two-week trial with the New York Giants, who sent him back, thinking he was too small to be a major league player. The Giants' mistake was Louisville's gain, as Barney Dreyfuss signed the diminutive third baseman for $650.

He hit .100 in 10 at bats for the Louisville Colonels in 1898, before being returned to the Worcester Farmers in the Eastern League. Leach once again came up with the Colonels in 1899, and this time stayed in the majors, hitting .288 in 406 at bats in his official rookie season. When the Colonels were contracted by the National League following his rookie campaign, he was sent to Pittsburgh, along with the likes of Wagner, Clarke, and Phillippe, to form the nucleus of what would be the first dynasty of the 20th century.

Tommy spent his first year in Pittsburgh as a utility infielder, appearing in only 51 games and hitting a mere .213, before finally cracking the starting lineup in 1901, after third baseman Jimmy Williams signed with the American League. He hit over .300 for the first time that season, with a .305 average, as he took over the starting spot at third.

With Leach finally emerging as a quality major league player, the young Pirates captured their first pennant in franchise history in 1901, setting up both the team and their third baseman with a season for the ages in 1902. The New York native led the National League in triples, with 22, and home runs, with six, the lowest total for a home run champion in the 20th century. The team again won the National League championship, with a remarkable 103–36 mark, a full 27½ games ahead of the second-place Brooklyn Superbas; it was a season Leach proudly remembered years after his retirement. Said Tommy, "In 1902 we won the National League pennant over the second-place team. Even in all the years that have passed since then no club in either major league has ever finished that far out in front."[2]

The club won their third consecutive pennant a year later and earned a spot in the inaugural World Series against the Boston Americans. In the first contest, the 25-year-old third baseman put himself in the record books when he not only had the first hit in series history, a triple to right field, but also scored the first Fall Classic run when Wagner knocked him in with a single. While the Bucs were upset by the Americans in the series, losing five games to three after taking a three-games-to-one lead, Leach played well, hitting .273, with a series-high seven RBIs.

When Clarke went out for six weeks in 1904, after suffering a serious spike wound, the diminutive third baseman added manager to his title, taking over while the Hall of Fame left fielder was recovering. While Leach was able to have a brief experience as skipper, the team was again unable to win the pennant, not only in 1904, but also in the next four seasons, with Leach hitting .272 during that time period.

Leading the league in runs, with 126, despite a subpar .261 average as he moved to centerfield, Pittsburgh once again rose to the heights of the National League, capturing their long-awaited fourth pennant before adding World Series champion to their résumé for the first time by defeating the Detroit Tigers in seven games. Tommy was phenomenal in the Fall Classic, with a .360 average.

While he was at the height of his career after the 1909 World Series, Leach only lasted in Pittsburgh for two and a half more seasons. After a poor 1911 campaign and struggling in the beginning of 1912, he was dealt to the Cubs with Lefty Leifeld at the end of May for King Cole and Solly Hofman. It turned out to be a poor trade for Dreyfuss, as the batsman had a resurgence with Chicago in 1913, with a .287 average and a league-leading 99 runs; however, it was his last good season in the majors, as age got the best of him. After going to the Reds in 1915, he was out of the game at season's end, hitting only .224.

But it was not the end of his major league career. Leach got one more chance in 1918, when he came back with the Bucs at the age of 40 due to the lack of personnel in the league, with many players going into the armed forces to serve their country during World War I. He hit a career-low .194 in 72 at bats for the Pirates before calling it quits for good.

Tommy Leach passed away in 1969, at the age of 91, and has been all but lost in time, as most forget about him when talking about the all-time great Pirates players. Fortunately, 39 years after his death, his home county finally recognized one of their most celebrated sons when the Chautauqua Sports Hall of Fame selected him as a member in 2008. Six years later, a website dedicated to the Pirates called Rumbunter.com chose him as the third-best third baseman in the history of the club, behind Pie Traynor and Richie Hebner (they claim that the fact that he spent a significant amount of time in the outfield kept him from a higher spot on the list). Finally, after so many anonymous years, Leach seems to be getting the recognition he deserves—including in the pages of this book as the 27th-best player in the history of the franchise.

MOST MEMORABLE PERFORMANCE

It was the first game of the first World Series, and while the players may not have realized it at the time, there would be many firsts that would put them in the record books in what would turn out to be one of the top events on the North American sports calendar. For the Pittsburgh Pirates, third baseman Tommy Leach would put his name in the books on three separate occasions.

Pittsburgh came into the series as prohibitive favorites, and while they would eventually lose the Fall Classics, on this day everything went well for the National League champions. They started early in the top of the first inning. With two outs, Leach came to the plate and promptly had not only the first hit in World Series, but also the first triple, nitting the ball deep to right field. Honus Wagner plated him in with a single to score the first run in World Series history to boot.

It would be a phenomenal day for the New York native. After flying out in the second, Leach knocked in Ginger Beaumont with a single in the fourth and singled again in the sixth, before smacking his second two-out triple of the day in the eighth. The Pirates won the first World Series game ever, 7–3, and Leach was the star, with a four-hit performance.

NOTABLE ACHIEVEMENTS (YEARLY LEADERS AND AWARDS ARE AS PIRATES ONLY)

Part of four National League championship teams (1901, 1902, 1903, 1909).

Part of one world championship team (1909).

Elected to the Chautauqua Sports Hall of Fame in 2008.

Finished in the top 10 for the National League batting title once.

Led the league in triples once (1902).

Led the league in home runs once (1902).

Led the league in putouts by a third baseman once (1904).

Led the league in assists overall and at third base twice (1902, 1904).

2nd in most inside-the-park home runs in major league history, with 49.

101st in most stolen bases in major league history, with 361.

103rd in most runs in major league history, with 1,355.

46th in most sacrifice hits in major league history, with 240.

23rd in most triples in major league history, with 172.

53rd in most putouts at third base in major league history, with 1,323.

83rd in most assists at third base in major league history, with 2,127.

Had the first hit in World Series history.

Hit the first triple in World Series history.

Scored the first run in World Series history.

28

AL OLIVER

There are many players in this book who deserve to be considered for election to the Hall of Fame, but there is one, Al Oliver, who experts bring up more than any other, perplexed about why he hasn't been more seriously considered. In 1994, when Bill James wrote the book *Whatever Happened to the Hall of Fame?*, examining the Hall of Fame election procedures, he made the point that Oliver was the only man to have 2,500 hits and 200 home runs, and hit .300 for his career, not to be included in the Hall of Fame.

In looking at the all-time hit leaders, Oliver ranks 55th, with 2,743. The following players above him are not in the Hall of Fame: Pete Rose, Derek Jeter, Rafael Palmeiro, Alex Rodriguez, Barry Bonds, Ichiro Suzuki, Omar Vizquel, Harold Baines, Ivan Rodriguez, Ken Griffey, Johnny Damon, and Vada Pinson. Rose is ineligible for the time being; Palmeiro and Bonds are embroiled in steroid allegations; Alex Rodriguez will be embroiled in steroid allegations when he retires; and Vizquel, Ivan Rodriguez, Griffey, Suzuki, Jeter, and Damon are not yet eligible. This leaves Harold Baines, Vada Pinson, and Oliver as the only players in the group who would be eligible not to be included.

Table 28.1 lists the two players who are directly above Oliver in hits and the two directly below who are in the Hall of Fame, as well as Pinson and Baines, with a career comparison of the group (years played in parentheses). Table 28.2 shows the Hall of Fame voting for each.

The stats of the three players do not necessitate automatic inclusion into Cooperstown and are not meant to diminish the accomplishments of those who have been elected, but they should prove that Al deserves more serious consideration. He spent only one year on the

Table 28.1. Career totals for Al Oliver and the players ranking above and below him.

Player	HR	RBI	2B	3B	OPS	AVE	WAR	Hits
Pinson (18)	256	1,169	485	127	.769	.286	54.1	2,757
Baines (22)	384	1,628	488	49	.820	.289	38.5	2,866
Oliver (18)	219	1,326	529	77	.795	.303	43.3	2,743
Appling (20)	45	1,116	440	102	.798	.310	74.5	2,749
Dawson (21)	438	1,591	503	98	.806	.279	64.5	2,774
Goslin (18)	248	1,612	500	173	.887	.316	66.1	2,735
Perez (23)	379	1,652	505	79	.804	.279	53.9	2,732

ballot, garnering a mere 4.3 percent of the vote, even though his career statistics are comparable to the other men included in this book. Despite the fact that Oliver had little support, James predicted that the former Pirate would be elected in 1998; unfortunately he was wrong.

Even though he hasn't been seriously considered for baseball's highest honor, it doesn't take away from the Portsmouth, Ohio, native's incredible career. Drafted by the Pirates in the 1964 Amateur Draft out of Kent State, Oliver showed what a special prospect he was, hitting .309 for the Gastonia Pirates of the Western Carolina League in his first season of professional baseball.

After struggling at the Double-A level with Macon in 1967, with a .222 average, Al was nonetheless promoted to the Columbus Jets in 1968, a team that included several future members of the 1971 world champion Pittsburgh Pirates, including Manny Sanguillen, Dock Ellis, Richie Hebner, and Bob Robertson, who was on injured reserve for the season. The Kent State alum hit .315, with a minor league career

Table 28.2. Hall of Fame voting for Al Oliver and the men above and below him in career totals.

Name	Highest Voting, Percentage, Plus Years on the Ballot
Pinson	1988, 15.7 percent, 15 years on ballot
Baines	2010, 6.1 percent, 5 years on ballot
Oliver	1991, 4.3 percent, 1 year on ballot
Appling	1964, 94 percent (runoff election), 7 years on ballot
Dawson	2010, 77.9 percent (elected), 9 years on ballot
Goslin	1956, 13.5 percent, 9 years on ballot (elected in 1968 by Veteran's Committee)
Perez	2000, 77.2 percent (elected), 9 years on ballot

CHAPTER 28

high of 14 home runs. It would be his last year in the minors, as the Bucs promoted him for the 1969 campaign.

While he had difficulty settling on a position, Oliver started his career at first base in 1969, despite being dubbed "Scoops," a sarcastic nickname for his knack for committing errors there in the minors. He improved with a .991 fielding percentage but was more impressive at the plate, hitting more homers in a season than he ever had in the minors, with 17, while knocking in 70 and hitting .285. Scoops finished second in the National League Rookie of the Year voting, tied with the Expos' Cocoa Laboy, behind the Cardinals' Ted Simmons.

Being moved around in the field to make space for Robertson at first, Oliver finally found a home in center field in 1971. Continuing his consistency at the plate, the left-handed line-drive hitter was an important part of the eventual world champions, although he was not effective offensively in the post season. Hitting .250 in the National League Championship Series and .211 in the Fall Classic, Oliver hit perhaps the most important home run of his career in the fourth game against the Giants in the NLCS, smashing a three-run shot that helped clinch their eighth National League title.

While he did well, he was angry with the front office that he wasn't playing more, only appearing in 116 contests in center. Claiming he "wanted to find out why I haven't played every day," and that "I've proven myself and I know there are teams that want me if the Pirates can't use me,"[1] the confidence he expressed paid off during his remaining years in Pittsburgh, as he began to play more, becoming not only one of the best hitters on the team, but also for the league. Al hit .312 in 1972, with 89 RBIs, being selected to play in his first All-Star Game, while finishing seventh in the Senior Circuit's Most Valuable Player voting.

Throughout the next five seasons, Oliver remained consistent, averaging 16 home runs, with 82 RBIs and a .303 average. He played in two more All-Star Games during that period, while garnering votes in the MVP race in four of the five campaigns, coming in seventh again in 1974. Not always having the best relationship with management, Al was unsurprisingly traded to Texas following the 1977 season. In a complicated four-team deal, Pittsburgh received Bert Blyleven from the Rangers and John Milner from the Mets, two important pieces of their 1979 world championship team.

The Portsmouth native had a successful run the remainder of his career with Texas, Montreal, San Francisco, Philadelphia, Los Angeles, and Toronto, winning his lone batting title in 1982, with the Expos, posting a .331 mark, with National League highs in hits (209), doubles (43), and RBIs (109). He also secured his best placing in the MVP vote, finishing third. While successful, Oliver would have had a real chance for 3,000 hits and a guaranteed spot in the Hall of Fame if not for bone spurs in his left shoulder. The spurs eventually rendered him ineffective in the field, as he was unable to throw the ball efficiently. Scoops retired prematurely in 1985, leaving him short of the statistics he could have achieved.

Whether his often-argumentative relationship with the media caused the lack of respect pertaining to his Hall of Fame consideration, it is hopeful that the Veteran's Committee will correct the error and give Al Oliver the honor many experts say he deserves.

MOST MEMORABLE PERFORMANCE

It certainly wasn't the best game of Al Oliver's career, as he went only 1-for-4, but when it comes to the impact of that one hit, few have been bigger in the history of the Pittsburgh Pirates.

The date was October 6, 1971, and the place, Three Rivers Stadium, as the Bucs were facing off against the San Francisco Giants in Game Four of the NLCS. Pittsburgh had rebounded after a Game-One loss to win the next two contests, needing one more victory to capture their eighth Senior Circuit crown.

Unfortunately, future World Series hero Steve Blass gave up eight hits and five runs, four earned, in two innings of work, as the Giants got off to a quick 5–2 lead. The Bucs battled back to tie the game in the bottom of the second on Richie Hebner's three-run homer, but the two teams failed to score again, with the game still tied going into the bottom of the sixth.

Roberto Clemente gave the Pirates their first lead of the day, singling in Dave Cash, but with the strong Giant lineup, one run was not a comfortable lead. With two outs and Clemente on second, San Francisco did not show Oliver any respect, walking Willie Stargell to face the center fielder; the move would prove to be a huge mistake. Al ripped a Jerry Johnson pitch over the fence for a three-run homer, all but clinching the pennant with a 9–5 advantage. The dejected Giants were out of it and scored no more, with the Bucs celebrating a return to the World Series thanks to the clutch home run by Al Oliver.

NOTABLE ACHIEVEMENTS (YEARLY LEADERS AND AWARDS ARE AS PIRATES ONLY)

Part of five National League Eastern Division championship teams (1970, 1971, 1972, 1974, 1975).

Part of one National League championship and one world championship team (1971).

Played in three All-Star Games.

Finished in the top 10 for the National League batting title three times.

Finished in the top 20 voting for the National League MVP four times.

68th in most at bats in major league history, at 9,049.

39th in most doubles in major league history, with 529.

55th in most hits in major league history, with 2,743.

62nd in most singles in major league history, with 1,918.

99th in most extra-base hits in major league history, with 825.

80th in most total bases in major league history, with 4,083.

100th in most RBIs in major league history, with 1,326.

29

JESSE TANNEHILL

In the first decade of the 20th century, the Pittsburgh Pirates had not only the strongest starting rotation of the time period, but also the best in the long history of the franchise. Between 1900 and 1902, the Bucs finished in second place for the second time in franchise history in 1900 and then proceeded to win two pennants. The starting rotation of Jack Chesbro, Deacon Phillippe, and Sam Leever was dangerous enough, but add to it a five-foot, six-inch, 150-pound southpaw from Dayton, Kentucky, who was one of the greatest hitting pitchers in the modern era by the name of Jesse Tannehill and manager Fred Clarke had what amounted to an ace on the mound on just about every day.

Chesbro, Leever, and Phillippe are probably better known in Pirates lore, but Tannehill may have been the best of the group. Table 29.1 lists the stats of the four men, along with their ranking in the National League from 1900 to 1902. The numbers in parenthesis indicate their position in the category in the National League during the time period.

It's incredible how they compare looking at the rest of the National League; it becomes even more impressive when considering the fact that in 1902, they were still relatively young, with Phillippe and Leever being 30, while Chesbro was 28 and Tannehill only 27. More championships seemed imminent with this foursome leading the way; the only problem was that Tannehill, who, again, was arguably the best in the group, was focused on jumping to the rival American League in 1903, and hell bent on taking others with him. It's hard to justify that the 29th-best player in Pirates history was a man who was

Table 29.1. Stats for Jack Chesbro, Deacon Phillippe, Sam Leever, and Jesse Tannehill from 1900 to 1902.

Name	Wins	ERA	Winning Percentage	H/9 Inn	BB/9 Inn
Tannehill	58 (4)	2.33 (1)	.725 (1)	8.66 (10)	1.30 (2)
Leever	45 (8)	2.64 (6)	.643 (4)	8.90 (NR)	1.68 (6)
Chesbro	64 (1)	2.66 (7)	.688 (2)	8.24 (3)	2.20 (NR)
Philippe	62 (2)	2.37 (3)	.646 (3)	8.64 (9)	1.13 (1)

single-handedly responsible for curtailing the team's dynasty, but if one concentrates on the stats, it's easy to see why he's here.

With an arsenal led by a slow curveball and pinpoint control, Tannehill was signed by the Cincinnati Reds in 1894, at 19 years of age, straight off the sandlots of Cincinnati. He immediately went to the major leagues but showed he wasn't ready for such a promotion, finishing with a 1–1 mark and an unimpressive 7.14 ERA.

Following his disappointing major league debut, the Dayton native was sent back to the minors, pitching for two seasons with the Richmond Blue Birds of the Virginia State League, where he was able to learn his craft. Tannehill was spectacular for the Blue Birds, winning 49 games in two years, while lowering his ERA by almost five earned runs, to 2.15. The Pirates were impressed with the southpaw and drafted him following the 1896 campaign.

In 1897, now 22 years old, Jesse was more effective for the Bucs, but he still struggled, finishing 9–9, with an ERA of 4.25. Worse yet was his hits per nine-inning ratio, as he allowed 172 hits in only 142 innings. While he still had issues on the mound, the smallish hurler showed he was a good hitter, and manager Patsy Donovan had no problem using him in the outfield, where he played 33 games and hit .266; however, a year later playing Tannehill in the outfield was no longer an option, as he finally began to live up to his potential.

The man from Kentucky was phenomenal, with a 25–13 mark on a sub-.500 team. No other Bucs pitcher came close to his output, with Billy Rhines having the second-highest win total, with 12. Jesse showed he was no fluke in 1899, again leading the club in victories, with 24, losing only 14 for a club that, while showing signs of improvement, was still hovering around the .500 mark, at 76–72.

In 1900, Tannehill and Leever were joined in the starting rotation by Chesbro, who was a spot starter in 1899, as well as Phillippe, who came over from Louisville after the Colonels were contracted by the National League. The quartet quickly lifted the franchise, helping the Bucs to a second-place finish. Phillippe and Tannehill both led the club with 20 wins, with Jesse being more impressive, losing on only six occasions, compared to Phillippe's 13. Tannehill also shined at the plate, hitting a career-high .336.

For the first time in four seasons, the southpaw failed to win 20 games in 1901, going 18–10, as the Bucs continued to improve, capturing their first National League crown. While Tannehill didn't win 20, he was nonetheless successful, winning the ERA crown for the only time in his career, with an average of 2.18.

In 1902, he had his best campaign in a Pirates uniform, winning 20 games once again, with a 20–6 record and a career-low 1.95 ERA. It should have been the beginning of great things for the young team, but mutiny was alive in the clubhouse, and Tannehill was at the forefront of it. The southpaw was secretly negotiating with American League president Ban Johnson, and there was a promise of a $1,000 bonus for jumping leagues in 1903. Rumors were swirling, and backup catcher Jack O'Conner was thought to be the ring leader and promptly suspended by Pirates president Barney Dreyfuss. Then came Tannehill's unveiling as a co-conspiritor.

During a fight with Jimmy Burke, a reserve third baseman for the team, Tannehill suffered a dislocated shoulder. He was taken to the hospital and put under ether so doctors could put the shoulder back in. While under anesthesia, Dreyfuss was in the room with him, and Tannehill confessed that he was leading the negotiations for as many as six Pirates to leave the team. But only three—Tannehill, O'Connor, and Chesbro—departed for the New York Highlanders (Yankees). Despite the fact that the Pirates won one last time in 1903, the loss of two of their four starters was too much, and the club's pennant-winning days drew to a close.

Playing in New York for one season, Jesse was sent to Boston at the end of the 1903 campaign and won 20 games twice for the Americans (Red Sox). In 1907, he developed a sore arm and was traded to Washington, where his injuries continued to plague him. Another separated shoulder and injured ribs limited him to a 2–4 mark in 1908. He did no better for Washington in 1909, and after a season with Minneapolis of the American Association in 1910, he ended his major league career where it began, in Cincinnati, where he pitched in four games in 1911.

Tannehill spent a few years in the minors after that and managed there for three more seasons. He retired in Cincinnati, where he worked in a machine shop, passing away in 1956. The hurler is remembered more for the way he finished his Pirates career than the success he had during it. While Jesse was in a Pittsburgh uniform, however, there was no mistaking that he was one of the best players in the league and a worthy addition to this list.

MOST MEMORABLE PERFORMANCE

As the 1900 season was coming to an end, it was becoming apparent that the young squad assembled by Barney Dreyfuss had the potential for greatness. Battling the Philadelphia Phillies for second place behind the Brooklyn Superbas, the team held on for a second-place finish and earned a spot in a postseason series, a preamble to the World Series called the Chronicle-Telegraph Cup, against the Superbas.

For the Pirates, it would be a momentous occasion, as, except for a second-place finish in 1893, they had never come closer than fifth in the 13 years the team had existed in the National League. They faced the St. Louis Cardinals on October 8, in a doubleheader, and if they swept the two games they would have a 4½-game lead over Philadelphia, with only four games left to play. The Bucs shut down the Cards in the first game, 8–0, as manager Fred Clarke sent Jesse Tannehill to the mound in the second contest to try to wrap it up.

Tannehill had become one of the aces for both the Pirates and the league. He finished the season 20–6, winning 20 or more for the third consecutive season, and was dominant in this contest. But things didn't start out well, as left fielder Tom McCreery had a first-inning error that led to two St. Louis runs and an early 2–0 lead. Nevertheless, McCreery made up for it at the plate, with two hits and three runs, while Claude Ritchey contributed three hits as the Pirates offense scored six runs in the last four innings to secure an 8–2 victory.

Jesse was unhittable after allowing the two first-inning runs, striking out three, while allowing only seven hits and a walk. He may have pitched better games in his career, but as the winning pitcher in the contest where the Pirates clinched a spot in their first postseason series in team history, none could have been more meaningful.

NOTABLE ACHIEVEMENTS (YEARLY LEADERS AND AWARDS ARE AS PIRATES ONLY)

Part of two National League championship teams (1901, 1902).

Won more than 20 games four times.

Finished in the top 10 in the National League for ERA five times.

Finished in the top 10 in the National League for winning percentage four times.

Led the league in ERA once (1901).

75th in home runs allowed per nine innings pitched in major league history, at 0.131.

83rd in most shutouts in major league history, with 34.

27th in walks per nine innings pitched in major league history, at .627.

57th in highest winning percentage in major league history, with .667.

103rd in lowest ERA in major league history, at 2.80.

30

DOUG DRABEK

A prospect of the New York Yankees when he came to the Pirates in a trade in 1987, Doug Drabek quickly became one of the best pitchers in the game, helping the Bucs capture three consecutive Eastern Division crowns. He led the league with 22 wins in 1990, capturing the Cy Young Award.

Photo courtesy of the Pittsburgh Pirates.

In a lonely yet proud fraternity, Vern Law and a right-handed hurler out of Victoria, Texas, by the name of Doug Drabek are the only two pitchers for the Pittsburgh Pirates who have won the coveted Cy Young Award. Both had many similarities in their marquee seasons, and both were young pitchers on teams mired in multiple losing seasons yet among the top in their profession when their clubs finally climbed out of the doldrums and won championships.

While Law was at his best when the Pirates were coming off losses, going 9–3 in such situations, Drabek was spectacular down the stretch. After starting off with a 7–2 record in 1990, the Texas native had a difficult June, going 1–3, with a 4.29 ERA and batters hitting .308 against him. Looking quite the opposite of a winner of the Cy Young Award on July 1, he went on an incredible roll, posting a 12–2 mark for the remainder of the season, with a more superstar-like 2.41 ERA. The same National League hitters who had been beating him in June were suddenly struggling, hitting only .202.

Perhaps the other big difference was that while Law was a career Pittsburgh Pirate, Drabek began his journey with the most successful franchise in major league history, the New York Yankees. He was thought to be an important piece of their future, until Pirates general manager Syd Thrift somehow convinced the Yanks that they were better off with Rick Rhoden, Cecilio Guante, and Pat Clements.

After originally being selected out of high school by the Cleveland Indians in the fourth round of the 1980 Major League Baseball Draft, the young hurler decided to attend the University of Houston in hopes of improving his draft stock. Instead, he went in the 11th round to the Chicago White Sox three years later. While pitching well for their Class A teams in Niagara Falls and Appleton, before posting a 12–5 mark, with a miniscule 2.24 ERA, at their Double-A club in Glen Falls, Doug was the infamous player to be named later in a deal to the New York Yankees in 1984.

The right-hander continued his minor league success in 1985, with Albany-Colonie, leading the Eastern League in strikeouts and innings pitched before finally getting his shot in the majors a year later, despite the fact that he had a poor start with Columbus in his first Triple-A venture, with a 7.29 ERA in eight starts. Drabek struggled his first month and a half with the Yankees, before winning his first major league game on July 11, allowing a single run in six innings against the Twins. Showing that his future was indeed bright, he was 6–6 during the rest of his rookie campaign, with a 3.60 ERA, far below the 5.80 he had sported before his first win.

While giving New York a hint of his potential, they nonetheless dealt him to the Pirates, along with Brian Fisher and Logan Easley, in the off-season. While the trade would turn out to be in favor of the Pirates, early in the 1987 season it appeared that Thrift had been taken advantage of by the Yankees.

Off to a 1–8 start in 1987, after allowing five earned runs in a loss to the Giants on July 6, things looked bleak for Drabek, as well as his young teammates, who looked like they were continuing the poor baseball they had played throughout the mid-1980s; luckily July 6 would prove to be the beginning of better days for the hurler.

Finishing the season 10–4, with a 2.24 ERA, following the July 6 debacle, Drabek demonstrated that he was ready to assume the mantle of ace. The team as a whole was also indicating that they were ready to challenge for the division title, with a 27–11 mark in the club's final 38 games in 1987.

Going 29–19 in the next two seasons, as the team surprised the league in 1988 with a second-place finish, the Bucs were one of the best young teams as of 1990, although few could have foreseen what was about to take place for the moundsman and his team during the first year of the decade.

After 11 seasons without a championship of any kind since winning the World Series in 1979, Pittsburgh captured the National League Eastern Division, while Drabek had a season for the ages. Winning 20 games for the lone time in his career and topping the National League in victories, with 22, and winning percentage, at .786, the Texas native took the game by storm. It was the first time in 32 years, since Bob Friend turned the trick in 1958, that a Pirate had led the National League in wins. Doug received 23 of 24 first-place votes for the Cy Young Award, capturing the well-deserved honor as the league's top pitcher.

In the National League Championship Series against the Reds, Drabek showed that his regular-season performance was not a fluke, with an ERA of 1.65 in his two starts and an incredible walks and hits per innings pitched of 0.98. But it was all for naught, as the team lost in six games to Cincinnati.

A year later, when the Bucs repeated with another title, Drabek, who had slipped quite a bit from 1990, with a 15–14 mark, again pitched wonderfully in the NLCS, only to lose a heartbreaking game. He limited the Braves with an 0.60 ERA in two starts, but a 1–0 loss in the sixth game, a contest that would have sent the Bucs to the World Series had they mustered up even minimal offense, proved to be the end of the road. The team came out listless in Game Seven after the difficult loss, with the Braves defeating them, 4–0.

Pittsburgh was not in a position to pay its players what they could get in the open market. Thus, stars began to jump the fence following the 1991 campaign, with John Smiley and Bobby Bonilla heading off to greener pastures. Despite the losses, the Pirates found a way to win a third consecutive division championship with the help of Drabek's fine rebound season. He was 15–11, lowering his ERA 30 points, to 2.77, in 1992. He finished fifth in the Cy Young voting and hoped for a better result in the 1992 NLCS, as most knew it would probably be the team's last shot at a title.

With Drabek pitching poorly in Games One and Four, the team found itself down three games to one before battling back to send the series to a seventh and deciding game against Atlanta. The right-hander took the mound for what would unfortunately be the last game of his Pirates career. He saved the best for last and was incredible through eight innings, as the Bucs appeared to be headed to the Fall Classic with a 2–0 lead going into the ninth. After appearing tired and loading the bases with no outs, manager Jim Leyland pulled Doug in the ninth. As most Pittsburgh fans know, but still try to forget, Stan Belinda came in, and the Braves scored three runs in arguably the worst moment in Pirates history. It was the end of the championships for the Bucs and Drabek's career in the Steel City.

He was never able to recapture the success he had found with the Pirates, summoning a 56–64 record between 1993 and 1998, playing for the Astros, White Sox, and Orioles. Wanting to enjoy his children rather than missing out on family life because of his grueling travel schedule, Drabek retired from the game in 1998. While his career had ended poorly, for six seasons in a Pittsburgh uniform he proved that

Thrift was an astute judge of talent, taking advantage of the Yankees in a very one-sided trade.

MOST MEMORABLE PERFORMANCE

During the 1990 campaign, a special season for the Pittsburgh Pirates, it was fitting that their ace and soon-to-be Cy Young Award winner, Doug Drabek, was on the mound as the Bucs had a chance to clinch their first division title in 11 seasons, facing the St. Louis Cardinals at Busch Stadium on September 30. After years of losing, the team was showing signs of progress, with a surprising second-place finish in 1988. Two years later, they were even better, closing in on the seventh division title in team history.

Drabek was at his best on this day, allowing only two singles and a double as of the end of the fifth inning, as the teams were battling in a scoreless tie. Knowing there was no room for error, the Texan retired the next nine Cardinal batters, and the Bucs scratched for two runs in the top of the eighth on a sacrifice fly by Gary Redus and a fielder's choice by Andy Van Slyke.

With a 2–0 lead in the bottom of the ninth, Drabek had retired the first two batters to make it 11 in a row and was facing pinch hitter Denny Walling with a one-ball count. Walling hit the next offering to Jose Lind, who tossed it to Sid Bream for the game's final out. Drabek jumped for joy on the mound, knowing he had given his team the division title they had been dreaming of with his three-hit performance.

NOTABLE ACHIEVEMENTS (YEARLY LEADERS AND AWARDS ARE AS PIRATES ONLY)

Part of three National League Eastern Division championship teams (1990, 1991, 1992).

Won the 1990 Cy Young Award.

Won the 1990 *Sporting News* Pitcher of the Year Award.

Finished in the top five for the Cy Young Award twice.

Selected to play in one All-Star Game.

Won more than 20 games once.

Finished in the top 10 in the National League in ERA three times.

Finished in the top 10 in the National League in wins three times.
Finished in the top 10 in the National League in WHIP three times.
Led the league in wins once (1990).
Led the league in winning percentage once (1990).
29th in most putouts for a pitcher in major league history, at 266.

CHAPTER 30

31

BRIAN GILES

There wasn't much to be happy about with Pittsburgh Pirates baseball between 1993 and 2012, but one highlight was slugger Brian Giles. Brought over from the Cleveland Indians in 1999, Giles became one of the game's preeminent sluggers, with 165 home runs in five seasons in a Pirates uniform. *Photo courtesy of the Pittsburgh Pirates.*

There are many sayings that can be used to describe a person, and in the case of former Pittsburgh Pirates outfielder Brian Giles, there are two that perfectly describe his career. The first is, "Timing is everything." If he had not come to the Steel City during the abyss that was Pirates baseball, his incredible power numbers and ability to get on base might have been more appreciated by the national baseball audience. The second is, "What goes around comes around," which would sum up his tale: A young prospect comes to Pittsburgh as part of a salary dump and then leaves the city as a star player the same way.

During his days in Pittsburgh, Giles was not only the best hitter on the team, but also one of the preeminent sluggers in the National League. But as phenomenal as his statistics were, there was another reason timing was not on his side, other than playing in Pittsburgh: he achieved such lofty numbers during perhaps the greatest offensive era in the history of the game, the steroid era.

Between 1999 and 2002, Brian averaged 37 home runs a year and 109 RBIs, while coming in with a remarkable 1.030 on-base plus slugging percentage and a .309 average. In most eras, he would be considered a future Hall of Famer, ranking at the top of most categories. During the steroid era, Giles was still considered one of the best hitters, but he was not at the top of any lists. Table 31.1 shows where he rated in the Senior Circuit during his time with the Bucs versus the leader in each category.

It was an amazing four-year peak in Giles's career, but he never came close to the leaders in the league. It was his rankings in the steroid era, the fact that his power numbers severely dwindled after his trade to the Padres (where he played in a hitter-unfriendly offensive

Table 31.1. Brian Giles's totals between 1999 and 2002 versus the leader in each category.

Category	Total	NL Rankings	NL Leader	Total
Home runs	149	6th	Sosa	226
RBIs	436	7th	Sosa	547
OPS	1.030	6th	Bonds	1.237
Slugging percentage	.604	7th	Bonds	.748
OBP	.426	5th	Bonds	.489

CHAPTER 31

facility) and perhaps his unseemly public misdemeanor battery case, where he was accused of hitting his girlfriend in a Phoenix bar, that led to Brian receiving not a single vote in his one and only year on the Hall of Fame ballot in 2015.

Sports Illustrated baseball writer Jay Jaffe does not think Giles belongs in the Hall of Fame, but he makes the case that Giles should not be a one and done on the ballot and warrants more consideration using Sabermetric statistics:

> His 50.9 career WAR ranks 30th among right fielders (he made 50 percent of his starts in right, 34 percent in left, and 16 percent in center), about 23 wins short of the average Hall of Famer at the position but still better than six of the 24 enshrined, all from prior to World War II. His 37.3 peak WAR ranks 25th among the same set, 5.6 wins below the standard but ahead of nine enshrined, including Enos Slaughter (34.9). He's just 0.4 behind Padres legend Dave Winfield in that category, and mere decimals ahead of Dave Parker and Dwight Evans, with Darryl Strawberry (34.7), Ken Singleton (33.6), and Roger Maris (32.3) below him. His 44.1 JAWS ranks 27th, 14 points below the standard but ahead of eight Hall of Famers, not to mention Golden Era Committee near-miss Tony Oliva (40.8).[1]

Before the El Cajon, California, native became a star in the Steel City, he was a member of the deep and fertile farm system of the Cleveland Indians in the early 1990s, after being selected in the 17th round of the 1989 Major League Baseball Amateur Draft. Giles had a successful run until being promoted to the Double-A Canton-Akron Indians, where he hit .216, with no home runs, in 84 at bats. He found his stroke again the following season, hitting .327, and continued to succeed after being sent to Buffalo, where Brian smacked a career-high 20 home runs in 1996, leading to his promotion to Cleveland as he continued his torrid pace, hitting .355 in 51 games.

Playing mostly left field with the Indians in 1997 and 1998, Giles fell to .268, with 33 home runs, prompting an off-season trade with the Bucs, who sent Ricardo Rincon in return; as it turned out,

Rincon was not nearly enough compensation for the muscular California native.

Becoming the starting center fielder with the Bucs, Brian immediately found Three Rivers Stadium to his liking, tying Hall of Famer Willie Stargell for most home runs in the facility's history, with 24. He smacked what would be a career-high 39 homers that season, including 28 while playing in center, two short of the franchise mark set by Frank Thomas in 1953. The only thing that kept the left-handed slugger from eclipsing 40 home runs in 1999 was a broken finger suffered while sliding into second base, which caused him to miss the final 11 games of the season.

Continuing his consistently strong performance, Giles helped the team bid adieu to Three Rivers with a 35-home run, 123-RBI campaign, only eight short of Paul Waner's Pirates RBI record. He led the club in just about every major category, and with the anticipated revenue that the new facility, PNC Park, was set to generate, the future looked bright for the team, who showed the outfielder their appreciation by inking him to a five-year, $45 million dollar deal, the richest in team history at the time.

The slugger continued his incredible run as a Pirate in PNC Park during the next two seasons. In 2001, he tied the all-time team mark in total bases for a left-handed hitter, with 340, before setting the franchise record for walks by a lefty the following season. He hit 75 homers during that two-year period, with 208 RBIs, and was more than living up to the lofty contract he signed in 2000. Unfortunately, the front office took the newfound wealth provided by PNC Park and actually made the team worse.

By 2003, the team was still struggling, as were their financial fortunes. With Giles enjoying another productive year in a Pirate uniform, the Bucs once again decided to rebuild and sent the outfielder to his native California, to the Padres, in exchange for Jason Bay, Oliver Perez, and Cory Stewart. It turned out to be another fine trade for the Bucs, as Brian hit only 83 home runs in seven seasons with San Diego, while Bay became the first Pirate in history to win the Rookie of the Year Award.

Regardless of the less-than-stellar way his career ended after leaving the team, Brian Giles will be remembered as one of the greatest sluggers in franchise history, even though his timing wasn't always the best.

MOST MEMORABLE PERFORMANCE

While suffering through one of the worst campaigns in franchise history, one in which there was much hope as the season began with the opening of PNC Park and much despair after the campaign ended with 100 losses, Brian Giles and the Bucs had a game for the ages on July 28, in the first game of a doubleheader against the Astros, scoring seven runs in the ninth inning for a dramatic 9–8 win.

In 2001, Houston was the class of the division, while the Bucs took up residence at the bottom. Despite the fact that they were 39–62 coming into the contest, 32.977 fans came to see the twin bill and were treated to nothing more than they had been throughout the entire season to that point—disappointment. Houston shot out to an early 4–1 lead against starter Bronson Arroyo and increased it to 8–2 with two runs in the top of the ninth.

In the bottom of the ninth, the first two Pirates were quickly retired, before a double by Kevin Young and a Pat Meares homer cut the advantage in half. Another run made the score 8–5, bringing the tying run to the plate in Jason Kendall. Kendall was hit by Houston closer Billy Wagner, who then faced Giles with the bases full. One of the best closers in the game, Wagner threw a one-ball, no-strike pitch to the lefty, who promptly placed it over the fence for a climatic 9–8 victory for the team, making it seven runs after two outs in the bottom ninth. The walk-off grand slam by Giles topped off a 3-for-5 performance in the most memorable game of his Pirates career.

NOTABLE ACHIEVEMENTS (YEARLY LEADERS AND AWARDS ARE AS PIRATES ONLY)

> Played in two All-Star Games.
> Finished in the top 25 for the Most Valuable Player Award four times.
> Hit more than 100 RBIs three times.

Finished in the top 10 in the National League in on-base percentage four times.

Finished in the top 10 in the National League in home runs twice.

Finished in the top 10 in the National League in OPS four times.

Finished in the top 10 in the National League in RBIs twice.

Led the league in assists by a left fielder once (2002).

Led the league in double plays by a left fielder once (2002).

Led the league in winning percentage once (1990).

62nd in highest OPS in major league history, at .902.

57th in highest OBP in major league history, at .400.

91st in highest slugging percentage in major league history, at .502.

64th in most walks in major league history, at 1,183.

32

JOHN CANDELARIA

Coming onto the scene in a huge way in 1975, by striking out 14 Cincinnati Reds in the NLCS during his rookie season, John Candelaria fought several injuries to become one of the team's best pitchers. A year later, Candelaria tossed a no-hitter on national TV against the Dodgers and won 20 games in 1977.

Photo courtesy of the Pittsburgh Pirates.

In the past 70 years there have been three seasons of note where a pitcher for the Pittsburgh Pirates has been considered among the best in the game: Vern Law in 1960, Doug Drabek's 1990 campaign, and 1977, when John Candelaria, a 23-year-old southpaw from the heart of New York City, fashioned one of the great performances in franchise history. Two of these hurlers were given the Cy Young Award in honor of their excellence, but the one who missed out, Candelaria, may have had the best season of all. Table 32.1 is a comparison of the three seasons. National League rankings are in parentheses.

While it's true that Drabek and Law played for championship teams and the "Candy Man," as Candelaria was known, did not, he ranked in the top three in all major pitching categories, and unlike the Most Valuable Player Award, the Cy Young is supposed to go to the best pitcher. The injustice of the 1977 Cy Young vote is that Candelaria not only lost, but also finished fifth. Table 32.2 is a comparison of the top five vote-getters.

It seems inconceivable looking at these statistics that the Pirates hurler was not at least given more consideration for the award, much less emerge victorious in the voting. Regardless of the fact that he didn't win, Candelaria had a season for the ages with the Bucs in 1977, the culmination of a three-year run that had all the makings of a potential Hall of Fame career, lofty heights that injuries and a bad back would unfortunately derail.

Standing at six feet, seven inches, unusually tall for a pitcher, the New York native began his sports career as a basketball player for the Quebradillas Pirates of the Puerto Rican Basketball League before playing winter baseball for Bayamon, also in Puerto Rico. He was drafted by Pittsburgh in the second round of the 1972 Amateur Draft and quickly rose through the Pirates system. Candelaria was 21–10

Table 32.1. A comparison of John Candelaria's 1977 campaign, Doug Drabek's 1990 season and Vern Law's 1960 outing.

Player	Wins	Winning Percentage	ERA	WHIP	Cy Young Vote
Candelaria	20 (3)	.800 (1)	2.34 (1)	1.071 (2)	5th
Drabek	22 (1)	.786 (1)	2.76 (6)	1.063 (3)	1st
Law	20 (3)	.690 (3)	3.08 (7)	1.126 (2)	1st

     CHAPTER 32

Table 32.2. A comparison of the top five vote-getters for the 1977 Cy Young Award.

Player	Wins	Winning Percentage	ERA	WHIP	Cy Young Pts.
Carlton	23	.697	2.64	1.124	104
John	20	.741	2.78	1.248	54
Reuschal	20	.667	2.79	1.218	18
Seaver	21	.778	2.58	1.014	18
Candelaria	20	.800	2.34	1.071	17

in two seasons of A ball before making the jump two levels to the Charleston Charlies of the International League in 1974 and 1975, where he was 7–1, with a minuscule 1.75 ERA.

His phenomenal record in Triple-A prompted a call up to the Bucs on June 8, as the southpaw continued his strong season, dominating National League hitters by allowing only 95 hits in 125 innings, with an impressive 2.76 ERA. As good John was then, it was in a losing effort against the Cincinnati Reds in the National League Championship Series that he showed a national audience just how good he was. The 21-year-old struck out a NLCS record 14 men in only 7 ²/₃ innings, allowing only three hits. It was a prelude to the next two seasons, during which time he would become one of the best hurlers in the game.

While Candelaria had an impressive 16–7 mark in the 1976 campaign, it was more memorable for a feat he performed for a national TV audience on August 9, doing something no Pirate had done since 1907: pitch a no-hitter in the city of Pittsburgh. He defeated the Los Angeles Dodgers that evening, 2–0, in a game where he loaded the bases without a hit in the third before dominating Los Angeles the rest of the way.

Continuing to improve, 1977 proved to be Candelaria's marquee season. He posted a remarkable 20–5 record, leading the Senior Circuit in winning percentage and ERA, with a 2.34 mark. He was the first Pirates left-hander to win 20 games in 53 years, also becoming the first southpaw since Sandy Koufax 12 years earlier to win 20 games and the ERA title in one campaign. It was a shame that John only finished fifth in the Cy Young voting for such a notable performance. Sadly, it would be the only time in his 19-year career that the Candy Man would receive votes for this prestigious honor.

Struggling somewhat in 1978, with a 12–11 mark, Candelaria rebounded in the Bucs' world championship campaign of 1979, with 14 wins. He was also called upon in Game Six of the Fall Classic, with the team trailing the Baltimore Orioles three games to two. He threw seven shutout innings that evening to help tie the series and send it to a seventh and deciding game, which the Pirates won.

Going 70–38, with a 2.94 ERA, in his first five seasons, the future looked bright for Candelaria, but an 11–14 record in 1980, coupled with a torn bicep muscle suffered a year later that limited him to six games, derailed his march to superstardom.

The Candy Man returned to form in 1982 and went 39–26 during the next three seasons, with an ERA below 3.00. It was at that point injuries again cropped up. John underwent surgeries to remove bone spurs from his left elbow and repair a chronic bad back, conditions that would hamper him his entire career, prompting manager Chuck Tanner to send his now-disgruntled lefty to the bull pen in 1985. The angry Candelaria demanded a trade. With the team losing, Pittsburgh gave in to his wishes, sending him to California, along with George Hendrick and Al Holland, for Pat Clements, Mike Brown, and Bob Kipper.

Candelaria pitched for eight more seasons with seven different teams, returning to Steel City in 1993, where he ended his major league career with his poorest season in professional baseball, fashioning an 8.24 ERA in 24 games.

John currently lives in Pittsburgh and has been an avid world traveler since leaving the game. It was a fine career despite the injuries, one where he might have had the greatest season a Pirates pitcher has enjoyed in the modern era.

MOST MEMORABLE PERFORMANCE

In 1907, Nick Maddox tossed the first no-hitter in Pirates history in front of a home crowd at Exposition Park. It was a great moment and one that no one would have guessed would be the last no-hitter the city would see for 64 years, until Bob Gibson threw one against the Bucs in 1971. While Gibson's game was nice, it wasn't a Pirate who tossed the gem; that streak would end five years later, when John Candelaria took the mound on August 9, 1976, against the Dodgers at Three Rivers Stadium.

CHAPTER 32

The game was being televised on ABC and the Candy Man was dominant early, retiring the first seven Dodgers in order until walking Steve Yeager in the third. Davy Lopes and Ted Sizemore would reach base on errors, loading them up with Bill Russell coming to bat with two outs. Candy was tough, getting Russell to ground out to short and ending Los Angeles' only threat of the evening.

Pittsburgh was having an equally tough time scoring but plated two in the fifth, when Bill Robinson doubled in Richie Zisk and Dave Parker to give them their only runs of the contest. It would be enough, however, as Candelaria retired the final 18 Dodgers in the game, getting Russell to fly out to Al Oliver in the top of the ninth to finally end a 69-year streak and allowing Pirates fans to witness someone on their team tossing a no-hitter.

NOTABLE ACHIEVEMENTS (YEARLY LEADERS AND AWARDS ARE AS PIRATES ONLY)

Part of two National League Eastern Division championship teams (1975, 1979).

Part of one National League championship and one world championship team (1979).

Finished fifth in the voting for the 1977 National League Cy Young Award.

Finished 18th in the voting for the 1977 National League MVP Award.

First Pirates left-hander to win 20 games since 1924 (Wilbur Cooper).

Selected to play in one All-Star Game

Won 20 games once.

Led the league in ERA once (1977).

Led the league in winning percentage once (1977).

Led the league in strikeouts per walks once (1984).

Led the league in fielding percentage for pitchers five times (1976, 1978, 1979, 1983, 1984).

112th in walks and hits per innings pitched in major league history, at 1.184.

125th in walks per nine innings in major league history, at 2.110.

66th in strikeouts per walks in major league history, at 2.826.

33

VIC WILLIS

In the Hall of Fame, pitcher Vic Willis is listed as a member of the Braves, which is correct, as he spent eight of his 13 major league seasons with Boston's entry in the National League. But if one considers only his time in Boston, Willis's credentials to enter Cooperstown would be highly compromised, as he was four games over .500 there, including a 30–54 mark his final two seasons. It becomes apparent in looking at his totals in the Steel City with the Pittsburgh Pirates that his time there was what actually prompted the Veteran's Committee to include him in their hallowed ranks 85 years after he pitched his last game.

The numbers in table 33.1 not only show that Willis was seemingly done in the majors at the end of his tenure with Boston, but also that his record with the team may have been better than indicated with Boston. They also demonstrate that the total effect he had on Boston's total team record was not far from his effect in the Steel City.

Regardless of the fact that his effect on each team's total records was similar, there is no doubt that his impressive comeback after coming over from the Beaneaters impressed the Veteran's Committee.

Born in Cecil County, Maryland, Willis signed a contract with the Harrisburg Senators of the Pennsylvania State League in 1895, before moving on to the Lynchburg Hill Climbers after the Senators folded. Despite only going 10–15, he impressed many, and even after missing the 1896 campaign due to illness, he was signed by Syracuse in 1897, where he had a phenomenal 21–17 mark, with an incredible 1.16 ERA.

Vic's phenomenal season prompted Boston's entry in the National League to purchase him for $1,000, a generous amount for the time.

Table 33.1.   Vic Willis's career and team records with Boston and Pittsburgh.

Seasons	Record	Winning Percentage	Team Record	Winning Percentage
1898–1903	121–93	.565	463–389	.543
1904–1905	30–54	.357	106–201	.345
Total Boston	151–147	.507	569–590	.491
1906–1909	89–46	.659	392–221	.639
Total Pittsburgh	240–193	.554	961–811	.542

During his rookie season with the Beaneaters, he showed he was worth every penny. He combined with Kid Nichols, Ted Lewis, and Fred Klobedanz to form an outstanding starting rotation that led Boston to their fourth National League crown in seven seasons, with a 102–47 mark.

The Maryland native, with his wonderful control and an off-speed pitch and curveball that were at times unhittable, had a wonderful rookie campaign, with 25 wins, and went on to become an effective force for the team in the next five seasons. He won 20 or more games three times, including a career-high 27 in both 1899 and 1902, while leading the circuit in ERA in 1899.

Almost jumping ship to the Philadelphia A's in 1901 and the Detroit Tigers of the American League in 1902, Willis nonetheless decided to stick with Boston but had several salary disputes with the club throughout the next couple of seasons before having the worst campaigns in his major league career. Going 12–18 in 1903, prior to leading the circuit in losses during the next two seasons, with 25 and 29, respectively, the moundsman began to wear out his welcome with the Beaneaters. While his records were poor, it was the quick demise of the team that was probably the reason, as his secondary statistics remained good.

With Vic's career on a downward trend, Barney Dreyfuss sent Dave Brain, Del Howard, and Vive Lindaman to Boston for the right-hander. Willis was thrilled to be sent to a contender and reassured fans and teammates alike that he was not as bad as his record indicated. He commented, "Don't believe those tales you hear about my being all-in. Wait until you see me in action for your team and then form your opinion of my worth to your team. I assure you that I am delighted to be a Pirate and that I will do my best to bring another pennant to the Smoky City."[1]

CHAPTER 33

The results were phenomenal. He once again became a 20-game winner in each of his first three seasons with the Bucs, as manager Fred Clarke tabbed his 32-year-old hurler to pitch the most important game of the season for the club in 1908, with the pennant on the line. Battling with the Cubs and Giants, Pittsburgh took on Chicago on the last day of the season with a simple chore: beat the Cubs and win the National League crown. Willis had a 23–10 mark going into the contest, and the teams were tied at two going into the bottom of the sixth. Unfortunately, the Cubs scored three in the next couple innings and won the contest, 5–2, ending the season for the Bucs.

A year later, the club won 110 games, with Willis having another phenomenal campaign, at 22–11, despite his being embroiled in yet another contract dispute at the beginning of the season, before losing the first contest played at Forbes Field. The team won their first pennant since 1903 and secured a spot in the World Series against the Tigers.

An alumnus of the University of Delaware, Vic was not at his best in his lone Fall Classic. He pitched twice, with a 4.63 ERA, losing his only decision, a 5–4 defeat in Game Six and a missed chance at securing the world championship, blowing an early three-run lead.

Even though Willis was a 20-game winner in each of his four seasons with the team, Dreyfuss seemed frustrated with his demands and reported disciplinary issues with manager Fred Clarke and put him on waivers following the 1909 campaign. Picked up by St. Louis, he was 9–12 for the Cardinals before being sold to the minor league Baltimore Orioles. After a dispute with the sale, he was awarded to the Chicago Cubs but decided to retire instead of reporting to the Windy City.

Dying of a stroke in 1947, at 71 years of age, Willis never had the chance to see that he would eventually be recognized with the greats of the game. In 1995, 48 years after his death, he was given baseball's ultimate honor of being elected to the Hall of Fame by the Veteran's Committee, an honor he most certainly would have never received if not for his time with the Pirates.

MOST MEMORABLE PERFORMANCE

The most memorable player performances in the pages of this book chiefly involve inspiring victories or feats, but in the case of Vic Willis, who won 66 percent of his games with the Bucs, yet seemingly came up on the losing end of many of the clutch encounters he pitched for the team, it is a contest he lost that he may be most remembered for.

Until 1909, the Pirates played in a facility called Exposition Park, which was on the North Side of the city, not far from where PNC Park now stands. The park was constantly flooding, necessitating special ground rules to combat the water. No longer wanting to deal with these issues, Pirates president Barney Dreyfuss opened the first steel and concrete stadium in the National League, Forbes Field, constructed in the Oakland section of the city, and on June 30, 1909, the magnificent facility opened to a sellout crowd of 30,338 fans.

Manager Fred Clarke called on Willis to start in this important contest, and while the veteran pitched well, allowing only four hits, the Pirates offense did not show up on this celebratory day, as he allowed two Chicago runs in the top of the eighth en route to a 3–2 loss. It was a defeat that crushed Dreyfuss, who would later say, "What a shame we had to lose that one. I'd have given my share of the gate to have won on this day."[2] For a pitcher who came up winless for the Pirates in the World Series and lost the pivotal contest of the 1908 pennant race, this was probably his most memorable big-game loss.

NOTABLE ACHIEVEMENTS (YEARLY LEADERS AND AWARDS ARE AS PIRATES ONLY)

Elected to Baseball Hall of Fame by Veteran's Committee in 1995.
Part of one National League championship and world championship team (1909).
Won 20 games four times.
Led the league in wins above replacement for pitchers once (1906).
Led the league in games started once (1909).
Finished in the top four in the National League in wins four times.
48th in most wins in major league history, with 249.
42nd in most innings pitched in major league history, at 3,996.
19th in most shutouts in major league history, at 50.
19th in most complete games in major league history, at 388.
28th in most putouts as a pitcher in major league history, with 271.
15th in most assists as a pitcher in major league history, with 1,124.

CHAPTER 33

34

MANNY SANGUILLEN

In the early 1970s, only one other catcher could be compared to Cincinnati Red Hall of Famer Johnny Bench; his name was Manny Sanguillen. Taking over the starting reigns behind the plate for the Pirates in 1969, Sangy hit .305 in his first five seasons with the team.

Photo courtesy of the Pittsburgh Pirates.

In most eras, Manny Sanguillen would have been considered the greatest catcher of his time. He had it all. He was a great hitter and a fast runner, and had a gun for an arm, with a quick release that would be a deterrent to even the greatest of base stealers, including Lou Brock, who felt he was the hardest catcher to steal against. Sanguillen would have been considered the best in the game behind the plate if only he hadn't played in the 1970s, the same era as Johnny Bench.

Even with Bench on the field, for the first three years of the 1970s, Sangy was in the conversation. Former Pirates pitcher and longtime team announcer Steve Blass felt that except for Bench's impressive power, Sanguillen was every bit his equal. Table 34.1 gives the stats of both backstops between 1970 and 1972. The numbers seem to back up Blass's sentiments. Bench was certainly a more dominant power hitter, but Sangy hit 37 points better, threw out 11 more runners, and was almost his equal in caught stealing percentage.

During the course of his career, Bench was able to maintain his excellence and is deservedly included in the short conversation of the greatest catchers in the history of the game, while Sanguillen's productivity both behind the plate and offensively slipped, as he eclipsed .300 only one more time the rest of his 13-year career. Nonetheless, for a short period of time when both men were in their prime, it seemed like a two-man race for best in the game.

Sangy had an amazing start to his career, especially considering that he wasn't even sure he'd play baseball. Impressive in several sports, particularly boxing, he was signed by legendary Pirates scout Howie Haak in 1964, as an amateur free agent. After a less-than-stellar first season in professional baseball in 1965, with the Batavia Pirates of the New York-Pennsylvania League, where he hit .235, the Colon, Panama, native quickly became a top prospect. He raised his average

Table 34.1.   Manny Sanguillen and Johnny Bench stats between 1970 and 1972.

Player	HR	RBI	AVE	OPS	CS	SBA	CS%	LG AVE CS%
Bench	112	334	.267	.860	87	93	48.3	35.0
Sanguillen	21	213	.314	.761	98	121	44.7	35.0

CHAPTER 34

to .328 with Raleigh a year later, before making the jump two levels from A ball to the Triple-A Columbus Jets in 1966.

In his first full season with the Jets, Manny slipped to .258 but was called up to the majors in mid-July, where he was more than respectable, with a .271 average in 96 at bats. Despite his good debut, Sanguillen spent the entire 1968 campaign in Columbus, once again eclipsing the .300 plateau, at .316. His fine performance prompted Bucs general manager Joe L. Brown to call up the 25-year-old backstop for good in 1969, and he immediately became the starting catcher for a young Pirates club that was about to become one of the best teams in the game.

Sanguillen was a legendary free swinger who never met a pitch he didn't like. He treated walks as if they were his enemy, only accruing 223 free passes in 13 seasons. Remarkably, while most hitters with his philosophy would strike out more than 150 times a year, Manny struck out a mere 331 times, with a career-high 45 of them coming during his official rookie campaign in 1969.

It was probably the most remarkable fact of the Panamanian's fine career, one that saw him hit .296 with his aggressive approach, including a .303 mark his first season as a starter behind the plate. Sangy also had unique speed for a catcher, finishing in the top 10 in triples in the National League on three occasions. After many seasons of trying to find a star-like presence behind the plate, Brown knew they now had one, as the young Pirate was about to ascend to one of the best in the game.

Manny's second season would prove to be phenomenal. He compiled a .325 average, finishing third in the National League, behind Rico Carty, and in a virtual tie with Joe Torre. The Baseball Writers' Association of America gave him the respect he deserved, as he finished 11th in the voting for the Most Valuable Player Award.

Showing that his first two years had not been an aberration, Sangy had another great season in 1971, finishing sixth in the batting race, while securing his first selection to play in the All-Star Game. With Johnny Bench suffering through his worst season to that point, with his batting average slumping to .238, with only 27 home runs, while throwing out what was then a career-low 41 percent of runners, Sanguillen was now arguably the best backstop in the game, helping lead the Bucs to their first National League pennant in 11 seasons.

Getting to his first World Series that season, the catcher went into the Fall Classic with below-average performances in his two National League Championship Series appearances, hitting only .222, with one RBI and no extra-base hits. But Manny quickly made people forget about that with a stellar World Series, accumulating 11 hits, including five in the final two games against the heavily favored Baltimore Orioles.

He continued his run as one of the best catchers in the game throughout the next two seasons, despite the fact that he fell below .300 for the first time since 1967, hitting .298 in 1972, before dropping to .282 a year later, although hitting a career-high 12 home runs. Sanguillen showed a rare glimpse of power in 1973, but it was a poor year for him personally, as he had trouble dealing with the death of his dear friend Roberto Clemente. The grieving catcher even went scuba diving in the waters in Puerto Rico, looking for the body of Clemente, which was never found after the plane the famed right fielder was flying in went down while trying to deliver relief supplies to earthquake-ravaged Nicaragua. Manager Bill Virdon tabbed Manny to replace Clemente in right field, an experiment that lasted only 59 games before he returned behind the plate.

He continued to hit below .300 in 1974, with a .287 average, prompting Zander Hollander to describe Sanguillen in his 1975 baseball annual by saying that his "once smoking bat has cooled."[1] Proving the preview wrong, the backstop hit a career-best .328, making his third All-Star Team, while the Bucs captured their fifth National League East crown in six seasons. The season proved to be Sangy's last run as a star, as he spent one more season in the Steel City before being dealt to the Oakland Athletics in a blockbuster, yet unique, deal that brought the team manager Chuck Tanner.

Manny stayed one season in Oakland before being returned to Pittsburgh in 1978, for Miguel Dilone, Mike Edwards, and Elias Sosa. For the next three seasons, he was nothing more than a little-used reserve, with only 342 at bats during his final years. Although no longer a starter, Sangy had one final great moment in a Pirates uniform in Game Two of the 1979 World Series. With the game tied at two and the Bucs already down a game in the series, he smacked a pinch-hit single in the ninth to give the team a dramatic 3–2 win.

Sanguillen retired from the majors following the 1980 campaign, playing one more season in professional baseball, in 1982, with the Reynosa Broncos of the Mexican League. He now spends his summers at PNC Park, sitting in a barbeque stand that bears his name, talking with the fans, many of whom have no idea that he was once a victim of circumstance, playing in the same era as Johnny Bench, which made him only the second-greatest catcher in the game during his prime.

MOST MEMORABLE PERFORMANCE

Manny Sanguillen had many great games during his Pittsburgh Pirates career, but it was one of his last postseason performances, in a pinch-hitting role, which helped the team win their last world championship to date, that may have been his most memorable.

In the opening contest of the 1979 series, starting pitcher Bruce Kison never made it out of the first inning, allowing five runs in what would turn out to be a 5–4 defeat. After taking an early 2–0 lead off a single by Bill Madlock and a sacrifice fly by Ed Ott, the Orioles battled back, tying the score at two, as Eddie Murray homered in the second and smacked an RBI double in the sixth.

Falling behind two games to none would have made Pittsburgh's run at a fifth world championship difficult indeed as the team came to bat in the top of the ninth inning. With two outs, Ed Ott singled and Phil Garner walked, putting men on first and second with pitcher Don Robinson coming to the plate. Manager Chuck Tanner decided to send in his 35-year-old former star catcher to bat to see if he could provide one more great moment for the team. True to form, the free-swinging Sanguillen was on the wrong end of a one-ball, two-strike pitch when he hit the next pitch into right field for a solid single, plating Ott as the team went on to even the series at one game apiece. It was a classic moment by the catcher and a pivotal one in the Bucs' world championship run.

NOTABLE ACHIEVEMENTS (YEARLY LEADERS AND AWARDS ARE AS PIRATES ONLY)

Part of six National League Eastern Division championship teams (1970, 1971, 1972, 1974, 1975, 1979).

Part of two National League championship and world championship teams (1971, 1979).

Finished in the top 16 in the National League MVP vote four times.

Played in three All-Star Games.

Finished in the top six in the National League batting race three times.

Led the league in assists by a catcher once (1971).

Led the league in double plays by a catcher once (1971).

Led the league in runners caught stealing once (1974).

88th in most defensive games at catcher in major league history, at 1,114.

75th in most putouts at catcher in major league history, at 5,996.

35

KENT TEKULVE

It's a small fraternity in the long and storied history of the Pittsburgh Pirates, those men who were on the mound as the team won a world championship. The Bucs have won five Fall Classics, but since the one in 1960 ended in the only walk-off seventh-game home run in the history of the event, that leaves only the following four men who belong to this special group: Babe Adams; Red Oldham; Steve Blass; and a string thin, sidearm hurler who stood at six-feet-four inches tall from Cincinnati, Ohio, named Kent Tekulve. And Tekulve faced the most difficult situation of the four. Table 35.1 is a listing of the famous four and the situations they were faced with.

In Game Seven of the 1909 World Series, Adams was masterful, garnering a record-tying third victory in a single Fall Classic with a one-sided 8–0 masterpiece. Game Seven of the 1925 Fall Classic was an incredible comeback victory, but Oldham entered the game in the ninth inning with a two-run lead and retired the side in order in a driving rainstorm as evening was descending on an unlit Forbes Field. Steve Blass tossed a clutch performance in Game Seven of the 1971 Fall Classic but was only in trouble once, in the bottom of the eighth, when he allowed his only run of the contest, retiring the last man of the inning with the tying run on third.

With the Pirates leading 2–1 in the bottom of the eighth of Game Seven of the 1979 World Series, Tekulve entered the contest with men on first and second and one out. The lanky hurler, who was nervous, remembered Willie Stargell coming to the mound to calm him down. "Eighth inning of that game and I'm pitching to Eddie Murray with the bases loaded," he recalled. "Willie comes over to me from first

Table 35.1. Pitchers who have been on the mound when the Pirates have won the World Series and the batters they retired and the final scores.

Season	Pitcher	Opponent	Batter Retired	Final Score
1909	Babe Adams	Detroit	Tom Jones	8–0
1925	Red Oldham	Washington	Goose Goslin	9–7
1971	Steve Blass	Baltimore	Merv Rettenmund	2–1
1979	Kent Tekulve	Baltimore	Pat Kelly	4–1

base and says, 'If you're scared, you play first and I'll pitch.' I figured if he can stay calm, so can the rest of us."[1] Kent got Terry Crowley on a ground out, which put men on second and third, and then walked Ken Singleton to load the bases, facing Eddie Murray, who was in the midst of a difficult slump. Stargell, knowing the game was on the line, came to the mound to give the reliever the memorable speech. Tekulve gave up a lazy fly to deep right field, but Dave Parker slipped on the poor Memorial Stadium turf, steading himself just in time to catch the final out of the eighth. The Cincinnati native returned to the mound in the ninth with a more comfortable 4–1 advantage and retired the Orioles in order to give him his moment in time.

It was the highlight of a wonderful 16-year career, which started when Tekulve was signed by Pirates scout Dick Coury as an amateur free agent out of Marietta College. He was passed on in the draft because, strangely enough, he had an unconventional running style. He had an effective sidearm delivery that scouting director Harding Peterson tried to convince him to abandon. Luckily, his running style never came into play, and as a pitcher he stuck with his delivery. After a successful professional baseball debut with the Geneva Pirates in the New York-Pennsylvania League, where he was 6–2, with a 1.70 ERA in seven starts, six of which were complete, he was inserted in the bull pen with the Salem Rebels in 1970 and spent the next six campaigns there, starting only 11 more times in 246 games.

Tekulve had a long yet successful minor league stay, going 53–31, with a 2.25 ERA. He was available for the Rule 5 Draft after the 1974 campaign and once again went unchosen, which proved to be quite advantageous for the Bucs. Teke returned to the organization in 1975 and quickly became an important part of the Pirates bull pen.

The reliever was 16–6 in his first three full seasons with the Bucs as a setup man, which included a 10–1 campaign in 1977. He sported a 2.65 ERA, and while he pitched in almost 60 games a season those three years, he was frustrated that he hadn't been given a more important role. That came to an end in 1978, when Kent was given the opportunity to be the teams closer after Goose Gossage left for free agency.

He quickly showed Pittsburgh what a great decision it was, leading the National League in games pitched, with 91, while saving 31. It was a phenomenal first season as a closer and one that saw him not only finish second for the Fireman of the Year Award, behind Rollie Fingers, but also fifth in the Cy Young voting and 13th in the race for the Most Valuable Player Award.

A year later, Tekulve was an important part of the team that would eventually win the franchise's fifth world championship. His 1979 campaign was a mirror image of the previous one, with the moundsman once again leading the circuit in games pitched, with 31 saves. Kent was on top of the world. The speakers at Three Rivers Stadium would blast the song "Rubber Band Man" when he entered the game. He ironically finished in exactly the same spot as in the 1978 Cy Young Award race but moved up five spots, to eighth, for the Senior Circuit's MVP Award.

Tekulve finished his marquee campaign in a fitting manner, saving three games in the World Series and allowing only four hits in 9 $^1/_3$ innings of work, while striking out 10. He appropriately finished the remarkable season on the mound in Game Seven of the World Series.

Kent was now near the top of the charts when it came to relief pitchers. Sadly, mechanical difficulties derailed his storybook career. He lost 10 consecutive games between 1980 and 1981, and, in 1982, gave up 11 runs in the course of two games. Despite his sporadic troubles, the hurler ended up winning 12 contests in 1982, once again leading the league in games pitched.

It was the beginning of a resurgence for the sidearmer. In 1983, he had the best season since 1979, with a career-low 1.64 ERA and 18 saves. Not wanting to lose their 36-year-old closer, the Bucs signed him to a four-year contract following his successful season. Tekulve once again slipped in 1984, with a 3–9 mark and only 13 saves, and he was again unhappy with how he was being used. After three poor performances for the team in 1985, he was dealt across state to the rival Philadelphia Phillies for Frankie Griffin and Al Holland.

Teke lasted four seasons as a setup man for the Phils before ending his career in 1989, with his hometown Cincinnati Reds. He retired as the all-time record-holder for games pitched in relief, with 1,050 (since broken by Jesse Orosco) and currently holds the all-time mark for games pitched without starting a contest. Kent spent five years as a broadcaster for the Phillies and is currently the studio host for the Pirates pregame and postgame shows. In 2014, he had a heart transplant and made a remarkable recovery, inspiring Pirates fans yet again, much as he did so many times on the mound, especially on a cold 1979 October evening in Baltimore when he became a permanent member of a special fraternity.

MOST MEMORABLE PERFORMANCE

Kent Tekulve is the all-time saves holder for the Pittsburgh Pirates, pitched more games without a start than any man in major league history, twice set the saves record in consecutive seasons for the team, and was on the mound when the Bucs won the 1979 World Series. But despite so many notable moments, it is a game on September 1, 1979, that lanky reliever Kent Tekulve may be most remembered for.

Ushering in September in San Francisco's Candlestick Park, Teke was on the mound before surprisingly being sent to left field by manager Chuck Tanner so Grant Jackson could pitch to a left-handed batter. With the Bucs up 5–3, Tanner brought Teke in to try and close out the victory in the eighth inning. He gave up a single to Terry Whitfield and walked catcher Dennis Littlejohn but got out of the inning unscathed. He returned in the bottom of the ninth, giving up a two-out single to Jack Clark. At that point left-handed slugger Darrell Evans came up to bat, and Tanner surprisingly came to the mound, replacing Teke with the southpaw to face Evans.

Instead of pulling Tekulve, Tanner wanted him to remain in the game in case Evans reached base, so he placed the reliever in left field. Odds were against the left-handed batter hitting the ball to left field, but that's exactly what happened, as a fly ball came barreling toward Teke. Luckily, he made the play, ending the game. By placing him in the outfield, the save ironically went to Jackson, costing the Cincinnati native a save that eventually would have been his 32nd and a Pirates record at the time.

NOTABLE ACHIEVEMENTS (YEARLY LEADERS AND AWARDS ARE AS PIRATES ONLY)

Part of three National League Eastern Division championship teams (1974, 1975, 1979).

Part of one National League championship and world championship team (1979).

Finished in the top 13 voting for the National League MVP twice.

Selected to play in one All-Star Game.

Finished fifth for the Cy Young Award twice.

Finished in the top 10 in saves in the National League five times.

Led the league in games finished three times (1978, 1979, 1983).

Led the league in games pitched three times (1978, 1979, 1982).

9th in most games pitched in major league history, at 1,050.

2nd in most games pitched by a reliever in major league history, at 1,050.

Holds the all-time major league record for most games pitched without a start, with 1,050.

12th in most games finished in major league history, at 638.

58th in most saves in major league history, at 184.

Holds the all-time Pittsburgh Pirates record for most saves, with 158.

Holds the all-time Pittsburgh Pirates record (tied) for most games pitched in a season, with 94.

Holds the all-time Pittsburgh Pirates record for most games finished in a season, with 67.

Holds the all-time Pittsburgh Pirates record for most innings pitched by a reliever in a season, with 135.

36

BOBBY BONILLA

The Rule 5 Draft in Major League Baseball has been both cruel and kind to the Pittsburgh Pirates. In the 1950s, they built their future championship squad through it, picking up both Roberto Clemente and Roy Face. In the latter half of the 20th century and early part of the 21st, it was not as good. In 2004, during the height of their record-setting losing streak, when the farm system should have been their most valuable commodity, they lost five players through the draft, almost six, but the Tampa Bay Rays backed off of Daryl Ward. The Bucs also lost two other players after they went unprotected. The front office was forced to rescue them by giving up other players in a trade. Brought back to the organization were Jose Bautista and an outfielder from the Bronx who would help lead them to consecutive Eastern Division titles by the name of Bobby Bonilla.

In high school, Bonilla was adept at working with computers, and after not being taken in the major league Amateur Draft, he decided to attend trade school. Luckily for the man they would eventually refer to as Bobby Bo, he went to a baseball clinic in Europe, where he was discovered by the Bucs and signed to a minor league contract.

At the beginning of his professional baseball career, it was not readily apparent that Bobby would be a future star for the Pirates and a pivotal part of their championship teams. Hitting only .235 in his first two seasons for the Pirates affiliate in the Gulf Coast League, he didn't show the impressive power that he would display in the majors, with only five long balls during that time period.

After a promotion in 1983, he started to show his power more prominently, with 22 home runs between Alexandria and Nashua, and he looked to be ascending the ladder as a top prospect in the

Pittsburgh organization. Regrettably, just as he was becoming a star in the minors, Bo broke his leg during spring training in 1985, and was on the disabled list until mid-July. He returned to Class A ball to work himself back into playing shape, hitting only .262, with three homers.

During the off-season, while the team still considered him an important prospect, they left him unprotected in the Rule 5 Draft, hoping teams would bypass the slugger because of the injury, not wanting to keep an injured player on their major league roster for the season. Unfortunately, the Chicago White Sox were not one of them and selected the Bronx native. While Pittsburgh hoped he would not be able to contribute to the Sox and Chicago would offer him back instead of keeping him on the roster for the entire season, Bobby was more successful than anyone thought he would be.

Bonilla hit higher than he ever had in the minors, posting a .269 average, and had one of the leading on-base percentages on the team, with a .361 mark. Knowing they had made a terrible mistake, the Bucs sent one-time phenom Jose DeLeon to Chicago to get him back. It turned out to be a fortuitous move, as Pittsburgh kept him on the roster rather than give him his initial Triple-A experience. While he only hit .240 that season after the trade, a year later he exceeded everyone's expectations.

The switch-hitter broke the .300 plateau for the first time in his professional career, and while he hit only 15 home runs, three of them were of record proportions. On July 3, 1987, he became the first Pirate to hit home runs from both sides of the plate in a single game, and nine days later he became the seventh player in franchise history to reach the upper deck of Three Rivers Stadium, hitting a prodigious shot off San Diego's Eric Show.

His confidence at its peak, the 1988 campaign would prove to be Bonilla's coming-out party. By the end of the season he would be considered one of the best in the game. Smacking 24 home runs, while garnering 100 RBIs, Bobby Bo again hit home runs from both sides of the plate and was voted as a starter at third base to play in his first All-Star Game. He also captured the Silver Slugger Award as the league's most proficient offensive player at third. Writer Tom Boswell said of Bonilla,

> When you're six feet three and swish the bat menacingly
> across the plate in a low golfer's arc, then rock back, hands
> low, swaying just a touch to some internal rhumba, it brings

CHAPTER 36

back memories of those great right-handed line-drive hitters.
. . . It's just as rare when a player reminds the game's oldsters
of both Willie McCovey and Willie Stargell.[1]

As good as the infielder was at the plate, he was inconsistent in the field. While he led the league in assists and total chances at the hot corner, he was also at the top with 32 errors, oftentimes booting easy grounders, while making spectacular plays on some of the more difficult ones.

Bonilla had another fine season in 1989 and, a year later, a campaign worthy of Most Valuable Player status, with the Bucs capturing their first division title in 11 seasons. He eclipsed 30 home runs for the first time, with 32, while accumulating what would be a career-high 120 RBIs. He would have captured the highest seasonal award the game has to offer if not for teammate Barry Bonds, finishing second to the all-time home run champion for the National League's MVP Award. The third baseman struggled in his first postseason experience, as did most of his teammates, with a subpar .190 average.

Once again knocking in 100 in 1991, with what was at the time a career-best .302 average, the switch-hitter spent the majority of his season in right field. He came in third in the MVP race, helping the Bucs win another Eastern Division crown. Unlike the rest of his team, Bonilla did not suffer at the plate in the National League Championship Series, posting a .304 average. Unfortunately, following the season he became a free agent. With the Pirates still on weak financial footing, they couldn't afford to beat the New York Mets' offer of five-years, $29 million, which made him the highest-paid player at the time.

Coming home was not the dream scenario the Bronx native had envisioned, and he was dealt to the Baltimore Orioles in 1995, where he reestablished himself as one of the game's best. In 1997, he inked a deal with the Florida Marlins, reuniting with manager Jim Leyland, and together they captured their first world championship. The financially strapped Marlins traded him back to the Mets in May 1998, and once again New York did not mesh well with Bobby Bo. After a poor 1999 campaign, the Mets released him and made what is considered one of the worst contractual mistakes in the history of the game. Not wanting to pay the $5.9 million buyout, they made a deal with him, deferring payment until 2011, and then paying him $1.1 million a year until 2035, turning a $5.9 million buyout into a more than $25 million one. Not a

BOBBY BONILLA

bad return of investment for a player who was thought so little of that he had been left unprotected for the Rule 5 Draft 30 years earlier.

MOST MEMORABLE PERFORMANCE

Never in the first 100 years in the history of the Pittsburgh Pirates had a switch-hitter smacked a home run in a game from both sides of the plate, that is, until July 3, 1987, when Bobby Bonilla, a slugger from the Bronx, became the first to turn the trick.

Going up against Los Angeles Dodger Fernando Valenzuela, Bobby Bo hit an innocent ground out in the second, plating Pittsburgh's first run of the game. An inning later, he ripped a three-run shot, batting right-handed against the southpaw to increase the Bucs' advantage to 5–0.

With the game firmly under control, the switch-hitter came up in the seventh inning, batting from the left side against the right-handed Ken Howell. On cue, Bonilla took the first pitch over the fence for his sixth homer of the year and a permanent spot in the Pittsburgh Pirates record book.

NOTABLE ACHIEVEMENTS (YEARLY LEADERS
AND AWARDS ARE AS PIRATES ONLY)

Part of two National League Eastern Division championship teams (1990, 1991).
Finished in the top three voting for the National League MVP twice and top 16 four times.
Selected to play in four All-Star Games.
Finished in the top 10 in home runs in the National League three times.
Led the league in doubles once (1991).
Led the league in extra-base hits once (1991).
Led the league in assists at third base once (1988).
Led the league in double plays at third base once (1989).
Eclipsed 100 RBIs three times.
36th in most sacrifice flies in major league history, at 97.
145th in most extra-base hits in major league history, with 756.
152nd in most home runs in major league history, at 287.
Only Pittsburgh Pirate to hit a home run from both sides of the plate in a game.

CHAPTER 36

37

BILL MADLOCK

Throughout the course of a world championship run, a general manager usually inevitably makes one in-season trade that seems to tip the scales in the club's favor and guide them to a title. In each of the Pittsburgh Pirates' five World Series title seasons, they made one in-season move that pushed them over the top. Perhaps the most impressive of those decisions occurred on June 28, 1979, when GM Harding Peterson obtained a two-time batting champion from the San Francisco Giants by the name of Bill Madlock, who solidified the team's infield and was an important part of their world championship squad. Table 37.1 is a list of the best in-season transactions for each of the five World Series championship teams.

In retrospect, looking at table 37.1, the only trade that came close to the Madlock deal was the Vinegar Bend Mizell trade in 1960, as the hurler won 13 games down the stretch for the Bucs. Considering the fact that "Mad Dog," Madlock's nickname, would go on to win two batting titles for the Pirates, this is clearly the best in-season deal Pittsburgh has made in a world championship season.

Madlock was born in Memphis, Tennessee, and selected in the 11th round of the 1969 Amateur Draft by the St. Louis Cardinals. Refusing to sign with the team, he enrolled at Southeastern Illinois College. In the January secondary draft seven months later, he was taken in the fifth round by the Washington Senators. Bill decided to ink a contract with them and went on to have a fine minor league career that included a .338 average for Spokane during his final campaign in 1973, with 22 home runs.

Table 37.1. Best in-season transactions for each of the five Pittsburgh Pirates World Series championship teams.

Year	Date	Trade (Results)
1909	August 19	Bobby Byrne from the St. Louis Cardinals for Jap Barbeau and Alan Storke. (Byrne hit .256, with seven RBIs, the rest of the season and hit .250 in the series.)
1925	May 30	Tom Sheehan from the Cincinnati Reds for Al Niehaus. (Sheehan was 1–1, with a 2.67 ERA, and third best in the National League with three saves in 23 relief appearances in 1925. Did not pitch in the World Series.)
1960	May 28	Wilmer "Vinegar Bend" Mizell and Dick Gray from the St. Louis Cardinals for Ed Bauta and Julian Javier. (Mizell went 13–5 for the Bucs in 1960, with a 3.12 ERA. Lost his only start in the World Series and had a 15.43 ERA. Gray, a hometown Jefferson-Morgan High School grad, never played for the Bucs and spent the season in Columbus.)
1971	August 10	Bob Miller from the San Diego Padres for Ed Acosta and Johnny Jeter. (Miller was 1–2, with a 1.29 ERA in 16 games in relief. Lost his lone World Series decision and had a 3.86 ERA in three games.)
1979	June 28	Bill Madlock, Lenny Randle, and Dave Roberts from the San Francisco Giants for Fred Breining, Al Holland, and Ed Whitson. (Madlock hit .328 the rest of the season, with seven homers and 44 RBIs, and .375 in the World Series. Roberts was 5–2, with a 3.26 ERA in 21 games, which included three starts. He walked the only batter he faced in the NLCS and did not pitch in the World Series. Randle went to the Bucs' Triple-A team in Portland and was sold to the Yankees on August 3.)

Mad Dog had a solid first season, hitting .351 with the Texas Rangers in 85 plate appearances. Instead of beginning a bright future with Texas, however, he was inexplicably traded to the Chicago Cubs for Fergie Jenkins after the season, which turned out to be a fabulous move for the Cubs. Madlock finished third in the Rookie of the Year voting in 1974, and proceeded to capture two consecutive batting titles in 1975 and 1976.

As good a player as Bill was, he also had a fiery personality and a reputation as a moody player, which would cause problems at times. This was perhaps the reason the two-time batting champion was dealt to the San Francisco Giants for Bobby Murcer, among three players, at season's end. Madlock's being upset about being moved from third to second base, along with other issues he had with the team, prompted the deal Peterson made for him in 1979, as the Bucs were fighting for their first division title in four years. It was a perfect move for both player and team, allowing manager Chuck Tanner to move Phil Garner to second base, while the Memphis native took over his more preferred position at third.

With the addition of Madlock and shortstop Tim Foli, the infield was now solidified, as the former Giant, who had gotten off to a slow start with San Francisco, hitting only .261, ended up batting .328 for the Bucs. He excelled in his first World Series, with a .375 average and magnificent .483 on-base percentage, as the club captured its fifth world championship, thanks in no small part to Bill's acquisition earlier in the season.

While both the team and Madlock expected greater things in 1980, they never materialized. Numerous injuries ended the Pirates quest for a repeat championship, and Mad Dog's temper curtailed the third basemen's campaign. Following a strikeout with the bases loaded, he shoved his glove in the face of umpire Jerry Crawford, being suspended for 15 games and fined $5,000. It was the low point of a season that saw him not only suffer knee issues, but also have his average drop to .277; luckily his game would soon reemerge.

In the strike-shortened 1981 campaign, Madlock won his third batting title, with a .341 average, and two years later would capture number four. The 1983 season began with concerns for the future of the 32-year-old slugger, as he had surgery to remove fragments from his left knee. He recovered enough to beat out the Cardinals' Lonnie Smith by two points in the batting race, becoming the 11th player in major league history to win four titles. Between 1971 and 1984, Bill was one of two right-handed hitters, Carney Lansford being the other in 1981, to win a batting title. Coupled with the fact that he was accepted by his teammates for his leadership, being named team captain following Willie Stargell's retirement, the three-year stretch would be one of the most satisfying of his career.

Unfortunately, Madlock's career began to spiral downward soon thereafter. He played another season and a half in Pittsburgh, never coming close to .300 again, and was traded to the Dodgers toward the end of the 1985 campaign. The infielder was also implicated in the 1985 Pittsburgh drug trials by former teammate Dale Berra but later cleared of any wrongdoing by Commissioner Peter Ueberroth. Madlock remained in Los Angeles for two years and was released in May 1987, before being signed by the Tigers, where he ended his major league career after the season. He spent the 1988 campaign in Japan, playing for the Lotte Orions, where he hit .263 and retired for good at season's end.

After he retired, Mad Dog had legal issues in Nevada, passing $12,000 worth of bad checks, but he eventually settled his debts and reentered the game of baseball. His leadership skills would help him, as he was hired as a coach for the Tigers under Phil Garner and managed the minor league Newark Bears for two seasons.

While he is the only man to win four batting titles not enshrined in Cooperstown, mostly because his career stats are not up to Hall of Fame standards, Madlock is remembered in Pittsburgh as not only the last captain of the Pirates, but also an important component of the team's last world championship to date.

MOST MEMORABLE PERFORMANCE

With the Pittsburgh Pirates down three games to one in the 1979 World Series, the team came into the fifth game at Three Rivers Stadium desperate for a win to keep their season alive. Aging veteran Jim Rooker was on the mound, and after falling behind 1–0 in the fifth inning, even the most supportive of Pirates fans were coming to grips with the idea that the magical season would likely be ending with a less-than-desirable result. But thanks to Bill Madlock and the strong Pirates offense, the Bucs made a dramatic comeback to send the series back to Baltimore.

Through the fifth inning, Madlock had singled in each of his two at bats to account for half of the Pirates offensive output; in the bottom of the sixth, he had a chance to put the Bucs ahead. Tim Foli had walked, and Dave Parker singled to start the inning. With Foli on third and one out, Stargell hit a sacrifice fly to tie the score. The team's third baseman then came up and smacked a single to center, scoring Parker to give the team the lead for the first time in this important ball game.

With momentum on their side, Madlock came up to bat again in the eighth and got his fourth hit in four attempts, eventually scoring

CHAPTER 37

the team's sixth run of the afternoon on a single by Foli. Pittsburgh eventually won the game, 7–1, and would outscore the Orioles 8–1 in the last two contests to capture a title that had looked completely out of reach. Thanks to Madlock's four hits, the Bucs survived for another day.

NOTABLE ACHIEVEMENTS (YEARLY LEADERS AND AWARDS ARE AS PIRATES ONLY)

Part of one National League Eastern Division championship and world championship team (1979).

Finished in the top 20 voting for the National League Most Valuable Player Award four times.

Selected to play in two All-Star Games.

Won two batting titles, one of five Pirates to win multiple titles (1981, 1983).

One of 11 players in major league history to win four batting titles in a career.

151st in highest batting average in major league history, at .305.

81st in most intentional walks in major league history, with 121.

46th in most games at third base in major league history, at 1,440.

72nd in most double plays turned at third base, with 200.

38

TRUETT SEWELL

After a long trip to his debut in the major leagues, Rip Sewell overcame many hurdles, including hurting his foot in a hunting injury. While rehabbing after the injury, Sewell ironically developed his signature throw, the eephus pitch. He went on to pitch 143 games in his 13-year career, including two 21-win seasons.

Photo courtesy of the Pittsburgh Pirates.

Truett Banks "Rip" Sewell is probably the most unique player included in this revered list. Without his incredible performance for the Pittsburgh Pirates during the height of World War II, an era when most of the game's greatest players were in the armed forces, he probably would not be included in this book.

Aside from Sewell's record during the war years and qualifications that put him on this list, his is perhaps one of the most interesting stories in franchise history. During an off-season hunting trip following the 1941 campaign he shattered the bones and damaged nerves in his right foot in a tragic accident. The date was December 7, a day more famous in U.S. history for the Japanese attack on Pearl Harbor. Having to learn to walk again before even thinking about getting back on the mound, Rip worked hard. Once he got to the point where he could throw, he developed a unique pitch in spring training that turned out to be his calling card. He tossed the pitch 25 feet in the air, almost like a softball pitch, having it come down at such an angle that it would entice hitters, making them swing at the slow pitch, oftentimes missing it. Teammate Maurice Van Robays named it the eephus pitch. When asked what the term meant Van Robays responded that the term *eephus* meant nothing because the pitch was nothing. A truly unique player indeed.

Born in Decatur, Alabama, in 1907, Sewell pitched for Vanderbilt University's freshman team but was actually at the school on a football scholarship. He was signed by the Detroit Tigers, making his debut for them in the majors in 1932. While he was of great lineage—his cousins Joe, Luke, and Tommy Sewell all played in the majors—Truett did not impress many that season, with a 12.66 ERA in five contests in relief. He was sent to the minors and cut from the team two years later after an altercation with Hank Greenberg at spring training. Sewell would remain there for six seasons before being purchased by the Boston Bees (Braves) in 1936, and was sent back to the minors a year later.

The Alabama native had not been successful in his professional baseball career up to that point, accumulating a record of 58–73 in seven minor league campaigns. But after a 16–12 mark with the Buffalo Bisons in the American Association, he was purchased by the Bucs in September 1937. Rip was given a shot at the major league team in 1938 and made the most of his opportunity, being placed on the major league roster and remaining there for the next 10 seasons.

He lost his only decision that first season in 17 relief appearances and found his way into the rotation a year later, starting 12 of 52 contests, with a 10–9 mark, winning his first major league contest with a 1–0 shutout of the Reds at 31 years of age. In 1940, as he was approaching 33, Sewell finally showed what a remarkable pitcher he could be. Going 16–5, with a 2.80 ERA, the right-hander was becoming the best hurler the Pirates had to offer. His .762 winning percentage was good enough for second in the National League, while his win total was fourth best. For his efforts, he received votes in the Most Valuable Player race, finishing 25th.

A year later, Truett lost 17 games, a league high, although his other stats were not bad, with a 3.72 ERA and 1.241 walks and hits per innings pitched. The off-season, when he injured his foot while hunting, would not be kind to him, but the gritty veteran hurler found a way to return after a tough rehabilitation.

It was initially difficult for Rip to throw off his injured right foot, so he had to change his mechanics, opting for a more overhand delivery. It was through this development that the eephus pitch was born. He held the ball on the seams while throwing it off three fingers to get backspin, with the ball floating 25 feet in the air. Done correctly, the pitch would enter the strike zone as it was coming down at the end. Pirates Hall of Fame catcher Al Lopez encouraged the injured pitcher to work on it, while his manager, Frankie Frisch, wasn't as sold on its effectiveness. When Sewell threw it for the first time in a game situation against the Tigers' Dick Wakefield in spring training, Wakefield was confused, flailing at it helplessly. And it was then that the memorable pitch became part of the hurler's repertoire. It became so successful that even Frisch couldn't argue with its use.

Batters were caught flat-footed when Rip would throw the 40-mile-per-hour toss, and he was once again one of the best hurlers in the league. Winning 17 games in 1942, the 36-year-old pitcher emerged victorious in a league-high 21 games in 1943. With a record of 21–9 and a 2.54 ERA in a National League-best 25 complete games, if there had been a Cy Young Award in 1943, Sewell would have been in a two-man race with Mort Cooper of St. Louis for the honors. His sixth-place finish in the MVP race, only three points behind Cooper, showed that to be probable.

Winning 21 games again a year later and finishing 11th in the MVP race, Sewell slipped in 1945, inking only 11 victories. As the game's greats began to return from the war, Rip's spot among the best pitchers in the National League began to falter. Whether it was age—he would be 39 in 1946—the fact the Bucs were not a good team, or that so much talent was returning, his stats were diminishing, as he won only eight times that season. While not impressive, Truett was nonetheless selected to play in his third All-Star Game. Up to that point, he had never surrendered a home run while throwing the eephus pitch, with Stan Musial's triple being the most productive hit against it. But that streak was about to end.

The great hitter Ted Williams warned Sewell not to throw it to him in the 1946 Midsummer Classic, but the headstrong southerner would not listen. Using advice he received from Bill Dickey, who told Williams to take a couple steps forward to generate more power, the Hall of Famer ripped the pitch 380 feet over the right-field fence for one of the event's most memorable home runs.

A year later, Rip had a bit of a resurgence, with a 13–3 record and a National League-best .813 winning percentage. He was 6–1 the following year, mostly out of the bull pen, but at 42 years of age, his days were numbered. He retired after the season and eventually moved to Florida, where he pursued his love of golf, playing deep into his 70s. He shot a 78 in 1976, when he was 69 years old, four years after he had his legs amputated due to blood clots.

Sewell was truly an amazing man, and his story is equally so, down to him being an early critic of the players' union, feeling that the men were ungrateful for the chance they had at playing in the majors. Rip is the most unlikely player to make this vaunted list—and perhaps the most interesting.

MOST MEMORABLE PERFORMANCE

Rip Sewell's most memorable moment came in one of the game's premier events, the 1946 All-Star Game, at Fenway Park in Boston. During the game he featured his calling card, the eephus pitch, one of the most unique pitches in the history of the sport.

Having one of his worst seasons as a major leaguer, Sewell was still selected to play in the game and entered the contest in the bottom of the eighth with the National League on the bottom end of an 8–0 score. He struggled, allowing singles by Stuffy Stirnweiss, Jack Kramer, and Vern Stephens to load the bases. Truett was able to coerce two fly outs in between and had the opportunity to get out of the inning unscathed as Ted Williams, the hometown boy, came up to bat. Williams was a proud man and one of the best hitters the game had ever seen. He had warned Sewell not to throw his famous eephus pitch, but considering the fact that he had never given up a homer with it, the moundsman decided to go ahead and challenge the Hall of Famer.

The problem with the pitch for hitters, other than the backspin and high angle, was that since it came in so slow, the hitter had to provide all the power, which was difficult. Yankee Hall of Fame catcher Bill Dickey suggested that Williams take a couple of steps forward before swinging to generate more power. The Splendid Splinter took his advice and smacked it 380 feet over the right-field fence for the first home run ever against the eephus, and a grand slam to boot, to make the score 12–0.

It was not Sewell's best moment but certainly his most memorable. While the ball went over the fence, the pitch had been mighty successful prior to the famous blast. The homer remains one of the most memorable in the history of the All-Star Game.

NOTABLE ACHIEVEMENTS (YEARLY LEADERS AND AWARDS ARE AS PIRATES ONLY)

Finished in the top 25 voting for the National League MVP three times.

Selected to play in four All-Star Games (played in three).

Led the league in wins once (1943).

Led the league in winning percentage once (1948).

Led the league in complete games once (1943).

Led the league in wins above replacement for pitchers once (1944).

Led the league in putouts by a pitcher three times (1941, 1942, 1944).

Won more than 20 games twice.

Finished in the top 10 in the National League in wins five times.

Finished in the top 10 in the National League in winning percentage four times.

128st in highest winning percentage in major league history, at .596.

CHAPTER 38

39

MATTY ALOU

Matty Alou was a reserve outfielder for the Giants, hitting only .260 in his first six seasons. When he came to the Pirates, manager Harry Walker turned him into a hitting machine. With Pittsburgh, Alou went on to win the National League batting title in 1966, and hit .327 during his five years with the Bucs.

Photo courtesy of the Pittsburgh Pirates.

There has always been a debate in baseball as to the true importance of a manager. Some feel you can put anyone in a dugout of talented players and they have as much of a chance at a championship as John McGraw did. There are others who think the manager has a huge effect on a game; a bad one can lead a potential world champion to the bottom of the standings, while a great one can make even the most mundane team a title contender. In reality, the answer likely comes from somewhere in the middle. When it comes to the effect Pittsburgh Pirates manager Harry Walker had on the new center fielder general manager Joe L. Brown obtained from the San Francisco Giants in 1966, it becomes clear that a manager can have a tremendous impact. That center fielder was Mateo Rojas Alou, better known in Pirates lore as simply Matty Alou.

A reserve outfielder with San Francisco, no one could have known what Walker had in store for Alou. A fine hitter himself, with a .296 career average that included a batting title in 1947, when he hit .363 for the St. Louis Cardinals, Walker began to work his magic on the contact hitter. When he came to the Bucs, Alou would try to pull every pitch. Walker, with the help of Pirates superstar Roberto Clemente, taught him to choke up and hit the ball down and to the left, allowing the slap hitter to better use his speed. He also was given a much heavier bat that weighed 38 ounces. The results were astonishing, as Matty won the National League batting crown his first season in the Steel City, with a .342 mark, 15 points better than his brother Jesus, who was the runner-up. Matty was able to maintain that level throughout his five years with the Bucs. Table 39.1 is a comparison of his time with the Giants and Bucs.

Born in the Dominican Republic, Alou was one of eight children, three of whom turned out to be talented baseball players. Playing for a Dominican Air Force team sponsored by the son of the country's

Table 39.1. Matty Alou's stats during his time with the Giants and Pirates.

Team	Hits	2B	3B	AVE
Giants (1960–1965)	272	32	7	.260
Pirates (1966–1970)	986	129	34	.327

dictator, Rafael Trujillo, he eventually signed with the San Francisco Giants before the 1957 campaign, joining his brother Felipe, who had signed with the organization in 1955, and soon Jesus, who would ink a contract a year later. Like the other Latin players in the era, Alou would face double-edged discrimination, both for the color of his skin and his Latin heritage. He once remembered, "The ballplayers always treat us good. The only trouble we had was in the streets, the restaurants, the hotels, all those things. We used to cry, but we didn't fight."[1]

Brought up to the majors in 1960, Matty got the opportunity to play in his first World Series in 1962, and was on third base in the bottom of the ninth of Game Seven, via a bunt hit, when Willie McCovey hit a line drive that would have won the game and the series if the ball hadn't landed in the glove of Bobby Richardson.

A year later, he and his brother Felipe were joined on the Giants by Jesus, and on September 10, they became the first trio of brothers to play in the outfield at the same time. It came on the heels of a game earlier in September when they had all batted in the same inning, ironically making all three outs.

While they would play a record 5,000 games by brothers in the majors, most would not be with the same team. Felipe was dealt to the Milwaukee Braves in 1964, and two years later, Matty would also leave San Francisco. Stuck on the bench with the Giants, not able to consistently crack the starting lineup, Alou went to the Bucs for Joe Gibbon and Ozzie Virgil.

Walker tried several times in vain to teach players his hitting method of choking up and hitting to the opposite field; Alou proved to be his masterpiece. Winning the batting title by a significant margin in 1966, his first season with the Pirates, many wondered if his sudden success, which saw him finish ninth in the Senior Circuit's Most Valuable Player voting, was a fluke. During the next four seasons, he would prove it was not.

Even though he had great success in the batter's box in 1966, it mostly came against right-handed pitching, as Walker would use Manny Mota, Alou's best friend on the team, against southpaws. Matty came to the plate 476 times that year against righties, while only 40 at bats came against left-handed pitching. He ironically hit .450 when facing southpaws.

The trend would continue a year later, with a mere 55 at bats versus left-handers, accumulating only a .236 average against them, but his overall average remained high, as he hit .338, good enough for third in the league.

While Alou maintained his status a year later with a National League second-best .332 average, by 1969, after Mota had been selected by the Montreal Expos in the expansion draft, the position was all his, and the results continued to be spectacular. He had arguably his best overall season in a Pirates uniform in 1969. He led the circuit in plate appearances; at bats, where he set a major league record, with 698; hits, with 231; and doubles, with 41. Matty also hit .331. In the All-Star Game that season, he was 2-for-4, with a walk.

A bona fide star, with a .335 average in four seasons in Pittsburgh, Alou slumped a bit in 1970, coming in under .300 for the only time as a Pirate, with a .297 average, while hitting only .250 in his first National League Championship Series appearance. With a more powerful Al Oliver looking to crack the lineup, Brown dealt the slugger to the St. Louis Cardinals before the 1971 campaign, along with George Brunet, for Nelson Briles and Vic Davalillo.

Alou was sent to the soon-to-be world champion Oakland A's a year later, hitting .381 in the 1972 American League Championship Series, with four doubles. Throughout the next few seasons, he would play with the Yankees, Cardinals again, and Padres, retiring in 1974.

After he retired, Matty became a Dominican scouting director for the Giants, before passing away in 2011, at the age of 72, from a stroke after suffering for years from the effects of diabetes. He had a short but important career with the Pittsburgh Pirates, being known as the star pupil in Harry Walker's school of hitting.

MOST MEMORABLE PERFORMANCE

The level of consistency in Matty Alou's five-year Pittsburgh Pirates career was remarkable. For a two-day period from June 17–18, 1967, he took his game to a new level; accumulating eight hits against the Philadelphia Phillies.

After defeating the Phillies 6–5 the day before, with Alou going 4-for-5, the Bucs entered Connie Mack Stadium for a contest the next day. Before this series, the center fielder had been in a bit of a slump, hitting only .284; his two-day output would quickly return him to the .300 plateau.

He led off the Sunday contest with an infield single, scoring the game's first run on a Willie Stargell single. An inning later, he had his second hit of the contest, with a single to right, scoring Jerry May and making the score 3–0.

Matty had his third hit in three innings with a clean single to center before lining out in the sixth inning. With the Bucs ahead 5–3 in the top of the ninth, the slap hitter came up for the final time and smacked a single to center, giving him his eighth hit in two days and raising his season average to .309. The slump had definitely ended, as he would accumulate five more hits in the next two days, eventually hitting .338 by season's end.

NOTABLE ACHIEVEMENTS (YEARLY LEADERS AND AWARDS ARE AS PIRATES ONLY)

Part of one National League Eastern Division championship (1970).

Finished in the top 25 voting for the National League MVP three times.

Selected to play in two All-Star Games.

Won the 1966 National League batting title.

Led the league in at bats twice (1969, 1970).

Led the league in doubles once (1969).

Led the league in hits once (1969).

Led the league in singles twice (1969, 1970).

Led league in at bats per strikeouts once (1970).

Had more than 200 hits in a season twice.

Finished in the top four in the National League in batting four times.

Set the major league record for at bats in a season in 1969, with 698.

40

FRANK KILLEN

One of the joys of baseball versus other sports is its lack of change throughout the years. Football is unrecognizable when compared to the game of the 1940s, as is basketball, and, to an extent, hockey. Even today when the powers that be in the sports world are trying to come up with ways to increase TV ratings, they are not immune to making rule changes that will alter the way the game is played. Except for a few minor changes made since the Live-Ball Era began in the 1920s, baseball still looks almost exactly as it did years and years ago.

During the 19th century, the game was somewhat different. A portion of the bat could be flat, it took eight balls for a walk, batters were out if they were hit by a pitch, and the distance from the pitching mound to home plate was only 50 feet. Thanks to fastball pitchers like Frank Killen, it was becoming impossible for hitters to get the bat on the ball with such a short distance between pitcher and batter. In 1893, to get more offense into the game, the distance was increased to 60 feet, six inches. While some pitchers hurt their arms making up the difference, others became less efficient trying to maneuver the extended ten and a half feet. Killen was one hurler who thrived, as the southpaw quickly became one of the best in the game.

Born in Pittsburgh in 1870, the left-hander started his amateur career as a catcher, becoming a player of note in the city. Moving to the mound at 18, Killen became just as successful, if not more so, signing a contract to play in the Michigan League in 1890. Midway through the season he moved to the International Association with the Grand Rapids Shamrocks and won three of his four appearances to end the year.

The man nicknamed "Lefty" received a contract with the Minneapolis Millers of the Western Association, where he accumulated 18 wins in 31 starts, although he had a less-than-impressive walks and hits per innings pitched of 1.512. Despite a minor league season that was not his most successful venture, the Milwaukee Brewers thought enough of the 20-year-old's potential to sign him after they moved from the Western League to the American Association. The shift, which caused Minneapolis to fold, was fortuitous for the Pittsburgh native. He took advantage of the opportunity to pitch in the majors, garnering a 7–4 mark in 11 starts, with a 1.68 ERA.

For the second time in two seasons, the team Killen was pitching for folded when the season ended, this time because the American Association and the National League merged, causing Milwaukee to lose its franchise. But he would not be out of work for long. The moundsman was quickly picked up by the Washington Senators. Lefty continued his improvement, becoming one of the stars in the game. The Senators were a poor collection of talent in 1892, finishing 58–93, 10th in the 12-team circuit.

Their pitching staff was among the worst in the game, with Phil Knell being the second-best pitcher on the squad, with nine wins. The best hurler proved to be Killen, who won exactly half the games Washington did during the season, with a 29–26 record. His 29 victories were good enough for seventh best in the circuit.

It was a tremendous season that should have been nicely rewarded by the Senators; instead, Frank was offered only $1,800 for the 1893 campaign. The 22-year-old southpaw considered it disrespectful and became disgruntled with management. He decided to hold out in spring training, looking for better riches. Luckily his hometown team, the Pirates, had a third baseman named Charley "Duke" Farrell who was also unsatisfied with his salary offer, despite the fact that he hit a paltry .215 during the 1892 campaign. The two teams came together to trade their unhappy players, giving Pittsburgh what would become one of the best left-handed pitchers in the game.

The 1893 campaign was a significant one, as it was during that season that the distance from home plate to the mound was increased in an attempt to make the game more offensive. The results were dramatic, as runs per game went from 5.10 per team to 6.57. Batting averages shot up 35 points, from .245 to .280, while ERA rose from 3.28 to 4.66 on average.

Many pitchers who had been successful from 50 feet were now substandard, but Frank Killen was not one of them. Thanks to the acquisition of their hometown hurler, the Pirates went from sixth place to within five games of the pennant, with a franchise-best 81–48 record. The southpaw was spectacular, compiling a National League-best 36 wins, a mark that remains the most wins by a left-hander since the mound was moved to its current standards. He was 36–14, as his ERA only increased by .33, compared to the massive average increase by Senior Circuit hurlers of 1.38 per game.

While Killen had the look of a potential Hall of Famer at this point in his career, his impressive output would be curtailed during the next two seasons due to injuries. In July 1894, he was hit by a line drive off the bat of Patsy Tebeau of the Cleveland Spiders, which broke Frank's arm and ended his season. He was not pitching well at the time of the injury, with a 14–11 record and 4.50 ERA. Without their star pitcher, the team slumped to 65–65.

The following season in June, Lefty was spiked during a play at home by the Giants' Parke Wilson. Not known for being able to keep his temper under control, an angry Killen punched Wilson and was almost suspended. He pitched one more game, defeating the eventual champion Baltimore Orioles, but developed blood poisoning and was once again done for the season.

Finally healthy a year later, the southpaw reemerged as a star, winning 30 games, with a 30–18 mark, one that could have been better if he hadn't lost his last five decisions of the year. It was also a campaign that saw Killen's legendary temper flare up when he caused a riot at a home game by punching umpire Daniel Lally over a disputed pitch.

The 1896 season proved to be the final successful one of the Pittsburgh native's career. While he was able to stop Wee Willie Keeler's 44-game hitting streak in 1897, he dropped to 17–23. A year later, the downfall continued, as he signed with the Washington Senators after being released by Pittsburgh following a 10–11 start for the Bucs. A year and a half later, Frank was out of the major leagues and back to the minors, where he played four more seasons, accumulating a 39–34 record. He retired from professional baseball for good after an 8–15 combined campaign with Indianapolis and Atlanta in 1903.

Following his retirement, Killen stayed in his hometown, first becoming an umpire and then running a saloon, while making some investments in real estate. He passed away in 1939, at the age of 69, from a heart attack, and to this day remains the last left-handed pitcher in the National League to win 30 games.

MOST MEMORABLE PERFORMANCE

The date was June 19, 1897, the year after Pittsburgh Pirates southpaw pitcher Frank Killen had become what would be the National League's last left-handed 30-game winner. Killen was not pitching well during the campaign, as the Bucs were about to face the greatest team in the game at the time, the Baltimore Orioles. He wanted the opportunity to pitch and not only beat the best the game had to offer, but also stop the 44-game hitting streak of Wee Willie Keeler.

Keeler didn't know it at the time, but the streak Frank was on would be an impressive historical mark, one that wouldn't be bested until Joltin' Joe DiMaggio's legendary 56-game streak in 1941. It was the streak by DiMaggio that would rekindle the greatness that was Keeler in 1897. If not for Killen's magnificence on this day, Keeler may have made it much harder on DiMaggio 44 years later.

Before the game, the Orioles stood at 33–9, meaning that Keeler had managed a hit in every game during the 1897 campaign to that point. Patsy Donovan scored the game's first run in the top of the second, before Baltimore tied it in the bottom of the frame. The Bucs' lefty was dominant from that point onward, allowing only five hits, while shutting down Keeler.

Pittsburgh was able to plate one in the eighth to break the tie and five more in the ninth to make the close game a rout. The loss threw the Orioles in a bit of a tailspin, as they lost eight of their next 10 games, costing them the defense of their pennant, with the team finishing two games behind Boston. For Killen, it was probably his last hurrah in a Pirates uniform. He promised his teammates cigars if he beat the Orioles, which his teammates happily accepted. For Keeler it was the end of a record, one that took 44 years to get the true respect it deserved.

NOTABLE ACHIEVEMENTS (YEARLY LEADERS AND AWARDS ARE AS PIRATES ONLY)

Led the league in wins twice (1893, 1896).

Led the league in games pitched once (1896).

Led the league in games started once (1896).

Led the league in complete games twice (1896, 1897).

Won more than 30 games in a season twice.

207th in most wins in major league history, with 164.

76th in most complete games in major league history, at 253.

Holds the major league record for wins by a left-handed pitcher in 1893, with 36 (record is for pitchers after the mound was moved back to 60 feet, six inches).

Last National League left-handed pitcher to win 30 games in a season, with 30 in 1896.

FRANK KILLEN

41

HOWIE CAMNITZ

When the Pittsburgh Pirates won their first World Series in 1909, Howie Camnitz was their star on the mound. The Covington, Kentucky, native won 25 games that season, with a league-high .806 winning percentage. Camnitz went on to become a 20-game winner two other times with the Bucs, finishing his Pirates career with a 116–84 mark.

Photo courtesy of the Pittsburgh Pirates.

During the first decade of the 20th century, the Pittsburgh Pirates possessed the best starting rotation in the game, formulating the first dynasty of the century and winning three consecutive pennants. Chesbro, Tannehill, Leever, and Phillippe were the early-day fearsome foursome. Chesbro and Tannehill left in 1902, and Phillippe and Leever, who were older players when they entered the majors, were past their prime toward the end of the decade. Luckily, Pirates president Barney Dreyfuss was developing another superior foursome to hopefully bring the Bucs more pennants. Veteran Vic Willis combined with youngsters Nick Maddox, Lefty Leifield, and a right-hander from Covington, Kentucky, by the name of Samuel Howard Camnitz, better known as Howie Camnitz. In 1909, Camnitz was perhaps the best the National League had to offer, as he helped lead the club to its long-awaited fourth pennant.

One of the games preeminent curveball specialists in his prime, Rosebud, as he was called due to his red hair, played at Centre College in Danville, Kentucky, before signing his first professional contract with the Vicksburg Hill Billies in the Cotton State League in 1903. He was spectacular, with a 26–7 mark, which impressed Dreyfuss. He was drafted by the Bucs in the fall of 1903, in the Rule 5 Draft, and spent the first part of the 1904 campaign in Pittsburgh.

Camnitz was ahead of his time in how he prepared for a game, often studying the box scores or whatever rudimentary scouting reports were at his disposal. He once said,

> I always inspect very closely the box score of the club we are about to meet next. My object is to ascertain what players are doing the hitting. Every student of baseball knows that players hit in streaks. If a pitcher has men on bases and a batsman facing him who has been having a slump in his hitting, he can take a chance on letting him line it out. On the contrary, if a player comes up who has been clouting the ball it may be the safest plan to let him walk.[1]

While well prepared, he found out in his short stint with the Pirates that season that there was a big difference between pitching to minor league competition and hitters in the majors.

Even though his curveball constantly confused batters in the Cotton State League, without a second pitch to complement it, the more talented major league hitters would time the delivery and anticipate where the ball would come over the plate. In 10 contests that season, mostly out of the bull pen, Howie was 1–4, with a 4.22 ERA and a 1.388 walks and hits per innings pitched. Not a humiliating start to his career for sure, but Dreyfuss felt he needed to perfect other pitches to make his curveball more effective and returned him to the minors.

Camnitz went to the Springfield Hustlers of the Illinois-Indiana-Iowa League and performed well, with a 14–5 mark, for the remainder of the 1904 campaign. He was then sent to the Toledo Mud Hens of the American Association for the next two seasons. He pitched often in 1905 and 1906, trying to perfect secondary pitches, with 300 innings pitched the first year and 309 following that. Winning 39 games during the two seasons, including 22 in 1906, Dreyfuss was convinced that Camnitz was ready to rejoin the Pirates and brought him back as the 1906 season was concluding.

The scouts were convinced he had developed his other pitches enough to make his curve more effective, which would allow him to stay in the majors. After tossing a seven-inning shutout against Brooklyn in late September in his second game of the year for the Bucs, Howie confirmed their opinions.

Camnitz did well in his first full season back with the Bucs, garnering a 13–8 record and a 2.15 ERA. More impressive was his WHIP, at 1.078, as he permitted only 135 hits in 180 innings pitched. As the Bucs were in the middle of a pennant race that they would lose on the final day of the season in 1908, Rosebud improved on his performance, with 16 wins, significantly reducing his ERA to a National League fourth best, at 1.56, which would prove to be his career low.

After five years without a pennant, the Bucs were ready to end the streak of futility in 1909. It would be a special season, one where they would not only win a franchise record 110 games, but also open their magnificent new facility, Forbes Field, the first concrete and steel stadium in the National League. Beginning with his first game of the season, during which he shut out the Cincinnati Reds on Opening Day, the Covington native was at his peak. By the end of the year he had tossed two one-hitters, won 25 games, and had a Senior Circuit-best .806, as well as a batting average against of .211 and on-base percentage against of .267.

As good as Camnitz's regular season was, conflicting reports on whether he had a throat ailment or had been drinking heavily surfaced as an explanation for his subpar World Series performance, when he lost his only start, with a 13.50 ERA. It seemed to be the beginning of a downward trend for the right-hander, who was only 28 years old in 1910. He was 12–13 that season, and while he was a 20-game winner the next two seasons, going a combined 42–27, both his ERA and WHIP were both higher than they had been during his peak years.

In 1913, a 6–17 start for the Pirates by Camnitz necessitated a trade to Philadelphia by Dreyfuss, as he dealt the hurler, along with Bobby Byrne, for Cozy Dolan. After the season concluded, the hurler signed with the Pittsburgh Rebels in the Federal League and tried to recruit Pirates players to the rival circuit in spring training, as an irritated Honus Wagner told him to leave the facility.

Rosebud looked well past his prime with the Rebels in 1914, and was kicked off the team the following season for violating team rules, as well as being involved in an altercation with a hotel guest in New York. While he continued to report to the Rebel facility at Exposition Park, claiming he was fulfilling his obligations and should be paid, he was never put back on the active roster, and his major league career was over.

After he retired, Camnitz managed for one season in the Blue Grass League, with the Winchester Dodgers in 1922, before entering the auto sales business in Louisville, where he worked for 40 years. He died in Louisville in 1960, at the age of 78.

MOST MEMORABLE PERFORMANCE

First impressions are important, especially when you get a second chance to make one. After a miserable trial run with the Pirates in 1904, Howie Camnitz was sent to the minors to refine his game. When he came back late in 1906, he wanted the Pittsburgh Pirates to know that he was a changed man. He made his comeback against the Brooklyn Superbas on September 28.

It was the second game of a doubleheader in Brooklyn, with the first contest going the Superbas' way, 5–4. They scored all their runs after the fifth inning, coming back from a 4–0 deficit for the victory. The second game was a shortened seven-inning affair, as Camnitz was spectacular. He allowed only three singles in the complete-game shut-out, a contest that was won with a run in the third by Tommy Leach.

Rosebud walked three, while striking out five, in showing the franchise and the city of Pittsburgh that he was back to stay in the major leagues. A second first impression that was the catalyst for one of the best three-year spans for a pitcher in franchise history.

NOTABLE ACHIEVEMENTS (YEARLY LEADERS AND AWARDS ARE AS PIRATES ONLY)

Played on one National League championship and world championship team (1909).

Led the league in winning percentage once (1909).

Led the league in homeruns per at bats twice (1907, 1910).

Led the league in putouts for a pitcher once (1910).

Won more than 20 games in a season three times.

Finished in the top 10 in the National League in winning percentage four times.

Finished in the top 10 in the National League in WHIP five times.

90th in lowest ERA in major league history, at 2.75.

147th in WHIP in major league history, at 1.203.

118th in hits per innings pitched in major league history, at 7.993.

42

GLENN WRIGHT

At the beginning of the 20th century, the Pittsburgh Pirates had what most experts consider the greatest shortstop in the history of the game, Honus Wagner. Wagner's credentials for that lofty title are well documented—blazing speed, incredible hitting, and phenomenal defense. Most important in franchise lore is that he was a pivotal part of four National League crowns and the franchise's first world championship. When Honus left the team in 1917, it left a huge hole in the Pirates infield that was difficult to fill. They tried to replace their star with men like Rabbit Maranville, a Hall of Famer who had few equals defensively, but he was not an offensive powerhouse. In 1924, team owner Barney Dreyfuss purchased a shortstop by the name of Glenn Wright from the Kansas City Blues in the American Association who proved to be closer to Wagner's ilk, as he forced Maranville to second base. It was a fortuitous move that would help give the Bucs their first pennant and world championship since the days of Wagner.

Born in Archie, Missouri, in 1901, Wright played for the University of Missouri before beginning his first professional season in 1921, with the Independence Producers of the Southwestern League, where he hit .316, with 22 home runs. The American Association's Kansas City Blues, who had wanted him right out of Missouri but sent him to Independence for more experience, signed him the following season. While Blues manager and former major leaguer Oscar Knabe was not a fan of Wright, he was quickly replaced in 1922, by Bill Good, who respected Wright's talent as much as Blues owner George Muehlebach and inserted him as his starting shortstop.

Their faith in the man who was nicknamed Buckshot, because his throws to first weren't always accurate, was well founded, as he hit .307 during his two seasons in Kansas City. This opened the door for him at Pittsburgh, who purchased him in 1924. Dreyfuss gave Muehlebach $40,000 for Wright, far less than the $100,000 the New York Yankees were willing to offer, but the Bucs had the option to purchase him and now had him in a Pirates uniform. The talented shortstop wasn't initially as thrilled, insisting on a portion of the money the Blues received. After Muehlebach refused his demands, Dreyfuss gave him $7,500 as part of the deal, and the Pirates were hoping they had their heir apparent to Wagner.

Writer Frederick G. Lieb describes Wright as a "rangy lad with an arm of steel."[1] In an interview with *Baseball Magazine*, former manager Fred Clarke said, "I consider Glenn Wright just as good a defensive player as Wagner. He isn't Wagner on the bases or at bat, but in the field he is the best shortstop in the game today."[2]

While he was a fine offensive player, Buckshot knew he had issues with his erratic arm and gave credit to Pirates first baseman Charlie Grimm for gathering up his throws at first. "I could throw hard, but no one could tell where. Charlie Grimm at Pittsburgh was my best first baseman in jumping around to catch the ball."[3]

It was an incredible rookie campaign. Wright hit .287, driving in 111 RBIs, while finishing 11th in Most Valuable Player race. Stabilizing the infield, he became an important part of a club that would restore the success it had experienced two decades earlier, capturing their long-awaited fifth National League crown. Glenn eclipsed the .300 plateau for the first time in his major league career with a .308 average, smacking 18 home runs, with 121 RBIs and a fourth-place finish for the National League MVP. As amazing as all that was, it was a game on May 7, against the St. Louis Cardinals, that may have been his most memorable moment in the major leagues. He had an unassisted triple play that day, a feat that only 15 players have accomplished in major league history, the fifth one at the time.

The Bucs earned a spot in their third World Series, against the defending world champion Washington Senators. After falling behind three games to one, the team battled back, winning the final three contests of the Fall Classic to capture the title. While he cracked a home run in a Game Two victory, Wright did not play well, hitting only .185 in the series.

Poor Fall Classic aside, Buckshot had become one of the best players in the game. He credited Rogers Hornsby for his offensive success, thanking him for the conversations they had about hitting at the Chase Hotel in St. Louis. Wright said that it was Hornsby who taught him to stand deeper in the batter's box so he could react to the pitches better.

As well as his career was going, it almost came to a screeching halt a year later, in 1926, when he was hit in the face by a Vic Keen fastball. He fell to the ground unconscious and was seriously injured. Wright remained unconscious for 32 hours, as many wondered if he'd survive. Luckily, he not only pulled through, but also returned to the lineup six weeks later to finish the season with a .308 average.

Now healthy, Glenn once again helped Pittsburgh capture a Senior Circuit pennant in 1927. His average fell to .281 that season, but he again topped 100 RBIs, with 105. The Bucs' prize for their 1927 championship was the opportunity to play the American League champion New York Yankees, one of the greatest teams in the history of Major League Baseball. Both the Pirates and Wright were helpless against Ruth, Gehrig, and company, being swept in four games, while the star shortstop hit only .154.

Buckshot played well after his poor series but sadly had another injury-plagued season in 1928, one where he hit what was then a career-high .310. After the season, he was surprisingly traded to the Dodgers for Jesse Petty and Harry Riconda. When he left the Bucs, he was third all-time on the franchise list in home runs, with 50, and seventh in RBIs, with 480, despite playing only five seasons.

With Brooklyn, the former Pirate had a big season in 1930, compiling career highs in home runs (22) and RBIs (126), as well as a career-high .321 average, but a series of injuries, including a separated shoulder, ended his career with the Dodgers when the team released him in 1933.

Wright played for Kansas City in 1934, and had one last chance in the majors in 1935, with the White Sox, where he was .125 in only 25 at bats, ending his major league career for good. He played with Syracuse, Seattle, and Wenatchee, where he was a player-manager for three seasons, but his professional career drew to a close in 1939.

After his playing days were over, Glenn managed the Spokane Indians and Corning Red Sox. He also served as a coach for the Pacific Coast League's San Francisco Seals. After years as a scout, he passed away in 1984, at 83 years of age. While his career in Pittsburgh was short, it was successful, as a fine replacement for the greatest shortstop there ever was.

MOST MEMORABLE PERFORMANCE

Noted for his bat and slick defense, although his arm wasn't always accurate, Glenn Wright put his name in the record books on May 7, 1927, when he achieved one of the rarest feats in the game—an unassisted triple play.

The Bucs were off to a bad start that year, standing at 6–9, and at home to play the St. Louis Cardinals. The game itself was exciting. Pittsburgh raced out to a 9–3 lead before the Cards rallied, scoring six in the eighth inning off starter Emil Yde and an aging Babe Adams to win the contest, 10–9.

Threatening to turn the game into a rout in the ninth inning, Vic Aldridge began the top half of the frame by walking Jimmy Cooney and Rogers Hornsby, before Jim Bottomley came to the plate. Bottomley took an Aldridge delivery and lined a shot at Wright. The Cardinals were in the midst of a hit-and-run as the shortstop snagged the line drive and ran to second to tag the base before tagging Hornsby, who was too close to second to run back to first.

At the time, only one other National League player, Ernie Padgett of the 1923 Braves, had performed the feat, while Neal Ball and Bill Wambsganss of Cleveland and George Burns of the Red Sox had achieved it in the Junior Circuit. Paul Hines also had one with Providence in 1878. As of 2015, only 15 players have managed the rare unassisted triple play, putting Wright in a small class of men.

NOTABLE ACHIEVEMENTS (YEARLY LEADERS AND AWARDS ARE AS PIRATES ONLY)

Played on two National League championship teams (1925, 1927).
Played on one world championship team (1925).

Finished in the top 11 voting for the National League MVP twice.

Led the league in at bats once (1924).

Led the league in games played once (1925).

Led the league in games at shortstop three times (1924, 1925, 1927).

Led the league in putouts for a shortstop once (1927).

Led the league in assists for a shortstop twice (1924, 1925).

Led the league in double plays for a shortstop twice (1924, 1925).

Eclipsed 100 RBIs three times.

89th in most putouts by a shortstop in major league history, with 2,156.

93rd in most double plays by a shortstop in major league history, at 695.

43

ELMER SMITH

Being both an effective pitcher and an everyday player is a rare occurrence. In the history of the game, only six players have had at least 100 decisions on the mound while playing a considerable amount of time at other positions. It's a feat that is not easy to achieve. While the Cardinals' Rich Ankiel was able to become a good outfielder after his bout with Steve Blass disease, the Pirates' attempts to turn John Van Benschoten from a power hitter into a pitcher never succeeded. Efforts to do the opposite with Stetson Allie have also not succeeded. Although recent endeavors have been met with failure, in the latter part of the 19th century, the Pirates had a pitcher who not only won an ERA title, but also became the franchise's most prolific hitter of the era after an arm injury forced him to the outfield; his name was Elmer "Mike" Smith.

Of the six pitchers with 100 decisions who spent a substantial amount of time at other positions, except for Babe Ruth, Smith may have been the best. Table 43.1 shows the pitching and offensive prowess of each player.

In looking at the statistics, Gleason and Ward pitched significantly more games than Smith, but the former Pirate was better on the mound compared to Gleason, while Ward was the superior pitcher. Offensively, Smith seemingly dominates both men on all accounts. He also looks comparable to Seymour offensively but was better as a pitcher. Coleman was a decent hitter but carries poor statistics in every category on the mound. There is really no argument when the great Babe Ruth enters the equation. Offensively, there is arguably no one better to ever play the game, and Ruth was also one of the best

Table 43.1. Pitchers with 100 decisions who spent a substantial amount of time at other positions.

Name	G	W	L	ERA	G	HR	RBI	AVE
Kid Gleason	299	138	131	3.79	1,672	15	824	.261
John Ward	293	164	103	2.10	1,579	26	869	.275
Elmer Smith	149	75	57	3.35	1,089	37	665	.310
Babe Ruth	163	94	46	2.28	2,273	714	2,214	.342
Cy Seymour	141	61	56	3.73	1,341	52	799	.303
John Coleman	107	23	72	4.68	549	7	279	.257

hurlers of his era and appears to have been on course to be a Hall of Fame pitcher had he stayed at the position.

Regardless of where Smith would rank among the elite in table 43.1, there is no question that he had a spectacular career no matter where he was on the diamond. He would have rated higher in this book had he reached his prime while wearing a Pittsburgh jersey.

A hometown boy, born in Allegheny City, which eventually merged with the city of Pittsburgh, Mike was a talented southpaw with an impressive fastball who signed his first professional contract at the age of 19. He played with the Nashville Americans of the Southern Association in 1886, where, while only 4–4 going, he was unhittable, with a miniscule 0.89 ERA. The American Association's Cincinnati Red Stockings were impressed and bought him for the rest of the campaign, and it was there that he matched his Nashville mark of 4–4.

Showing major league potential, Smith once again made the team in 1887, and went from a young left-hander at the bottom end of the staff to one of the team's star hurlers. He got off to a slow start but soon blossomed, winning 13 of 14 decisions on his way to a 34–17 mark, with an American Association-low 2.94 ERA.

With his future looking bright, the southpaw hurt his shoulder in spring training and suffered early on with a 5–9 start. He rebounded to win 22 games, but the sore shoulder never healed, as he slumped to 9–12 in 1889, with a ballooning ERA of 4.88. At only 21 years of age, his once-promising career seemed over when he was released by Red Stockings at season's end.

Smith went to Kansas City in the Western Association for the next two seasons and had massage treatments on his arm, which helped him recover. Even though his arm was still healing, the team couldn't find a catcher who could catch his fastball, making it difficult for him to pitch. And then a funny thing happened to Mike while he was with the Blues: He was developing into a good hitter, breaking the .300 plateau in both 1890 and 1891, which impressed many National League teams. Luckily for the Pittsburgh Pirates, he chose his hometown club, where he quickly demonstrated that his improved hitting could translate to the majors.

The moundsman could still pitch, going 6–7 in his first season for the Bucs, but his future was as an outfielder, even though he hit only .274 that year. Despite his less-than-stellar debut, the team's catcher at the time, Hall of Fame manager Connie Mack, knew he had a successful player in Smith. According to writer Frederick G. Lieb, the converted pitcher "became a hard and timely hitter and an early intimate of catcher Connie Mack."[1]

Mike was a well-rounded player, possessing decent power for the era, as well as exceptional speed. He used an extremely heavy bat, weighing 54 ounces, which was especially big when compared to Roberto Clemente, who used bats weighing anywhere from 40 to 42 ounces, and Willie Mays, who liked bats that weighed between 33 and 34 ounces. Smith had a breakout season in 1893, hitting .347, with 103 RBIs. Between 1893 and 1895, he proceeded to hit .335, knocking in 258.

It was an impressive prelude to his finest year in 1896. He finished the season with a career-high .362 average and 94 RBIs, scoring 121 runs. While the Pittsburgh native hit .310 in 1897, it would prove to be his last season in his first stint with the Bucs. During the off-season, Smith was dealt back to the Cincinnati Reds, along with Pink Hawley and $1,500, for Bill Gray, Jack McCarthy, Billy Rhines, Pop Schriver, and Ace Stewart.

As he had done in Cincinnati the first time, Mike got off to a fabulous start, posting a .342 average in 1898, but he would quickly go downhill. He never eclipsed .300 again and, in 1900, went to the Giants. The left-fielder returned to Pittsburgh in 1901, but was hitless in six at bats before ending his major league career with Boston, where he finished the season.

Smith went on to play five more campaigns in the minors, calling it quits in 1906, after a fine year with the Binghamton Bingoes in the New

York State League, where he had a .313 average. He stayed in Pittsburgh after he retired, passing away in 1945, at the age of 77. Each time Pirates fans see the failed experiment of trying to turn a pitcher into an everyday player and vice versa, they need only look back into franchise history, to the career of Elmer Smith, to see that it can be done.

MOST MEMORABLE PERFORMANCE

While he is on this list because of his offensive prowess, it was on the mound during his first season as a Pittsburgh Pirate that Elmer "Mike" Smith showed what made him special: his abilities as a great everyday player who at one time was also one of the game's most talented pitchers.

Mike won 34 games in his first full season in the majors with the Cincinnati Red Stockings, but a sore arm relegated him to the minors, where he learned how to play the outfield and become a good hitter. When the Bucs signed him in 1892, it was for his hitting, although he also got the opportunity to pitch that season for Pittsburgh, facing the Baltimore Orioles on September 2, with a chance to confirm what a good hurler he was.

Pittsburgh was on a four-game winning streak when they faced the last-place Orioles and dominated their opponents that day. Scoring two runs in each of four consecutive innings between the third and sixth, they won the game, 8–0, led by Lou Bierbauer's three hits and Patsy Donovan's home run.

Even though the offense was impressive, it was Smith who stole the show. He allowed only two singles in the complete-game shutout, while striking out four and walking three. It was truly a dominant performance and one that proved that while the Pittsburgh native would enjoy a successful offensive career in the majors, he was also a rare commodity in that he could also pitch with the best of them.

NOTABLE ACHIEVEMENTS (YEARLY LEADERS AND AWARDS ARE AS PIRATES ONLY)

Finished in the top 10 in the National League in batting average twice.

Finished in the top 10 in the National League in on-base percentage twice.

Finished in the top 10 in the National League in slugging percentage twice.

Finished in the top 10 in the National League in on-base plus slugging percentage twice.

Eclipsed 100 runs three times.

Eclipsed 100 RBIs once.

71st in most triples in major league history, with 136.

68th in highest on-base percentage in major league history, at .398.

106th in highest batting average in major league history, at .310.

97th in home runs per at bats as a pitcher in major league history, at .149.

44

JASON KENDALL

In the painful, record-setting 20-year run of losing seasons the Pittsburgh Pirates and their fans endured between 1993 and 2012, there were many so-called saviors that the Pirates faithful looked to in hopes of being led out of the doldrums: Jason Bay, Brian Giles, Kris Benson, and a gritty California catcher, the son of a former major leaguer who was the team's top pick in 1992, the last winning season before the streak, by the name of Jason Kendall.

A member of the original San Diego Padres, Fred Kendall was a light-hitting catcher with a career .234 average in his 12-year career. While he was a solid backstop, his son, born in 1974, in Manhattan Beach, California, would achieve whatever All-Star dreams Fred may have had, as the younger Kendall became one of the best catchers in the game during his time with the Bucs.

Kendall played for Torrance High School, making a national name for himself, not just for his spectacular .549 average, but also the fact he had a Joe DiMaggio-like achievement, setting a national high school record with a 43-game hitting streak. His national notoriety for his record, as well as his incredible talent, prompted the Pirates to take him with the 23rd pick in the first round of the 1992 Major League Baseball Draft.

Between 1992 and 2005, when the franchise drafted Andrew McCutchen, the actual savior of the franchise, the Bucs selected many false heroes who failed to make the team a winner. A team doesn't get that bad without making poor decisions in the draft, and the Pirates more than made their share of disastrous choices. The following list is a who's who of the greatest draft busts in the history of the game, which helped make Pittsburgh the laughingstock of baseball: Charles Peterson, Mark Farris, Chad Hermansen, J. J. Davis, Clinton Johnston, Bobby Bradley, John Van Benschoten, and Bryan Bullington. All were first-round draft picks, or, more succinctly, first-round busts, during that era for the Pirates. The one they were successful with was Kendall. Even those that made a contribution—Kris Benson, Sean Burnett, Paul Maholm, and Neil Walker—could not equal the Pirates catcher.

From the beginning, the California native showed the Pirates that he was the special player they thought he could be. After solid seasons with Pittsburgh's Gulf Coast League team and their Class A club in Augusta, where he was a midseason and end-of-season All-Star, Jason blossomed in his third professional season with the Salem Buccaneers, hitting .318, before being named the Southern League's Most Valuable Player with the Carolina Mudcats in 1995, hitting .326 in his first full season of Double-A ball.

There are many stories in the history of the game where a franchise has made a huge mistake bypassing Triple-A and sending a prospect straight to the major leagues from Double-A. The Pirates took that gamble in 1996, bringing their prize prospect straight to Pittsburgh. He had been named the 26th-best prospect in the game by *Baseball America* before the season began, and while many worried that he was being pushed too quickly, the 22-year-old backstop quickly calmed their fears.

Kendall hit exactly .300, getting stronger as the season went on. He was the first Pirates rookie to be named to the All-Star Team and only the 16th everyday player and fifth catcher in National League history at the time to have such a distinction for a rookie. While he finished third in the official National League Rookie of the Year vote, he won the *Sporting News* award and was placed on the Topps All-Rookie Team. Needless to say, the Bucs' front office made no mistake by pushing Kendall to the majors in a quick fashion.

The slugger continued his success the next two seasons, hitting .311, including a fine .326 campaign the latter year, breaking double digits for the first time in home runs, with 12. It was a prelude to what looked to be the finest season of his career, one that appeared to put him among the upper echelon of players in the league. Throwing out

46 percent of the runners trying to steal against him, Kendall also was hitting .332 going into a holiday game against the Milwaukee Brewers on July 4. A truly consistent offensive force who would hustle on almost every play, he laid down a bunt against the Brewers and was desperately trying to beat the throw to first base when he landed awkwardly on the bag and dislocated his ankle in a gruesome injury that those at the game and watching at home won't soon forget.

The injury ended the season for the young catcher, and many wondered if he could return to form after such a horrific experience. As in his rookie year, when many thought he had been brought up too quickly, Kendall answered his critics the next season by playing in 152 games, while hitting .320, with a career-high 14 homers. He was named the starting catcher in the All-Star Game for the injured Mike Piazza, the first Pirate to nab such a spot since 1961. While he broke his cheekbone during a pickoff attempt in mid-September, Jason continued to play the remainder of the season. It would be the only low point in a fabulous campaign that saw him become the only Pirate to hit for the cycle at Three Rivers Stadium.

Kendall signed a multiyear contract at the end of the 2000 season, as Pirates management was trying to shore up top players with the expected revenue generated by the new facility, PNC Park. Winning baseball never came to fruition, and Kendall went into a two-year slump that saw him drop more than 30 points from his averages in 2001 and 2002. Despite the fact that the veteran catcher would rebound with two fine seasons, hitting a combined .322, he unfortunately became a victim of a salary dump prior to the 2005 campaign. He and his soon-to-be eight-digit salary were dealt to the Oakland A's for Mark Redman, Arthur Rhodes, and cash—another in a long line of poor trades for the front office during that forgettable era.

With Oakland, the former Pirate not only finally had the chance to play postseason baseball, as they won a division title in 2006, but he also became only the eighth catcher in baseball history to eclipse the 2,000-hit plateau. He spent his last few years in the game with the Brewers and Royals, retiring with a .288 career average.

Since his retirement, Jason has been busy surfing and writing a book, called *Throwback: A Big-League Catcher Tells How the Game Is Re-*

ally Played. His latest venture is an attempt with former Royal teammate Willie Bloomquist to qualify for the two-man bobsled in the 2018 Olympics. Knowing how he has defied the odds so many times in the past, one shouldn't bet against Jason Kendall standing on the Olympic podium one day.

MOST MEMORABLE PERFORMANCE

Hitting for the cycle is one of the rarest occurrences in the game of baseball, on par with no-hitters. In the history of the game, players have only achieved the rarity 306 times, while there have been 288 no-hitters. A Pirate has only hit for the cycle 23 times since 1887, and in the 30-year history of Three Rivers Stadium through May 18, 2000, no Buc had achieved the difficult feat. With only a few months remaining until the facility was set to be imploded, chances for one were becoming slim, that is until catcher Jason Kendall took the field against St. Louis on May 19.

There were two opposing players to hit for the cycle in the memorable facility, Joe Torre in 1973 and Jeff Kent the season before. Kendall began his attempt to join the duo in the bottom of the first inning with a two-run homer, scoring Mike Benjamin in front of him to give Pittsburgh an early 2–0 lead.

Pittsburgh dominated the Cardinals, building an 8–1 advantage before the game was three innings old, as the catcher singled in the second to get halfway to his historic accomplishment. In the third, Jason doubled Benjamin in, leaving him only a triple short of the cycle.

After striking out in the fifth, Kendall received one more chance at making history in the eighth, with pitcher Kris Benson and Benjamin on base. With the count 2–2, he ripped the next offering into the right-field gap and hustled his way to third for the most difficult part of the journey, the triple.

The batsman managed four hits, five RBIs, and three runs, while placing his name somewhere no other man in Pirates history would ever be as the only Buc to hit for the cycle in Three Rivers Stadium.

CHAPTER 44

NOTABLE ACHIEVEMENTS (YEARLY LEADERS AND AWARDS ARE AS PIRATES ONLY)

Selected to play in three All-Star Games, starting in one.

Led the league in hit by pitch once (1998).

Led the league in games played as a catcher six times (1997, 1998, 2000, 2002, 2003, 2004).

Led the league in putouts as a catcher twice (1998, 2000).

Led the league in double plays as a catcher three times (1997, 1999, 2002).

Led league in assists as a catcher three times (1997, 2000, 2004).

Led league in caught stealing as a catcher three times (1996, 1997, 2004).

Had more than 100 runs in a season once.

Finished in the top 10 in the National League in batting three times.

5th in hit by pitch in major league history, at 254.

5th in most games as a catcher in major league history, at 2,025.

2nd in most putouts as a catcher in major league history, with 13,019.

11th in most double plays as a catcher in major league history, with 148.

50th in most assists as a catcher in major league history, with 989.

66th in most runners caught stealing as a catcher in major league history, at 495.

JASON KENDALL

45

GUS SUHR

Gus Suhr was an excellent first baseman for the Pittsburgh Pirates in the 1930s, hitting .279 in his career. While he was a good all-around player, it was his streak of 822 consecutive games played that put his name in Pirates history. When it ended in 1936, after Suhr missed a contest to attend his mother's funeral, the streak was a National League record.
Photo courtesy of the Pittsburgh Pirates.

Much has been made of the two most well-known iron men in the history of baseball, Lou Gehrig and Cal Ripken Jr., but in the 1930s there was another one, the first baseman from the Pittsburgh Pirates, who had played in more consecutive games than any other player in the history of the National League: Gus Suhr.

A good line-drive hitter who was one of the better offensive players for the team in the 1930s and played more games at first base than any Pirate ever has, Suhr's brush with history was going on at the same time as Gehrig's legendary streak.

The Bucs' left-handed first baseman's streak ended on June 5, 1937, when Suhr traveled to San Francisco to attend the funeral of his mother. As great as his streak was, it paled in comparison to Gehrig's, who, on that same date, was playing in his 1,742nd consecutive game. When it ended, Suhr's National League record stood at 822. Its greatness is still apparent some 79 years later, as it is currently the 10th-longest streak in major league history and the fourth-longest in the National League. Table 45.1 lists the players who have appeared in the most consecutive games in National League history, as well as Major League Baseball as a whole.

Born in San Francisco, California, in 1906, Suhr played at Polytechnic High School in the Bay Area before starting his professional career with the Quincy Red Birds in the Illinois-Indiana-Iowa League in 1925. Hitting .282, he impressed his hometown San Francisco Seals,

Table 45.1. Most consecutive games in National League history and Major League Baseball as a whole.

National League	Consecutive Games	Major League Baseball	Consecutive Games
Steve Garvey	1,207	Cal Ripken Jr.	2,632
Billy Williams	1,117	Lou Gehrig	2,130
Stan Musial	895	Everett Scott	1,307
Gus Suhr	822	Steve Garvey	1,207
		Miguel Tejada	1,152
		Billy Williams	1,117
		Joe Sewell	1,103
		Stan Musial	895
		Eddie Yost	829
		Gus Suhr	822

who signed him at the end of the 1925 campaign and moved him from first to second base.

Staying with the Pacific Coast League team for four seasons, Gus was eventually moved back to first base in 1929, and he rewarded them with incredible results. He had a marquee campaign, with 51 homers, 62 doubles, 176 RBIs, 196 runs, and a .382 average. It caught the attention of many in the major leagues, and luckily the Pittsburgh Pirates were able to secure his services.

The San Francisco native was thrilled to be playing in the majors, as was his family. "Going to the big leagues was an honor. My family visited by train every year in May or June, and I always went to San Francisco after the season," he recalled.[1]

Pittsburgh president Barney Dreyfuss had plans to erect a screen in right field of Forbes Field to stop what he felt were cheap home runs. He temporarily halted the measure, hoping that his new left-handed first baseman could take advantage of it. While Dreyfuss eventually recanted and went ahead with his plans to install the screen, Suhr nonetheless had a fabulous rookie campaign in 1930, with what would be a career-high 17 home runs and 107 RBIs, while hitting .286. The rookie was satisfied with his performance. "I felt good about my rookie year. My first day up I got two hits off Red Lucas of the Reds, who later became a teammate."[2]

During the next two seasons, the infielder struggled, injuring his knee in 1931, on a pickoff play, which contributed to a lowly .211 average, and the following year he had trouble against left-handed pitchers, as new manager George Gibson adjusted his stance. He improved to .263 but was far under his 1930 output; however, his defense at first was spectacular, which kept him in the lineup. His power returned in 1933, and Suhr was productive in the next three seasons, hitting .274, with 259 RBIs, including 103 RBIs in 1934.

Through it all, the first baseman remained in the starting lineup, continuing his impressive streak. In 1935, Suhr thought he had broken the National League mark when he played in his 618th straight game, breaking Eddie Brown's Senior Circuit mark, but when research credited Steve Brodie of the National League's Baltimore Orioles as playing in 722 consecutive contests in the 1890s, the record was no longer his. It was only a minor setback, as a year later he would play in his 723rd straight contest, and the record would be his again. That season, Gus enjoyed his most successful run as a Pirate, breaking the .300 plateau for the first time, hitting .312, with a career-high 118 RBIs.

While it was an impressive mark, there wasn't much press that went along with it; that would come 20 years later, when Stan Musial broke *his* mark. Suhr's son Gus Jr. confirmed this fact when he stated, "There was more fanfare when Stan Musial broke dad's record."[3]

Records aside, one of the highlights of the batsman's career came in 1938, when the Pirates were finally in a pennant race, losing it in the last week of the campaign to the Chicago Cubs, as Gus hit .294. It was the beginning of the end for Suhr in Pittsburgh, as he was dealt to the Philadelphia Phillies a year later, on July 28, for Max Butcher. Sad to leave the only major league team he had ever played for, the first baseman hit well for the Phillies the rest of the 1939 campaign, with a .318 average, but he was released in May, just one year later, after a .160 start. The 34-year-old never returned to the majors again.

Returning to the PCL during the war due to the lack of players, Suhr once again joined the Seals between 1943 and 1945, before finishing his professional career with the Pittsburg/Roseville Diamonds in the Far West League in 1948. He lived a long life after that, finally passing away in 2004, at the age of 98, following a brief illness.

MOST MEMORABLE PERFORMANCE

It was a fairly nondescript day for the Pittsburgh Pirates on June 4, 1937, coming into the ball game at 24–13 to face the Boston Braves. It would also be one for first baseman Gus Suhr, who did little to distinguish himself, with a single in four at bats during a 9–1 rout by the Braves. Sadly, it would be the last contest in his incredible consecutive games streak, the 822nd one he had played in.

The next day, Suhr was not on the bench for the matchup against the Giants at the Polo Grounds in New York, following the passing of his mother, necessitating that he travel to San Francisco to be with his family at her funeral. He missed three contests due to the unfortunate circumstance and then played in the next 132. If not for the funeral, his final number of 957 games would have been 62 more than Stan Musial's then-Senior Circuit mark.

CHAPTER 45

The contest was perhaps not as impressive as some of the moments in this book, but in what would become the foremost thing Suhr is known for in his career, it is certainly one of the most fitting.

NOTABLE ACHIEVEMENTS (YEARLY LEADERS AND AWARDS ARE AS PIRATES ONLY)

Selected to play in one All-Star Game.

Led the league in games played three times (1932, 1933, 1936).

Led league in games played at first base four times (1932, 1933, 1936, 1937).

Led the league in putouts at first base once (1938).

Led the league in double plays as a first baseman once (1930, 1938).

Led league in fielding percentage for a first baseman once (1936).

Had more than 100 runs in a season once.

Had more than 100 RBIs in a season three times.

Finished in the top 10 in the National League in triples eight times.

112th in most triples in major league history, with 114.

66th in most putouts for a first baseman in major league history, at 13,103.

70th in most putouts in major league history, with 13,104.

74th in most double plays as a first baseman in major league history, at 1,086.

94th in most assists for a first baseman in major league history, with 766.

72nd in most games for a first baseman in major league history, at 1,406.

Held the National League record for most consecutive games played until 1957, with 822.

10th in most consecutive games played in major league history, with 822.

4th in most consecutive games played in National League history, with 822.

Holds the all-time Pirates record for most consecutive games played, with 822.

46

TONY PENA

The Gold Glove is the ultimate honor the game of baseball can bestow on a defensive player. While there have been many great defensive players to take to the diamond in the history of the Pittsburgh Pirates, in the 68 years that the award has been given, only eight Pirates have captured the celebrated trophy on multiple occasions, a list that includes only one catcher, Tony Pena.

Born in the city of Monte Cristi, in the Dominican Republic, Pena had a unique stance behind the plate that allowed him to uncoil like a cobra to throw out opposing runners. He sat on the ground with one leg to his side and the other sticking straight out. One of the strongest—if not the strongest—arms behind the plate in the history of the Bucs, he was able to throw to second base with pinpoint accuracy. Whether leaping up from his unique crouch or throwing from the prone position, runners were often out upon arrival at the bag. To show the rarified position Pena holds in the franchise's history, table 46.1 lists the winners of multiple Gold Gloves for the Bucs.

Like current Pittsburgh catching prospect Elias Diaz, Pena was a young Latin American up-and-comer who was fabulous defensively but needed work offensively to become a more complete player. He was signed as an amateur free agent in 1975, at 18 years of age, and sent to the club's rookie league team in the Gulf Coast League before heading to the Charleston Patriots. Tony proved to be efficient behind the plate, but his .214 combined average did nothing to impress the front office that he could be anything more than a good defensive replacement in the majors.

A year later, Pena's stats had started to improve, as he showed some power, with 10 home runs in 1977, but by the time he was

Table 46.1. Winners of multiple Gold Gloves for the Pittsburgh Pirates.

Player	Position	Gold Gloves
Roberto Clemente	outfield	12
Bill Mazeroski	second base	8
Andy Van Slyke	outfield	5
Tony Pena	catcher	3
Barry Bonds	outfield	3
Dave Parker	outfield	3
Gene Alley	shortstop	2
Harvey Haddix	pitcher	2

promoted to Double-A ball in 1978, he had regressed to .230. The year the Pirates won the fifth and, thus far, last world championship, he finally seemed to be putting everything together. While with the team's new Double-A team in Buffalo, the young catcher exploded, with 34 home runs, 97 RBIs, and a batting average that was 83 points higher than the previous season, finishing fifth in the Eastern League, at .313. The 22-year-old backstop also continued to shine defensively, leading the circuit's catchers in putouts, assists, and double plays.

Ready for his final minor league promotion in 1980, Pena went to Portland, improving his average to .329, while being named to the Topps Triple-A All-Star Team. A late-season call up that season, the young catcher, nicknamed Jala by ESPN's Chris Berman, showed the Bucs' front office that he was ready to handle major league pitching, hitting .429 in 21 at bats, including a single in his second major league at bat against the Cubs' Doug Capilla on September 26.

The 1981 campaign would prove to be one of the most troubling in major league history. The season, cut short by a strike, was split in half, as baseball had what was in essence its first divisional series. While the Pirates did not fare well in the odd campaign, the momentum that the Monte Cristi native had garnered the previous two seasons continued in his official rookie year in Pittsburgh. He hit .300 and was named the Topps Rookie All-Star catcher, as well as selected to be on the United Press International All-Rookie Team.

In 1982, Pena's first full season, he began a three-year string of consistency that included averages near or above .300, along with double-digit home runs and a defensive peak that was among the best any catcher in the franchise's history has ever enjoyed. After hitting .296 in 1982 and being selected to play in his first All-Star Game, he had a season the following year that put him among the best in the game. Jala started off slowly, with a .244 average going into June, with only one home run. It was looking like his first two seasons might have been an aberration when he quickly turned around.

After hitting .307 in June, Tony went on a tear the rest of the campaign. His average between July 1 and the end of the season was .325, as he smacked 13 of his career-high 15 home runs in the year's final 88 games, while knocking in 51 during that time period. Pena was named to the *Sporting News* year-end All-Star Team and captured the first of three consecutive Gold Gloves with the Bucs.

The four-year vet continued his consistency in 1984, with a fine .286 average, while matching his career high in home runs, with 15, two short of the team record for a catcher held by Jim Pagliaroni, who had belted 17 in 1965. Pena achieved perhaps his best single-game offensive output in his major league career on August 31, with two home runs and six RBIs against the Reds. He led the Senior Circuit in just about every defensive category for catchers and was once again rewarded with a Gold Glove.

While his average dropped to .249 in 1985, his defense did not, becoming only the fifth player in Pittsburgh history to capture three Gold Gloves. Pena played one more season in Pittsburgh in 1986, raising his average back to .288, while being selected to play in his fourth All-Star Game, but less than a year later, on April Fools' Day 1987, he was surprisingly dealt to the Cardinals for, among others, Andy Van Slyke, who would join him in the near future as a multiple Gold Glove winner for the Bucs.

Jala would never reach the same level after leaving the Pirates, although he won a fourth Gold Glove with the Red Sox in 1991, and hit perhaps the most dramatic home run of his career, winning Game One of the 1995 American League Division Series against Boston while with the Indians, with a blast in the 13th inning of an exciting 5–4 victory at Jacobs Field.

Pena went on to play 18 seasons and hit .338 in 29 postseason games after his time with the Bucs. He became a manager following his retirement, leading the Royals to their only winning season between 1994 and 2013, in 2004, while being named Manager of the Year for the American League. He is currently a bench coach for the Yankees, and while he has been gone from the Pittsburgh organization for almost 30 years, Tony remains perhaps its greatest defensive catcher.

MOST MEMORABLE PERFORMANCE

For a player with moderate power at best, on August 31, 1984, Pittsburgh catcher Tony Pena was on par with the best power hitters in the game. Playing the Cincinnati Reds, managed by Pete Rose during the time he reportedly bet on the game, Jala was a one-man wrecking crew. After the Reds took a 1–0 lead in the second inning, the three-time Gold Glove winner came to the plate in the fourth with one out and Lee Lacy and Jim Morrison on base. Pena drove the one-strike pitch over the fence for his 11th home run of the season to give Pittsburgh a 3–1 lead.

Two innings later, the backstop was once again in the batter's box, after Johnny Ray had doubled and Jim Morrison had been hit by a Joe Price offering. With no one out, Pena ran the count to three balls and one strike before nailing Price's fifth pitch over the fence for his 12th home run, extending the Bucs' advantage to 6–1. Cincinnati tacked on a meaningless run off Pittsburgh starter John Candelaria in the seventh, as the team held on for a 6–2 victory, with Pena accounting for their entire offensive output.

NOTABLE ACHIEVEMENTS (YEARLY LEADERS AND AWARDS ARE AS PIRATES ONLY)

Won three National League Gold Glove Awards (1983, 1984, 1985).
Selected to play in four All-Star Games.
Finished 12th in the 1983 National League Most Valuable Player voting.
Led the league in games played by a catcher once (1985).
Led the league in putouts as a catcher twice (1983, 1984).
Led the league in double plays as a catcher once (1984).
Led the league in assists by a catcher twice (1984, 1985).
Led the league in runners caught stealing by a catcher twice (1984, 1985).
40th in most runners caught stealing by a catcher in major league history, at 656.
8th in most putouts for a catcher in major league history, with 11,212.
6th in most double plays as a catcher in major league history, with 156.
40th in most assists for a catcher in major league history, at 1,045.
6th in most games for a catcher in major league history, at 1,950.

47

FRANK THOMAS

When someone mentions the name Frank Thomas, most baseball fans think of the power-hitting hall of famer who spent the majority of his career with the Chicago White Sox, racking up 521 home runs and 1,704 RBIs. Introduce yourself to the heavy-hitting Pittsburgh Pirates of the 1950s by the same name and he will look you in the eye and make sure you know that he was the "original Frank Thomas." For those who were lucky enough to see him during his prime at Forbes Field, they will fondly remember the original version.

While the latter-day Frank Thomas was the better player throughout the course of his career, it's not preposterous to compare them, especially in their first six full seasons. Table 47.1 is a comparison of the two during that time period.

The White Sox version is better in every category but triples, but the Steel City Thomas was impressive too, especially considering the fact that Forbes Field was cavernous and rather unkind to right-handed power hitters. Despite the unfriendly facility, he averaged 26.8 homers per season and 91 RBIs during the full seasons he played in a Pirates uniform. In 1958, he smacked 35 home runs; no third baseman would hit more for the franchise until Pedro Alvarez led the league with 36 in 2013. If not for the fact that he played for some of the worst teams in major league history and that a Hall of Fame player bears the same name, the name Frank Thomas from the 1950s would resonate with Pirate and baseball fans alike.

Born in Pittsburgh in 1929, the original Frank Thomas was signed as an amateur free agent in 1947, after attending Mount Carmel College in Niagara Falls, Ontario, where he was studying to become a

Table 47.1. Statistics for Frank Thomas of the Chicago White Sox and Frank Thomas of the Pittsburgh Pirates.

Player	AB	H	2B	3B	HR	RBI	Slug	OPS	AVE
Thomas (CHC)	3,100	1,014	200	5	215	698	.603	1.054	.327
Thomas (PIT)	3,286	909	150	18	161	546	.480	.816	.277

priest. Deciding to pursue baseball as his life's calling, he started his professional career with the Bucs' Class D team in Tallahassee, where he hit 24 homers in his first year and a half, before being promoted to the Class B Waco Pirates.

Frank continued his ascent in the Bucs' system, finally ending up with their top team in New Orleans in 1950. He played with the Pelicans for three seasons, belting 35 long balls in his final year, while hitting .303. The Pirates were among the worst teams in baseball in the early to mid-1950s, and GM Branch Rickey could no longer afford to keep such potential in the minor leagues. After two short stints with the Bucs in 1951 and 1952, Thomas came up for good in 1953, and was given the starting nod in center field. He responded with a spectacular first full season in the majors, ripping 30 home runs, good enough for seventh in the National League, while knocking in 102. Both stats were records for rookie center fielders, better than Mickey Mantle and Willie Mays, who had debuted only two years earlier.

In 1952, the Pirates were suffering one of their worst seasons, winning only 42 games, with a horrific .273 winning percentage. While in eight short years they would be world champions, this lineup included Joe Garagiola, Tony Bartirome, Jack Merson, a young Dick Groat, Pete Castilione, Bobby Del Greco, Gus Bell, and Ralph Kiner, who, at 29, was aging quickly and would be traded the next season to the Cubs. It was hardly an intimidating collection of players. The influx of power Thomas brought to the team in 1953 did not significantly improve the club, as they won only eight more games, but it was the beginning of an incredible rebuilding project. And while he would not be present for the magnificent conclusion in 1960, Frank was still an important part of the effort.

Except for hitting .245 in 1955, the Pittsburgh native was remarkably consistent between 1954 and 1957, hitting 23, 25, 25, and 23 homers, respectively, despite having few good hitters to protect him in the lineup. "It was tough, but I did the best I could and let the chips fall where they may," Thomas once commented.[1] Even though he had a subpar average in 1955, he overcame the obstacles, hitting .280 during the four seasons, with 335 RBIs and an .800 on-base plus slugging percentage. As it turned out, it was just a prelude to his finest season in a Pirates uniform—a year that would ironically be his last.

After a decade of pathetic second-division performances, the young Bucs began to blossom, finishing second in the Senior Circuit, with an 84–70 mark. Thomas set career highs in just about every category. He ripped 35 home runs, knocked in 109 runs, and had a .528 slugging percentage and .863 OPS. He was selected to play in the All-Star Game and finished fourth in the National League Most Valuable Player voting, behind three of the greatest to ever play the game, Ernie Banks, Willie Mays, and Hank Aaron. It was Frank's greatest season for sure. Prior to the season, the batsman was signed to a $25,000 contract by GM Joe L. Brown, and he enjoyed everything about his successful campaign, traveling to the West Coast to play the new teams there—and especially the winning.

The Bucs now had a bright future, one that Brown would enhance with a trade to the Cincinnati Reds in January 1959, receiving Smoky Burgess, Harvey Haddix, and Don Hoak from their Ohio neighbors, all of whom would be integral in the world championship they would enjoy a year later. But to get the trio, Brown had to give up something big, which turned out to be the original Frank Thomas. When he left the Bucs, Frank was second to Ralph Kiner on the franchise's all-time home run list, with 163. Unfortunately for the Reds and Thomas, he was suffering from tumors that were growing at the ends of the nerves in his hand, affecting his play and causing him to hit only .225.

The slugger was traded to the Cubs and then the Braves, before ending up with a team that was worse than those he had played on in Pittsburgh in the mid-1950s—the 1962 New York Mets. Thomas was one of the few stars with the expansion team, hitting 34 homers that season. He spent two seasons in New York before being dealt to the Phillies in the middle of the 1964 pennant race. Frank hit well for the Phils and was heating up in August, with a .294 average, when he broke his thumb, ending his year. It was an injury that Philadelphia manager Gene Mauch felt cost the team the pennant, as they finished only one game out of first in a legendary collapse. It was Thomas's last highlight season.

After a few sluggish years, he retired following the 1966 campaign, when he was hitless in five at bats with the Cubs and hit .203 with their Triple-A affiliate in Tacoma, ending his career with 286 home runs, far off the total of the latter-day Frank Thomas. Nonetheless, if one sees the 87-year-old today he will still remind them of one thing: the fact that he is the original Frank Thomas.

MOST MEMORABLE PERFORMANCE

In 1958, the man who refers to himself as the original Frank Thomas was having his marquee season for the Pirates, achieving career highs in home runs, RBIs, slugging, and OPS. On August 16, while playing the Reds at Crosley Field, the place that he would ironically consider home following a trade after the season, Thomas would put an exclamation point on his phenomenal campaign with a three-home run effort in a 13–4 shellacking of Cincinnati.

After hitting a home run to lead off the second inning that gave Pittsburgh a 1–0 lead, Frank garnered his second RBI of the day on a sacrifice fly to left field in the third, increasing the advantage to three.

The Reds went on to tie the score before Thomas once again came to the plate as the first hitter of the inning, leading off the top of the sixth for the Bucs. He launched his second homer of the day deep over the left-field fence, as Pittsburgh once again took the lead, 4–3. With the Reds tying the score in the bottom half of the frame, the Pirates offense caught fire in the final three innings, scoring nine runs, three of them coming off the bat of the Bucs' third baseman in the top of the ninth. With Dick Stuart and Bob Skinner on base with leadoff singles, Frank once again ripped the ball over the left-field fence to give him three homers and six RBIs in a showing of perhaps the greatest offensive output of his fine career.

NOTABLE ACHIEVEMENTS (YEARLY LEADERS AND AWARDS ARE AS PIRATES ONLY)

Selected to play in three All-Star Games.

Finished in the top 25 voting for the National League MVP five times.

Led the league in hit by pitch once (1954).

Led the league in games played once (1956).

Led the league in games played as an outfielder once (1954).

Led the league in sacrifice flies once (1957).

Led the league in double plays as a left fielder twice (1955, 1957).

Led the league in assists as an outfielder once (1954).

Led the league in assists as a left fielder once (1957).

Eclipsed more than 100 RBIs in a season twice.

Finished in the top 10 in the National League in home runs and slugging twice.

89th in most assists by a left fielder in major league history, with 55.

156th in most home runs in major league history, with 286.

146th in most sacrifice flies in major league history, at 70.

FRANK THOMAS

48

GEORGE GRANTHAM

Coming over in a trade from the Cubs after the 1924 campaign, George Grantham went from a promising prospect to a superstar, helping lead the Bucs to the 1925 World Series championship. In his seven seasons with the Bucs, Grantham hit .315, with 508 RBIs.

Photo courtesy of the Pittsburgh Pirates.

The rule of thumb when trading a veteran superstar is to get a young prospect who will hopefully one day give you similar production as the seasoned player who just departed. More times than not, for every Brian Giles a team receives, there are many more Bobby Hill's. In 1924, when Pittsburgh Pirates president Barney Dreyfuss and manager Bill McKechnie sent the franchise's all-time leading hurler in wins, Wilbur Cooper, along with Charlie Grimm and future Hall of Famer Rabbit Maranville, to the Chicago Cubs for Vic Aldridge, Al Niehaus, and a young second baseman from Galena, Kansas, by the name of George "Boots" Grantham, they hoped the young players would finally be the missing pieces to give the Bucs their first pennant in 16 seasons.

While it eventually proved out to be a good trade for Pittsburgh, when it first happened, Pirates fans were highly irritated, while Cubs fans seemed to be rejoicing. Maranville had a history of being a troublemaker. Cooper, while successful, was extremely moody, as his attitude was not his best quality. And Grimm had held out for more money before the opening of the 1924 campaign. These factors made them prime candidates to be traded.

McKechnie was on the hot seat after the deal. He was badly criticized for it, and anything less than a pennant in 1925 likely would have been the end of his managerial tenure with the Pirates. As it turned out it, was one of the best maneuvers he had ever made, as Cooper fell to 12–14 with the Cubs, and Maranville hit .233. Grimm was the only one who succeeded, with a .306 average and 10 homers. Even though Niehaus had originally been the key to the trade, being considered one of the best prospects in the game, the other two would be the more productive players for the team. Aldridge won 15 games, losing only seven, while in Grantham, who moved to first base in 1925, they had an infielder with a .300 average who became one of the crucial components to the Pirates offense in the next seven seasons and helped lead them to the pennant and world championship they so desired; advantage Pittsburgh.

Before he became a hero for a world championship team, Grantham went to school in Flagstaff, Arizona, after his family moved there from Galena, Illinois. He dropped out in the seventh grade and began to play baseball. The family would eventually relocate to Arizona, in a small town called Kingman, where George became a star for some local teams.

Lying about his age, he entered the U.S. Navy during World War I and served on a submarine in the seas off Cuba. When Grantham returned, he signed his first professional contract with the Class B Tacoma Tigers of the Pacific Coast International League, where he hit only .225 in his initial campaign in 1920.

But it was only a temporary lapse, as he improved a year later, raising his average 134 points, to .359, before heading to Portland in the Pacific Coast League midseason. There he continued his great play, keeping his average over .300, at .305. Grantham played one more season in the minors, hitting .302, before the Chicago Cubs bought his contract and immediately placed him on the major league roster. The 22-year-old went one for seven in his abbreviated major league debut in 1922, and then .281 in his official rookie campaign a year later, showing off his speed with a National League second-best 43 stolen bases and 70 RBIs.

In 1924, George went from being an effective rookie to one of the best second basemen in the game. Breaking the .300 plateau for the first time in the majors, with a .316 average, while showing some power, with 12 home runs, Grantham's future looked bright in the Windy City—that is, before the surprising trade that sent him to the Pirates after the season ended. While his time in Chicago was over, his future remained bright.

Niehaus turned out to be a bust instead of an improvement over Grimm at first, hitting only .219 before being traded to Cincinnati on May 30. He would never play in the majors again. With Niehaus failing, McKechnie moved the former second baseman to first, and Grantham responded with a career-high .326 average, as the manager's critics were silenced. The trade did, in fact, lead to the pennant that Pirates fans had been looking for since 1909. The team faced the defending world champion Washington Senators in the World Series, and while Grantham only hit .133, the Bucs defeated Washington in an exciting seven-game series.

Hitting .311 in the next two seasons, the Kansas native moved back to his original position at second in 1927, and helped lead the club to their second National League pennant in three years. This time the

Bucs faced one of the greatest teams in the annuls of the game, the 1927 New York Yankees. While they were competitive at times, the Pirates were beaten in a four-game sweep, during which Grantham had a more effective series, with a .364 average. Even though it would be the last World Series for Pittsburgh with the former Cub on their roster, he enjoyed a consistent career in the Steel City, never falling below .300.

After two fine campaigns where he hit a combined .316, with 22 home runs, Grantham had his finest season in a Pirates uniform in 1930. The team had a good 80–74 record despite the fact that they had been outscored by 37 runs. The 30-year-old had career highs in home runs (18), RBIs (99), doubles (34), and slugging percentage (.534), while hitting .324. The left-handed hitter followed up with another successful year in 1931, hitting .305 as he split time between first and second base. But it would be George's last season with the Bucs, as they sold him to the Cincinnati Reds.

While Grantham had nominal success in 1932, he began a downward spiral the following season, and his major league career ended in 1934, following a short trial with the Giants. He resurfaced in the minor league for two years, hitting .286 with the Pacific Coast League's Seattle Indians in 1935, his final season.

George eventually became a manager in the men's department for the Central Commercial Company, passing away in 1954, at only 53. Although he is often forgotten, one only need look to baseball statistician Bill James for Grantham's place in baseball history, as James concludes that there have only been two players in the major leagues to play more than 1,200 games in an important defensive position and remain above average in every offensive category: Willie Mays and George Grantham. James also names him as the 62nd-greatest second baseman of all-time in his updated *Historical Baseball Abstract*,[1] as he was the key component in one of the greatest trades in Pirates history.

MOST MEMORABLE PERFORMANCE

Even though he was part of a heavily criticized trade at the beginning of the season, George Grantham's performance in 1925 would show that manager Bill McKechnie and owner Barney Dreyfuss knew what they were doing when they obtained him and Vic Aldridge from the Cubs for three key Pirates players. That fact would be emphasized on June 22, 1925, when Grantham led an assault on the St. Louis Cardinals at Sportsman's Park in St. Louis.

As the day began, the Pirates were 32–23 after a slow start and catching up to a New York Giant team that they would surpass by year's end. The game, for all intents and purposes, was over in the first inning, when the Bucs plated eight runs, leading 9–3 before the contest was two innings old. Led by two Pirates with four hits, Max Carey and Grantham, Pittsburgh garnered six home runs and 21 hits, including a 10-run eighth inning, in a 24–6 trampling of the home team.

The Kansas native was the star of the game, leading the way with two home runs and six RBIs in perhaps the greatest offensive output of his fine 13-year major league career, one that put an exclamation point on a season that saw the Bucs win their second world championship.

NOTABLE ACHIEVEMENTS (YEARLY LEADERS AND AWARDS ARE AS PIRATES ONLY)

Played on two National League championship teams (1925, 1927).
Played on one world championship team (1925).
Finished in the top 10 in the National League in on-base percentage six times.
Finished in the top 10 in the National League in walks five times.
Finished in the top 10 in the National League in triples three times.
Eclipsed 100 runs once.
93rd in highest on-base percentage in major league history, at .392.
128th in most sacrifice hits in major league history, with 168.
11th in highest batting average in Pittsburgh Pirates history, at .315.
10th in highest slugging percentage in Pittsburgh Pirates history, at .491.
6th in highest on-base percentage in Pittsburgh Pirates history, at .419.
5th in highest on-base plus slugging percentage in Pittsburgh Pirates history, at .901.

49

STEVE BLASS

Ask Pirates fans who followed the team in the early part of the 21st century and they will tell you a very different tale about Steve Blass than those who have been fans since the days he took the mound for Pittsburgh. Today's younger generation knows him as the insightful color man on the Bucs' local broadcasts, a position he has held since 1983. To others he's more famous for ending his career because of a malady that has been since named in his honor—a complete lack of control referred to as "Steve Blass disease." For the more astute Pirates aficionados, Blass was not only one of the greatest pitchers in the history of the franchise, but also one of the top hurlers in the game in the late 1960s and early 1970s.

Born in Canaan, Connecticut, Blass was a star player for Housatonic High School, tossing five no-hitters in his junior and senior campaigns, before being signed by the Pirates as an amateur free agent in 1960, for $4,000, after turning down a $2,500 offer from the Cleveland Indians. Following a solid season in Batavia in 1961, Steve showed the organization his future star potential with a combined 18–7 mark a year later, spending most of the season with the Kinston Eagles.

The hurler was promoted to Pittsburgh's Triple-A club in Columbus in 1963, and while struggling somewhat with a 13–11 record and a 4.44 ERA, the club thought enough to promote him to the majors in early 1964. The young 22-year-old pitcher credits roving minor league pitching coach Don Osborne for his success to that point. Said Blass, "He helped me with guidance in terms of how to handle pro ball. He preached the simplicity of pitching, because as a youngster you try to complicate things. He helped me to trust my stuff, get the ball over the plate, and find out if you're good enough."[1]

On May 18, Blass got his chance to start for the first time in the majors, but his first starting assignment would be anything but easy, as he was scheduled to face future Hall of Famer Don Drysdale. The sports books in Las Vegas would have given long odds on Steve's success in that contest, but he remarkably found a way to emerge victorious.

It was a dream come true. I had been around several days and had pitched a time or two in relief. Drysdale was 6–1 at the time, and I looked up at the scoreboard and he was leading the league in just about everything. What I remember about the game was Leo Durocher was their third base coach at the time and was screaming at me, using language I had never experienced before; he was trying to rattle me. It certainly ended up being a wonderful thrill.[2]

After finishing the season 5–8, Blass was looking forward to his second year in 1965, but he would have to wait, as he didn't make the team in spring training and spent the entire campaign in Columbus. Not wanting to spend another season in the minors, he made the squad in 1966, and pushed himself to prove to Pirates manager Harry Walker that he deserved to stay, with an 11–7 mark.

The team, as well as the pitcher, struggled in 1967, with the Pirates faltering with an 81–81 mark, while the Canaan native posted a subpar 6–8 record, although his ERA fell from 3.87 to 3.55. The club did no better a year later, but the same could not be said for Steve, as he had a breakout season, firmly placing himself among the best hurlers in the game. He went 18–6, for a league-leading .750 winning percentage, on a team that finished under .500, with a miniscule 2.12 ERA.

Blass continued to be one of the team's most effective hurlers the next two campaigns, winning 26 games before coming into a two-year streak where he once again established himself as one of the premier hurlers in the Senior Circuit. In 1971, he compiled a 15–8 record, with a 2.85 ERA and a National League-best five shutouts, to lead Pittsburgh to its second consecutive Eastern Division championship. While the moundsman was less-than-stellar in his National League Championship Series performance against the Giants, allowing nine earned runs in seven innings in two starts, the Bucs nonetheless defeated San Francisco in four games to earn a shot against the Baltimore Orioles in the 1971 Fall Classic.

As he faced the Orioles in Game Three after Pittsburgh dropped the first two contests of the series, Blass used the lessons he had learned in his poor performance against the Giants to defeat Baltimore, 5–1, and give the Pirates momentum.

> I got my brains beat out [in the NLCS], and my confidence was a little eroded. This was my first postseason performance, and I thought I had to be different in the postseason, better than I was in the regular season. I tried to overpower hitters, and that wasn't my game. By Game Three of the World Series, I learned my lesson: Be yourself and go with what got you there.[3]

With his lesson well learned, the Pirates rebounded in the series, forcing a Game Seven, where Blass would have the chance to either be a hero or a goat in Pirates lore. Things did not start out well for the 29-year-old hurler, as he was a little wild from the outset. Orioles manager Earl Weaver, who was a master of mind games, decided he would try to put the nail in his coffin, protesting Rule 801, claiming Blass was not pitching from in front of the rubber. The ploy backfired, as Blass calmed down and focused on the task at hand. "I thank Earl every time I see him. . . . In the first inning I was all over the place, until Earl came out, and it calmed me down with his nonsense. As the game went on I got settled into the contest."[4]

Steve hurled a phenomenal game, defeating Baltimore, 2–1, to give the Bucs their fourth world championship. Wanting to make sure he remembered everything about the special occasion, Blass took time to appreciate the experience.

> I took a moment in the bottom of the seventh after I warmed up and before the first pitch. I took the baseball and went to the back of the mound to take in the whole scene. You don't know if you'll ever get back again, and I wanted to soak in the atmosphere and have an image to bring up whenever I need it. I made everyone wait until I soaked in my mental image, then we went back to work.[5]

STEVE BLASS

Now a national star, the right-hander used the momentum he had gained from the World Series to produce arguably his best season in the majors. He finished 19–8, with a 2.49 ERA, finishing second behind Steve Carlton in the Cy Young voting in 1972, and ending up on the cover of *Sports Illustrated*. At 30 years of age and with his future limitless, a funny thing happened on his way to superstardom: His career took a turn for the worse when he was afflicted with a condition that would eventually have his name attached to it: Steve Blass disease. It was at this juncture in his career that he became incredibly wild.

His pinpoint control now gone, many tried to cure him, but none succeeded. His ERA skyrocketed to more than seven runs per game, to 9.85, and Blass walked 84 hitters in only 109 innings pitched, while hitting a league-high 12 batters. It was a baffling situation for a man who only a few months earlier had been arguably the best pitcher in the game. Writer Kirk Robinson put it in perspective when he wrote,

In 1972, if you had to choose any pitcher in the world to start one big game, Steve Blass would have been on your short list. . . . In 1973, famously, the wheels came off of (his) career. He hit batters, he walked people, he threw pitches worthy of Nuke Laloosh, throwing behind hitters, bouncing pitches, terrifying mascots, and generally looking as lost as an Amish buggy on Broadway. . . . And then his career was over. A disease was born.[6]

Pittsburgh sent him to Charleston to see if he could find the solution there, but it was to no avail, as his ERA remained poor, at 9.74, walking almost two batters per inning. Allowing 25 more free passes in 14 innings during spring training in 1975, Blass called it quits. It was regrettably the end for one of the best players to ever take the mound for the Bucs. Fortunately, the malady happened to a man who not only handled it with class, but also went out of his way to help others afflicted by it in the years that followed.

After the sudden end to his career, Steve sold class rings and was a PR man for a beer distributor, before finally finding his second calling in 1983, as the color man for the Pirates on a fledgling cable network, a position he still holds today. He continues to entertain Pirates fans with analysis of the team he has been part of for 54 years.

Steve Blass disease still exists, even becoming part of the American landscape, being mentioned on such shows as *Northern Exposure*. For Blass, he has, in a way, managed to cure himself, becoming very accurate in another sport, garnering two holes-in-one in a single round of golf on a late summer afternoon in 2009. While he has been cured in one sport, but not the one he had dedicated his life to, Steve is nonetheless remembered as one of the greatest pitchers in Pirates history.

MOST MEMORABLE PERFORMANCE

Probably the most memorable performance in the career of Steve Blass is his Game-Seven masterpiece in the 1971 World Series, during which he helped the Bucs win their fourth world championship.

After a successful 15–8 campaign during the regular season, Blass was anything but in the NLCS against the San Francisco Giants. He gave up five runs in five innings in a Game-One loss and was even worse in the fourth game, surrendering another five runs, four earned, in only two innings, although his offense bailed him out in a dramatic 9–5 victory that gave Pittsburgh the National League pennant.

With the Bucs down two games to none against the Baltimore Orioles in the Fall Classic, Pirates fans were not exactly confident when manager Danny Murtaugh called on Blass to turn the tide in Game Three. Luckily, their worries were unfounded, as the righty was incredible, conjuring up a complete-game, three-hit, 5–1 win.

The two teams battled to a seventh game, where Murtaugh once again gave the ball to his 15-game winner. Many wondered which Blass would show up, the one who had struggled against San Francisco or the master who had stalled the Oriole bats in the series. Early on it looked as if the fans in Pittsburgh would be disappointed, when Blass walked Don Buford to start the contest. With the powerful Boog Powell at the plate, the Pirates hurler surrendered a long shot that fortunately went foul, before Powell ripped another impressive foul ball. Sensing that the pitcher was close to faltering, Baltimore manager Earl Weaver decided to try to completely destroy Blass's concentration, stepping out to argue that Blass was not pitching in front of the rubber, violating Rule 801.

Umpire Nestor Chylak called Murtaugh to the mound, making sure that both men knew that Blass must, in fact, pitch from in front of the rubber. Chylak gave the 29-year-old hurler time to warm up after the lengthy delay, and it initially looked like Weaver's ploy had worked, as Blass tossed a warm-up pitch high over catcher Manny Sanguillen's glove. Sensing the Pirates hurler was about done, Weaver again came out to complain, this time that Blass was going to his mouth too much. Unfortunately for the Orioles skipper and his team, the disruption seemed to settle Blass rather than push him over the edge. After bouncing the first pitch after the delay in front of the plate and throwing the next one high and outside, the third pitch was perfect, striking out Powell, and the rest, as they say, is history.

The moundsman limited Baltimore to four hits, while striking out five in the 2–1 victory. Even though his career would be in shambles two year later, it was his clutch performance in the most important game of his career that is undoubtedly the highlight of his tenure with the Bucs.

NOTABLE ACHIEVEMENTS (YEARLY LEADERS AND AWARDS ARE AS PIRATES ONLY)

> Played on one National League championship and world championship team (1971).
> Played on four Eastern Division championship teams (1970, 1971, 1972, 1974).
> Selected to play in one All-Star Game
> Finished in the top 22 voting for the National League Most Valuable Player Award twice.
> Finished second in the voting for the 1972 National League Cy Young Award.
> Led the league in winning percentage once (1968).
> Led the league in shutouts once (1971).
> Led the league in fielding percentage for a pitcher once (1968).
> Finished in the top six in the National League in ERA twice.
> Finished in the top seven in the National League in wins twice.
> 209th in highest winning percentage in major league history, at .575.
> 17th in most wins in Pittsburgh Pirates history, with 103.
> 7th in most strikeouts in Pittsburgh Pirates history, with 896.
> Compiled a 2–0 mark in the World Series
> Has spent 29 years as a Pirates broadcaster, second only to Lanny Fratarre's 33.

50

JASON BAY

As good as the Pittsburgh Pirates have been throughout their history, one oddity was that they had never had a player voted as the National League Rookie of the Year. Since the award's inception in 1947, there have been some great Pirates freshman, but none good enough to be so named—that is, until a young Canadian player obtained in the 2003 Brian Giles deal from San Diego by the name of Jason Bay ended the streak at 58 years.

While not an official Major League Baseball award, prior to 2004, four Pirates had been honored by *Sporting News* with their Rookie Pitcher of the Year and Player of the Year awards: Don Robinson and Mike Dunne for Rookie Pitcher of the Year, and Johnny Ray and Jason Kendall for Player of the Year. Table 50.1 lists the winners of the Player of the Year Award, plus Bay, who was also given the honor, while table 50.2 gives the Rookie Pitcher of the Year honorees. Also included are their stats and finish in the Baseball Writers' Association of America vote for the MLB Rookie of the Year.

Robinson, Dunne, Ray, and Kendall had wonderful rookie seasons, but all paled in comparison to Bay, who was certainly deserving of being the Pirate to break the streak. The only other player who was comparable was Robinson, who also finished eighth in the Cy Young Award voting after falling behind Bob Horner and Ozzie Smith for Rookie of the Year. The most important aspect of Bay's status as a pioneer in Pirates history is the fact that he was able to maintain his excellence throughout his stay in the Steel City, making him more than just a one-year fluke.

Table 50.1. Pittsburgh Pirates who have been honored as *Sporting News* Player of the Year.

Year	Player	HR	RBI	Slugging Percentage	OPS	AVE	ROY Finish
1982	Ray	7	63	.382	.700	.281	2
1996	Kendall	3	42	.401	.773	.300	3
2004	Bay	26	82	.550	.907	.282	1

Born in Brail, British Columbia, Bay represented his country in the 1996 Junior Olympics before starting his collegiate career at North Idaho College, where he was a star, before transferring to Gonzaga University. He led the West Coast Conference in batting and was named to the All-Conference team his two seasons with the Bulldogs.

With his stock on the rise, the Montreal Expos took their native son in the 22nd round of the 2000 Amateur Draft. Bay only remained in the Montreal organization for two seasons, before being dealt to the Mets, as Expo general manager Oscar Minaya thought the team would be contracted and sent many of his young future prospects away in deals in hopes of immediate wins. After playing well for the Mets in their farm system for most of the season, stealing 35 bases, Jason was traded to the Padres, along with two other players, for Steve Reed and Jason Middlebrook.

Playing for his third organization in three seasons, Bay hit .303, with 20 home runs, for the Portland Beavers in 2003, getting a short look with the Padres. Luckily for Pittsburgh fans, San Diego was interested in Brian Giles, who the Pirates were looking to deal in a salary dump, and sent Bay, Oliver Perez, and Corey Stewart in exchange. He hit .291 in 27 games for the Bucs the remainder of the 2003 campaign. As good as Bay's trial run was for Pittsburgh that season, few expected the offensive outburst the young Canadian left fielder would have a year later, in his official rookie season.

Table 50.2. Pittsburgh Pirates who have been named *Sporting News* Rookie Pitcher of the Year.

Year	Player	W	L	K	WHIP	ERA	ROY Finish
1978	Robinson	14	6	135	1.139	3.47	3
1987	Dunne	13	6	72	1.292	3.06	2

After having off-season shoulder surgery, Bay rehabbed for the Bucs' Triple-A club in Nashville before the season began and was incredible once he came back to Pittsburgh. Named the Rookie Player of the Month on three occasions, he was consistent throughout the season. His 26 home runs broke the franchise record of 23 for a rookie set by Ralph Kiner and Johnny Rizzo, and the slugger garnered his second eight-RBI performance of his young career, the first coming the year before. In beating the Padres' Khalil Greene for Rookie of the Year honors, receiving 146 vote points to Greene's 106, the Bucs' young left fielder also became the first Little League World Series participant (he played for Canada in 1990) to be so honored.

In 2005, proving he was the real thing, Bay became the first player in Pirates history to hit .300 with at least 30 home runs, 40 doubles, 20 stolen bases, 100 runs scored, and 100 RBIs. He followed that up in 2006, with then-career highs in home runs, at 35, and RBIs, with 109. Jason was also the first player in franchise history to hit 10 homers in 10 games. Perhaps his greatest honor in a Pirates uniform came in 2006, with the All-Star Game being played in Pittsburgh for the second time in 12 seasons. He was selected as not only the first Pirates starter in 13 years, but also the first Buc to start in All-Star Game in Pittsburgh since Bob Elliott in 1944.

While things looked great for Bay heading into 2007, he slumped as the season unfolded, finishing with a .247 average, as almost every offensive category suffered. Injuries also played a part in his decline. He played sparingly in September while battling tendonitis in his right knee. Jason rebounded in 2008 and was hitting .286, with 22 homers, as July was coming to an end, when the new GM, Neal Huntington, decided that the team once again needed to rebuild if it was to finally end its long losing legacy. He dealt his star to the Red Sox in a three-way trade that included the Dodgers, netting Andy LaRoche, Bryan Morris, Craig Hansen, and Brandon Moss in return.

Even though Huntington was eventually the right man to restore winning baseball to Pittsburgh, this was not his finest move, and none of the four would ever make significant contributions to the Pirates. Bay was phenomenal for Boston, with career highs in home runs, with 36, and RBIs, with 119, in 2009. He signed a four-year, $66 million contract with the Mets in 2010, but injuries, combined with the cavernous dimensions of Citi Field, which hurt his power, all but ended his career. After a short stint with the Mariners in 2013, Bay retired. Despite the fact that his 11-year major league career came to such a sudden end, it had been a successful one, one that ensures his place in Pirates history, as he remains the only player in franchise history to win the coveted Rookie of the Year Award.

MOST MEMORABLE PERFORMANCE

Coming to Pittsburgh as a key prospect in a trade in which the team gave up its star was certainly enough pressure on a young player, but doing so in a market where the city was looking for a baseball savior in the midst of a record-setting streak of losing seasons could have made it unfathomable. With everything that new Pittsburgh Pirate Jason Bay had going against him, he showed Pirates fans that he was the special player they had been hoping for when he drove in eight runs in a game on September 19, not long after his arrival from San Diego. It had been 53 years since a Buc had achieved such a feat, not since Ralph Kiner had equaled the production on June 25, 1950.

While it was a contest the Pirates lost, 10–9, to the eventual Central Division champion Chicago Cubs, it was a nice comeback effort in a game that saw the Cubs take an early 9–4 lead by the top of the third at PNC Park. After plating three in the top of the second, Pittsburgh was enjoying a temporary 4–3 advantage in the bottom half of the frame when the new Pirates left fielder smashed a one-out grand slam, scoring Matt Stairs, Jack Wilson, and Rob Mackowiak in front of him.

Chicago scored six in the top of the third, and it appeared it was going to be a blowout, but Bay would not allow it. He cut the lead to three in the fourth with his second homer of the day with Mackowiak on third after smacking a triple, and an inning later, after Kendall scored on a wild pitch to Bay, Jason tied the game at nine with a two-run double.

Chicago went on to score the game's last run in the sixth, off a sacrifice fly by Alex Gonzalez, but it didn't detract from the phenomenal effort by Jason Bay. He repeated the effort a year later, with eight RBIs against the Brewers, but in dealing with the pressure of being the city's savior directly after coming over from the Padres, September 19, 2003, has to be considered his most memorable performance.

NOTABLE ACHIEVEMENTS (YEARLY LEADERS AND AWARDS ARE AS PIRATES ONLY)

Selected to play in two All-Star Games, being named a starter in 2006, at PNC Park.

Became the first Pirate to win the National League Rookie of the Year Award in 2004.

Won the *Sporting News* Rookie of the Year Award in 2004.

Won the *USA Today* Rookie of the Year Award in 2004.

Named to the 2004 *Baseball Digest* All-Star Team.

Finished in the top 23 voting for the National League Most Valuable Player Award twice.

Led the league in games played once (2005).

Led league in fielding percentage for a left fielder once (2005).

Led league in stolen base percentage once (2005).

Eclipsed 100 runs in a season twice.

Eclipsed 100 RBIs in a season twice.

Holds the all-time Pirates record for home runs by a rookie, with 26.

Became the second Pirates right-handed hitter to eclipse 30 home runs in a season.

13th in highest fielding percentage for a left fielder in major league history, at .989.

83rd in highest fielding percentage for an outfielder in major league history, at .989.

11th in highest stolen base percentage in major league history, at 84.82.

41st in most putouts by a left fielder in major league history, with 2,183.

38th in most games by a left fielder in major league history, with 1,208.

ON THE OUTSIDE LOOKING IN
The Next 10 Pittsburgh Pirates

Bill Virdon won the Rookie of the Year Award with St. Louis in 1955, but a year later he had fallen out of favor with the Cardinal front office. Thankfully Pirates GM Joe L. Brown took advantage of the situation, bringing him to Pittsburgh, where Virdon patrolled center field for the Bucs for 11 seasons and was a pivotal part of their 1960 world championship team.
Photo courtesy of the Pittsburgh Pirates.

The following is a list of players who came close to making the top 50 all-time greatest Pittsburgh Pirates list but fell short. Consider these individuals to be numbers 51 through 60.

1. Jake Stenzel: A 19th-century outfielder, Stenzel was one of the first great offensive forces for the Pittsburgh Pirates. In his three full seasons in the Bucs' lineup, he hit .361, with 300 RBIs and 171 stolen bases. Unfortunately, his short stay in the Steel City kept him just out of the top 50 players in franchise history. He was traded to the Baltimore Orioles after the 1896 campaign, along with three other players, for Steve Brodie and Jim Donnelly. He ended his career with a .338 average, 21st highest of all-time.

2. Bob Veale: In the history of the Pittsburgh Pirates, there has perhaps been no more intimidating presence on the mound than six-foot-six, 212-pound lefty Bob Veale. He was a bespeckled southpaw whose hard delivery was not always consistent, leading the league in strikeouts once and walks four times. He still holds the all-time franchise record for strikeouts in a game, with 16, and is second in both career strikeouts and walks. He ended his career after a short stint with the Red Sox, winning 120 games.

3. Jay Bell: An unfulfilled prodigy at shortstop with the Cleveland Indians, shortstop Jay Bell was dealt to the Pirates in 1988. After continuing his struggles for a few seasons, he came into his own in 1991, with 16 home runs, finishing 12th in the National League Most Valuable Player balloting. He stayed with the Bucs for eight seasons, capturing the Gold Glove in 1993. With the team in rebuilding mode, the front office wanted to shed salary after the 1996 campaign, sending Bell and Jeff King to the Kansas City Royals. Bell eventually ended up in Arizona, where he found his power stroke, hitting 38 homers in 1999, and was finally part of a world championship team two years later. He has spent time as a coach for the Cincinnati Reds, after spending time on Clint Hurdle's staff in Pittsburgh.

4. Dave Giusti: Coming over from the St. Louis Cardinals in 1970, Dave Giusti had been a starting pitcher throughout his career with the Astros and Cards. When he arrived in Pittsburgh, manager Danny Murtaugh made a brilliant move, not only for

the team, but also for the hurler himself, switching Giusti to his closer, and the results were amazing. He saved 133 games in seven seasons for the Pirates, including a league-high 30 in 1971, the year he won the circuit's Fireman of the Year Award. Traded to Oakland in 1977, along with several players, for, among others, Phil Garner, Giusti spent the season with the A's and Cubs before retiring.

5. Smoky Burgess: A natural hitter who was also one of the greatest pinch hitters the game has ever known, Forrest "Smoky" Burgess was part of the mammoth trade with the Cincinnati Reds, along with Harvey Haddix and Don Hoak, that gave the Bucs the players they needed to win the 1960 World Series. He hit .296 in his six seasons with the Pirates and was selected to play in three All-Star Games. The slugger was superb in his only World Series, hitting .333 against the Yankees in 1960.

6. Jake Beckley: Signed by the Pittsburgh Alleghenys in 1888, at only 20 years of age, Jake Beckley became the franchise's first true offensive superstar after their move to the National League in 1887. Except for the 1890 campaign, during which time he played for the city's entry in the ill-fated Players' League, Beckley spent his first eight seasons in the National League with Pittsburgh, hitting .300, while eclipsing the 100-RBI plateau four times. He finished his 20-year major league career in 1907, with a .308 average, and was elected to the Hall of Fame in 1971, by the Veteran's Committee.

7. Pud Galvin: Beginning his career in the National Association in 1875, Pud Galvin was a star hurler with the Buffalo Bisons of the National League between 1879 and 1884, winning more than 40 games twice during that time period. He was sold to the Pittsburgh Alleghenys in 1885, playing for the team in its last two seasons in the American Association before moving to the National League. He won more than 20 games four times with the Pirates, for 126 wins in seven seasons in the Steel City. In 1892, he was traded to the St. Louis Browns, where he played his last major league campaign. Winning 365 contests in the course of his 15-year career, Galvin was selected by the Veteran's Committee for induction into the Hall of Fame in 1965.

8. Claude Ritchey: Born in Emlenton, Pennsylvania, Claude Ritchey was part of the haul that came over from the Louisville Colonels in 1900, including Honus Wagner, Tommy Leach, Deacon Phillippe, and Fred Clarke. This nucleus helped power the Pirates to four National League pennants and one World Series championship in the first decade of the 20th century. The second baseman hit .277 in seven seasons with the Bucs and was an important part of the championship era. Ritchey was sent to the Boston Doves (Braves) in 1907, finishing his major league career two years later.

9. Burleigh Grimes: After starting his career with the Pirates in 1916, in a less-than-stellar manner, with a 5–19 mark his first two seasons, Burleigh Grimes went to Brooklyn, where he became a star before returning to the Steel City in 1928. After returning from Brooklyn, he pitched in a more efficient manner, leading the National League with 25 wins that season. Following one more campaign in Pittsburgh, where he was 17–7, Grimes was dealt to the Braves in 1930. He returned to the Bucs in 1934, for his final major league season, going 1–2 in eight games. The moundsman retired with 270 wins and was elected to the Hall of Fame in 1964 by the Veteran's Committee.

10. Bill Virdon: Winning the Rookie of the Year Award with the St. Louis Cardinals in 1955, the team quickly gave up on him and dealt Bill Virdon to the Pirates a year later for Bobby Del Greco and Dick Littlefield. It would prove to be a very one-sided deal for GM Joe L. Brown. Virdon was a spectacular center fielder for the Bucs during the next 11 seasons, patrolling the vast wasteland that was center field at Forbes Field like no other. As good as he was defensively, he wasn't too bad on the offensive side either, hitting .267 in his 12-year career. After he retired following the 1968 campaign (he actually announced his retirement in 1965, but had six late-season at bats three years later), when he hit his final home run in his next to last at bat, Virdon became a successful manager with the Pirates, Yankees, Astros, and Expos, winning 995 games and three division crowns.

MOST LIKELY TO BREAK INTO THE TOP 50

While he wouldn't be in the top 60 Pirates at this point in his career, pitcher Gerrit Cole is perhaps the favorite to be included in this list in the near future. He has a breakfast campaign in 2015, with an 19–8 mark and a 2.60 ERA. Successful thus far in his short major league career, Cole has amassed a 40–20 mark in his two-plus seasons. With the potential for a Cy Young Award in his near future, he will certainly jump up into the top 50 if he ascends to that level.

WHAT COULD HAVE BEEN

The 10 Pittsburgh Pirates Who Became Stars after They Left

The Pittsburgh Pirates made many mistakes with Jose Bautista, losing him in the Rule 5 Draft and then, after reacquiring him, inexplicably trading him to Toronto for a catcher by the name of Robinzon Diaz. Bautista went on to hit 243 home runs with the Blue Jays, including 54 in 2010.

Photo courtesy of the author.

Just as many players became stars after being acquired by the Pittsburgh Pirates, there are many who left the team early in their careers as unheralded young players and became stars later down the road. The following is a list of the top 10 players whom, had they remained with the franchise, either would have been certainties to be named in the list of the top 50 Pittsburgh Pirates of all-time or would have serious credentials to be included in the conversation.

1. Joe Cronin: Signed as a free agent with the Pirates in 1925, management sold Joe Cronin to the Kansas City Blues of the American Association in 1928, after he appeared in only 50 games with the Bucs in two seasons. Had Bill McKechnie not been fired in 1926, Cronin may have taken over at second base, a move it appeared McKechnie was intending to make in 1927, and been a star for the Bucs for the bulk of his career. Donie Bush was hired and moved George Grantham to second, sending Cronin to the bench for most of the 1927 campaign. Once Kansas City purchased the infielder, they had sold his rights to the Washington Senators by mid-season, and he went on to hit .301 in his 19-year major league career and become one of the great defensive shortstops of his era. Cronin was elected to the Hall of Fame in 1955.

2. Rube Waddell: Rube Waddell's eccentricities are legendary to baseball fans and historians alike. When the Pirates obtained him in 1900, as part of the trade with the Louisville Colonels that also netted such luminaries as Honus Wagner and Fred Clarke, he was a young 23-year-old hurler who had only started in 10 games in his first two seasons. While going only 8–13 his first year in Pittsburgh, Rube won the National League ERA title, with a 2.37 mark. Clarke, who managed the Pirates, was a strict disciplinarian, and Waddell's personality did not mesh well with the Pirates skipper, so he was sold to the Chicago Orphans (Cubs) early in the 1901 campaign. He eventually landed with the A's and won 20 games on four occasions and finished his major league career with a 193–143 mark. He was elected to the Hall of Fame in 1946.

3. Red Faber: Urban "Red" Faber was drafted by the Pittsburgh Pirates in the Rule 5 Draft from Dubuque of the Illinois-Indiana-Iowa League in 1909. He made the Opening Day roster for the Bucs in 1911, but was never used. He was returned to Minneapolis and eventually sold by the Pirates to Des Moines in the Western League in 1912, after hurting his arm in a distance-throwing contest. As the story goes, Faber was taught the spitball, had his contract purchased by the White Sox before the 1914 campaign, and went on to win 254 games in the span of his 20-year career. He was elected to the Hall of Fame in 1964.

4. George Kelly: Batting only .125 in three abbreviated seasons with the New York Giants, the Pittsburgh Pirates picked up George "High Pockets" Kelly in 1917, on waivers. The Bucs were trying to give their 43-year-old first baseman, Hall of Famer Honus Wagner, a break at first with Kelly, but it proved to be a bad idea, as he hit poorly for the Pirates, with an .067 average in 30 at bats. They put Kelly on waivers, and the Giants picked him up. This time he did not disappoint, later moving on to Cincinnati, knocking in more than 100 runs on five occasions and 1,020 for his career. The backup for Wagner eventually joined him in Cooperstown in 1973.

5. Dazzy Vance: The Pittsburgh Pirates purchased Charles "Dazzy" Vance from Hastings in the Nebraska State League in 1915, but unlike Red Faber, he would play an official game with the team. During his major league debut in 1915, where he pitched 2²/₃ innings, he gave up three runs and three hits, losing the game for the Bucs. He was sold to the Yankees soon thereafter, and it was discovered that he had a sore arm after he struggled with a 0–3 record. Vance pitched only twice more until 1922, and after his arm healed he won 197 games with Brooklyn and St. Louis in the next 13 seasons. He was elected to the Hall of Fame in 1955.

6. Joe Kelley: After a short trial with the Boston Beaneaters in 1891, the Pirates purchased Joe Kelley midway through the 1892 campaign from Omaha of the Western League. He hit .239 in 205 at bats with the Bucs and was traded to the Balti-

more Orioles in September for George Van Haltren. While Van Haltren hit .338 in his one season with the Bucs, Kelley went on to hit .316 in 17 major league seasons, with 2,220 hits. He was elected to the Hall of Fame in 1971.

7. Jose Bautista: Jose Bautista was the first player to be left unprotected by the Pirates in the 2003 Rule 5 Draft and was picked up by Baltimore, and his career took several twists and turns after that. The Orioles put him on waivers in 2004, and he was picked up by Tampa Bay, who sold him to Kansas City, who traded him to the Mets, all in the space of two months. Pittsburgh then retrieved him, making up for their mistake by giving the Mets Kris Benson and Jeff Keppinger for Bautista, Ty Wigginton, and Matt Peterson. If this were the end of the story it would be great, but this was the Pittsburgh team smack dab in the middle of a 20-year streak of losing baseball. Three and a half years later, Bautista was dealt to the Toronto Blue Jays for a catcher named Robinzon Diaz, one of the worst trades in franchise history. He has hit 286 home runs to date, including 54 in 2010. Had the Bucs held on to him, the streak of losing seasons may never have reached 20 years.

8. Willie Randolph: Willie Randolph was an up-and-coming prospect with the Pittsburgh Pirates in 1975, batting .164 in 61 at bats in his first stint in the major leagues. Hoping to acquire a player who would be a stabilizing force in the starting rotation for the Bucs in the foreseeable future, GM Joe L. Brown inexplicably dealt him to the Yankees, along with Dock Ellis and Ken Brett, for Doc Medich. Medich won eight games for Pittsburgh in one season, while Randolph played in six All-Star Games, garnering 2,210 hits in 18 major league seasons.

9. Tim Wakefield: Tim Wakefield burst onto the scene in 1992, a converted first baseman who did such a great job of learning the knuckle ball that he made it to the major leagues as a pitcher. He was 8–1 that season for the Pirates, with a 2.15 ERA, finishing third in the Rookie of the Year voting, while winning two games against the Braves in the National League Championship Series. His bright future in Pittsburgh came to a quick end after a 6–11 finish in the 1993 campaign. Following a year in the minors, the Bucs released him. Wakefield was picked up

by the Red Sox and pitched for 17 years in Boston, emerging victorious 186 times for the Sox to reach the 200-win plateau in his career.

10. Dick Bartell: Dick Bartell was an incredible prospect for the Pittsburgh Pirates in the late 1920s, hitting .308 in his three full seasons with the team. Unfortunately he did not get along with Pirates president Barney Dreyfuss, who promptly dealt the infielder to the Phillies. He went on to hit .284 in his 18-year career, with 2,165 hits, receiving votes for the National League's Most Valuable Player Award six times.

While these players would have made strong cases for being included in the top 50 Pirates had they not been traded before they became stars, the following men were also with the team at a young age and went on to have impressive careers with other teams: Tony Armas, Bronson Arroyo, Gus Bell, Jay Buhner, Jack Chesbro, Bob Elliott, Gene Garber, Jose Guillen, Dick Hall, Julian Javier, Cookie Lavagetto, Hans Lobert, Don Money, Bob Purkey, Aramis Ramirez, Bobby Tolan, Wilbur Wood, and Gene Woodling. Drafted by the Pirates but never signing with the team were Greg Vaughan and Mickey Morandini.

NOTES

CHAPTER 1

1. "Honus Wager," *Baseball-Reference.com*, www.baseball-reference.com/players/w/wagneho01.shtml.

2. Quoted in Dennis DeValeria and Jeanne Burke DeValeria, *Honus Wagner: A Biography* (New York: Henry Holt & Co., 1995), 138.

3. Quoted in David Finoli and Bill Ranier, *When Cobb Met Wagner: The Seven Games of the 1909 World Series* (Jefferson, NC: McFarland, 2011), 37.

4. Quoted in William Cobb, ed., *Honus Wagner on His Life in Baseball* (Ann Arbor, MI: Sports Media Group, 2006), 3.

5. Finoli and Ranier, *When Cobb Met Wagner*, 128.

CHAPTER 2

1. Bruce Markeson, *Roberto Clemente: The Great One* (Champaign, IL: Sports Publishing, 1998), 8.

2. Stew Thornley, "Roberto Clemente," *Society for American Baseball Research*, http://sabr.org/bioproj/person/8b153bc4.

3. Markeson, *Roberto Clemente*, 109.

CHAPTER 3

1. Quoted in "Paul Waner," *Baseball-Reference.com*, www.baseball-reference.com/bullpen/Paul_Waner.

2. Quoted in Joseph Wancho, "Paul Waner," *Society for American Baseball Research*, http://sabr.org/bioproj/person/9d598ab8.

3. Quoted in Wancho, "Paul Waner."

CHAPTER 4

1. Quoted in James Forr, "Willie Stargell," *Society for American Baseball Research*, http://sabr.org/bioproj/person/27e0c01a.

2. Quoted in "Marking the 10th Anniversary of Willie Stargell's 2001 Death," *Miscellaneous Baseball: Gathering Assorted Items of Baseball History and Trivia*, April 4, 2011, https://miscbaseball.wordpress.com/2011/04/08/marking-the-10th-anniversary-of-willie-stargells-2001-death.

3. Quoted in "Marking the 10th Anniversary of Willie Stargell's 2001 Death."

4. Quoted in Forr, "Willie Stargell."

5. "Willie Stargell Quotes," *Baseball Almanac*, www.baseball-almanac.com/quotes/quostar.shtml.

CHAPTER 5

1. Ralph Kiner and Toby Mergler, "Ralph Kiner Was a Pilot before a Pirate," *ESPN.com*, November 9, 2009, http://sports.espn.go.com/espn/page2/story?page=mergler/091109.

2. Quoted in Mark James McNutt and Alan Jalowitz, "Ralph Kiner Biography," *Penn State Online Library*, http://pabook.libraries.psu.edu/palitmap/bios/Kiner__Ralph.html.

3. Quoted in Warren Corbett, "Ralph Kiner," *Society for American Baseball Research*, http://sabr.org/bioproj/person/b65aaec9.

4. "Ralph Kiner Quotes," *Baseball Almanac*, www.baseball-almanac.com/quotes/quokiner.shtml.

CHAPTER 7

1. Quoted in Terence Moore, "Van Slyke's Agony Realized through Revelations," *MLB.com*, April 27, 2011, http://m.mlb.com/news/article/18303456/.

2. John Schuerholz, *Built to Win: Inside Stories and Leadership Strategies from Baseball's Winningest GM* (New York: Grand Central Publishing, 2007).

3. Quoted in Michiko Kakutani, "Barry Bonds and Baseball's Steroid Scandal," *New York Times*, March 23, 2006, www.nytimes.com/2006/03/23/books/23kaku.html?n=Top%2FFeatures%2FBooks%2FBook%20Reviews&_r=1&.

CHAPTER 8

1. Frederick G. Lieb, *The Pittsburgh Pirates* (Carbondale, IL: Southern Illinois University Press, 2003).

2. Jim McCurdie, "Arky Vaughan: The Quiet and Talented Shortstop at Long Last Welcomed into the Hall of Fame—37 Years after Retirement and 33 Years after His Death," *Los Angeles Times*, January 13, 1986, http://articles.latimes.com/1986-01-13/sports/sp-27753_1_arky-vaughan.

3. Bill James, *The New Bill James Historical Baseball Abstract* (New York: Free Press. 2003).

CHAPTER 9

1. Quoted in James Forr and David Proctor, *Pie Traynor: A Biography* (Jefferson, N.C.: McFarland, 2010), 214.

2. Quoted in James Forr, "Pie Traynor," *Society for American Baseball Research*, http://sabr.org/bioproj/person/85500ab5.

3. Quoted in Bill James, *The New Bill James Historical Baseball Abstract* (New York: Free Press, 2003), 554.

4. Quoted in Forr, "Pie Traynor."

5. Bill Burgess, "How Good Was Pie? Is Pie Still a Top 10 3BMan?" *Baseball Fever*, August 14, 2004, www.baseball-fever.com/archive/index.php/t-37345.html.

CHAPTER 12

1. Quoted in Tom Simon, ed., *Deadball Stars of the National League* (Dulles, VA: Brassey's, 2004), 178.

2. Quoted in Simon, *Deadball Stars of the National League*, 177.

CHAPTER 13

1. Quoted in Bill James, *The New Bill James Historical Baseball Abstract* (New York: Free Press, 2003), 501.

CHAPTER 14

1. Bill James, *The New Bill James Historical Baseball Abstract* (New York: Free Press, 2003).

2. Quoted in Callan Bird, "Lloyd Waner," *Penn State Online Library*, 2009, http://pabook.libraries.psu.edu/palitmap/bios/Waner_Lloyd.html.

3. James, *The New Bill James Historical Baseball Abstract*.

4. Quoted in Bird, "Lloyd Waner."

CHAPTER 15

1. Quoted in Bill James, *The New Bill James Historical Baseball Abstract* (New York: Free Press, 2003), 881.

2. Quoted in James, *The New Bill James Historical Baseball Abstract*, 881.

3. Mike Hoban, *Defining Greatness: A Hall of Fame Handbook* (Bradenton, FL: Booklocker, 2012).

4. James, *The New Bill James Historical Baseball Abstract*.

5. Quoted in David Cicotello, "Wilbur Cooper," in *Deadball Stars of the National League*, ed. Tom Simon (Dulles, VA: Brassey's, 2004), 182.

6. Quoted in Cicotello, "Wilbur Cooper," 181.

7. "Clarke Has More Work for Cooper," *Pittsburgh Press*, September 7, 1912, p. 8.

CHAPTER 16

1. Quoted in Bill James, *The New Bill James Historical Baseball Abstract* (New York: Free Press, 2003), 665.
2. Quoted in Frederick G. Lieb, *The Pittsburgh Pirates* (Carbondale: Southern Illinois University Press, 2003), 61.

CHAPTER 18

1. Bill James, "Whatever Happened to the Hall of Fame?" (excerpt) *Baseball Library*, www.baseballlibrary.com/excerpts/excerpt.php?book=hall_of_fame&page=2.
2. Frederick G. Lieb, *The Pittsburgh Pirates* (Carbondale: Southern Illinois University Press, 2003), 106.
3. Quoted in Mark Armour, "Sam Leever," in *Deadball Stars of the National League*, ed. Tom Simon (Dulles, VA: Brassey's, 2004), 146.

CHAPTER 19

1. Quoted in Louis P. Masur, *Autumn Glory: Baseball's First World Series* (New York: Hill and Wang, 2003), 109.

CHAPTER 20

1. Quoted in Bill James, *The New Bill James Historical Baseball Abstract* (New York: Free Press, 2003), 812.

CHAPTER 21

1. Frederick G. Lieb, *The Pittsburgh Pirates* (Carbondale: Southern Illinois University Press, 2003), 199.

CHAPTER 22

1. Quoted in C. Paul Rogers III, "Vern Law," *Society for American Baseball Research*, http://sabr.org/bioproj/person/9266780c.
2. Quoted in David Finoli and Bill Ranier, *The Pittsburgh Pirates Encyclopedia*, 2nd ed. (Champaign, IL: Sports Publishing, 2015), 287.

CHAPTER 23

1. Quoted in Gregory Wolf, "A Friend of Pirate History," *Hardball Times*, April 6, 2012, www.hardballtimes.com/bob-friend.
2. Quoted in Wolf, "A Friend of Pirate History."
3. Quoted in Wolf, "A Friend of Pirate History."

CHAPTER 24

1. Quoted in Bill James, *The New Bill James Historical Baseball Abstract* (New York: Free Press, 2003), 746.

CHAPTER 25

1. Quoted in Johnny Moore, "An Interview with Former Two-Sport Star Dick Groat," *Go Duke.com*, June 6, 2014, www.goduke.com/ViewArticle.dbml?ATCLID=209518073.
2. Quoted in Moore, "An Interview with Former Two-Sport Star Dick Groat."

CHAPTER 26

1. Quoted in Joe Guzzardi, "Ginger Beaumont and His Baseball Feat That Will Never Be Matched," *Baseball: Past and Present*, May 11, 2011, http://baseballpastandpresent.com/2011/05/11/%E2%80%9Cginger%E2%80%9D-beaumont-baseball-feat-matched.

CHAPTER 27

1. Quoted in Lawrence Ritter, *The Glory of Their Times* (New York: Harper Perennial Modern Classics, 2010), 26.
2. Quoted in Ritter, *The Glory of Their Times*.

CHAPTER 28

1. Quoted in Associated Press, "Al Oliver Orders Pirates to Play Me or Trade Me," *Morning Record*, November 29, 1971, p. 11.

CHAPTER 31

1. Jay Jaffe, "JAWS and the 2015 Hall of Fame Ballot: Brian Giles," *Sports Illustrated*, December 24, 2014, www.si.com/mlb/2014/12/24/jaws-2015-hall-of-fame-ballot-brian-giles.

CHAPTER 33

1. Quoted in Daniel R. Levitt, "Vic Willis," *Society for American Baseball Research*, http://sabr.org/bioproj/person/3c061442.
2. Quoted in Frederick G. Lieb, *The Pittsburgh Pirates* (Carbondale: Southern Illinois University Press, 2003), 133.

CHAPTER 34

1. Zander Hollander, ed., *The Complete Handbook of Baseball* (Chicago: Signet, 1975), 223.

CHAPTER 35

1. Quoted in Gene Collier, "Obituary: Willie Stargell: Numbers Couldn't Measure the Man," Pittsburgh Post-Gazette, April 10, 2001, http://old.post-gazette.com/obituaries/20010410stargell2.asp.

CHAPTER 36

1. Quoted in "Bobby Bonilla," *Baseball Reference*, www.baseball-reference.com/bullpen/Bobby_Bonilla.

CHAPTER 39

1. Quoted in Mark Armour, "Matty Alou," *Society for American Baseball Research*, http://sabr.org/bioproj/person/3d8b257b.

CHAPTER 41

1. Quoted in Irv Goldfarb, "Howie Camnitz," *Society for American Baseball Research*, http://sabr.org/bioproj/person/cdcde915.

CHAPTER 42

1. Frederick G. Lieb, *The Pittsburgh Pirates* (Carbondale: Southern Illinois University Press, 2003), 199.
2. Quoted in Bill James, *The New Bill James Historical Baseball Abstract* (New York: Free Press, 2003), 629.
3. Quoted in Eugene Murdock, "Glenn Wright Last of the 1925 All-Stars," *Society for American Baseball Research*, http://research.sabr.org/journals/glenn-wright.

CHAPTER 43

1. Frederick G. Lieb, *The Pittsburgh Pirates* (Carbondale: Southern Illinois University Press, 2003), 24.

CHAPTER 45

1. Quoted in David Finoli and Bill Ranier, *The Pittsburgh Pirates Encyclopedia*, 2nd ed. (Champaign, IL: Sports Publishing, 2015), 333.
2. Quoted in Finoli and Ranier, *The Pittsburgh Pirates Encyclopedia*, 333.
3. Quoted in Finoli and Ranier, *The Pittsburgh Pirates Encyclopedia*, 333.

CHAPTER 47

1. Quoted in Harold Friend, "Frank Thomas Could Have Won the '64 Philadelphia Phillies the Pennant," *Bleacher Report*, July 23, 2010, http://bleacherreport.com/articles/424007-frank-thomas-could-have-won-the-pennant-for-the-1964-phillies.

CHAPTER 48

1. Bill James, *The New Bill James Historical Baseball Abstract* (New York: Free Press, 2003).

CHAPTER 49

1. Quoted in David Finoli and Bill Ranier, *The Pittsburgh Pirates Encyclopedia*, 2nd ed. (Champaign, IL: Sports Publishing, 2015), 344.
2. Quoted in Finoli and Ranier, *The Pittsburgh Pirates Encyclopedia*, 344.
3. Quoted in Finoli and Ranier, *The Pittsburgh Pirates Encyclopedia*, 344.
4. Quoted in Finoli and Ranier, *The Pittsburgh Pirates Encyclopedia*, 345.
5. Quoted in Finoli and Ranier, *The Pittsburgh Pirates Encyclopedia*, 345.
6. Quoted in Associated Press, "Curing Baseball's Dreaded Steve Blass Disease," *SportzEdge*, May 14, 2014, http://sportzedge.com/2014/05/14/curing-baseballs-dreaded-steve-blass-disease-2.

BIBLIOGRAPHY

BOOKS

Cobb, William, ed. *Honus Wagner on His Life in Baseball*. Ann Arbor, MI: Sports Media Group, 2006.

Cushing, Rick. *1960 Pittsburgh Pirates Day by Day: A Special Season, an Extraordinary World Series*. Pittsburgh, PA: Dorrance Publishing, 2010.

DeValeria, Dennis, and Jeanne Burke DeValeria. *Honus Wagner: A Biography*. New York: Henry Holt & Co., 1995.

Finoli, David, and Bill Ranier. *The Pittsburgh Pirates Encyclopedia*, 2nd ed. Champaign, IL: Sports Publishing, 2015.

———. *When the Bucs Won It All: The 1979 World Champion Pittsburgh Pirates*. Jefferson, NC: McFarland, 2005.

———. *When Cobb Met Wagner: The Seven Games of the 1909 World Series*. Jefferson, NC: McFarland, 2011.

Forr, James, and David Proctor. *Pie Traynor: A Biography*. Jefferson, NC: McFarland, 2010.

Hoban, Mike. *Defining Greatness: A Hall of Fame Handbook*. Bradenton, FL: Booklocker, 2012.

Hollander, Zander, ed. *The Complete Handbook of Baseball*. Chicago: Signet, 1975.

James, Bill. *The New Bill James Historical Baseball Abstract*. New York: Free Press, 2003.

Jones, David, ed. *Deadball Stars of the American League*. Dulles, VA: Potomac Books, 2006.

Lieb, Frederick G. *The Pittsburgh Pirates*. Carbondale: Southern Illinois University Press, 2003.

Markeson, Bruce. *Roberto Clemente: The Great One*. Champaign, IL: Sports Publishing, 1998.

Masur, Louis P. *Autumn Glory: Baseball's First World Series*. New York: Hill and Wang, 2003.

Parker, Clifton Blue, and Bill Nowlin, eds. *Sweet '60: The 1960 Pittsburgh Pirates*. Phoenix, AZ: Society for American Baseball Research, 2013.

Ritter, Lawrence. *The Glory of Their Times*. New York: Harper Perennial Modern Classics, 2010.

Schuerholz, John. *Built to Win: Inside Stories and Leadership Strategies from Baseball's Winningest GM*. New York: Grand Central Publishing, 2007.

Simon, Tom, ed. *Deadball Stars of the National League*. Dulles, VA: Brassey's, 2004.

Tiemann, Robert, and Mark Rucker, eds. *Nineteenth-Century Stars*. Phoenix, AZ: Society for American Baseball Research, 2012.

Travers, Steven. *Barry Bonds: Baseball's Superman*. Champaign, IL: Sports Publishing, 2002.

Waldo, Ronald T. *The Battling Bucs of 1925*. Jefferson, NC: McFarland, 2012.

Wolf, Gregory, ed. *Winning on the North Side: The 1929 Chicago Cubs*. Phoenix, AZ: Society for American Baseball Research, 2015.

NEWSPAPERS

Daily Minor, Kingman, Arizona

Morning Record, Meriden, Connecticut

Pittsburgh Press, Pittsburgh

Pittsburgh Post-Gazette, Pittsburgh

Tribune Review, Pittsburgh

WEBSITES

Al Oliver website, Al-oliver.com

Baseball Almanac, baseball-almanac.com

Baseball Fever, www.baseball-fever.com

Baseball Library, www.baseballlibrary.com

Baseball: Past and Present, http://baseballpastandpresent.com

Baseball Reference, www.baseball-reference.com

Bio, www.biography.com

Bleacher Report, http://bleacherreport.com

Chautauqua Sports Hall of Fame, www.chautauquasportshalloffame.org

CNN, www.cnn.com

Encyclopedia.com, www.encyclopedia.com

ESPN, http://espn.go.com

Google Books, https://books.google.com

Google News, https://books.google.com

Hardball Times, www.hardballtimes.com

Indiana Baseball Hall of Fame, www.indbaseballhalloffame.org

Los Angeles Times, www.latimes.com

Major League Baseball, http://mlb.com

Miscellaneous Baseball: Gathering Assorted Items of Baseball History and Trivia, https://miscbaseball.wordpress.com

National Baseball Hall of Fame, http://baseballhall.org

New York Times, www.nytimes.com

On Deck Circle, https://ondeckcircle.wordpress.com

Online Book of Baseball History, www.thisgreatgame.com

Penn State Online Library, www.libraries.psu.edu/psul/home.html

Rumbunter, http://rumbunter.com

Seamheads.com, http://seamheads.com

Society for American Baseball Research, http://sabr.org

Sports Illustrated, www.si.com

Sports on Earth, www.sportsonearth.com

SportzEdge, http://sportzedge.com

BIBLIOGRAPHY

INDEX

Aaron, Hank, 53, 289

Abbaticchio, Ed, 169

Abrams, Al, 66

Acosta, Ed, 230

Adams, Charles "Babe," 10, 69–73, 83, 109, 125, 219–220, 262

Adams, Sparky, 134–135

Addis, Bob, 38

Aguilera, Rick, 119

Aikens, Tom, 2

Aldridge, Vic, 104, 262, 294, 297

Alicea, Luis, 158

All-American Girls Professional Baseball League (AAGPBL), 84

Alley, Gene, 284

Allie, Stetson, 265

Alou, Felipe, 243

Alou, Jesus, 243

Alou, Matty, 241

Alvarez, Pedro, 287

American Tobacco Company, 10

Ames, Red, 102

Anderson, Greg, 53

Ankiel, Rich, 265

Anson, Cap, 107–108

Antonelli, John, 15

Appling, Luke, 180

Archie, Missouri, 259

Arizona State, 50–51

Armas, Tony, 321

Arroyo, Bronson, 201, 321

Atwell, Toby, 38

Auten, Phil, 7

Avery, Steve, 119

Babe Adams Highway, 72

Baines, Harold, 179–180

Baker Bowl, 67

Ball, Lucille, 37

Ball, Neal, 262

Banks, Ernie, 162, 289

Barbeau, Jap, 230

Barger, Carl, 52

Barnhart, Clyde, 141

Barr, Jim, 150

Barrow, Edward, 64

Barry, Shad, 123

Bartell, Dick, 66, 321

Bartirome, Tony, 288

Baseball America, 77, 272

Baseball Digest, 309

Baumholtz, Frank, 153

Bauta, Ed, 230

Bautista, Jose, 225, 317, 320

Bay, Jason, 77, 200, 271, 305–309

Bearsville, West Virginia, 103–104

Beaumont, Clarence "Ginger," 167–171, 176

Beaver Valley News Tribune, 21

Beckley, Jake, 313

Belinda, Stan, 194

Bell, Gus, 288, 321

Bell, Jay, 312

Beloit College, 168–169

Bench, Johnny, 213–215, 217
Benjamin, Mike, 274
Bennett Park, 9
Benson, Kris, 76, 271–272, 274, 320
Berman, Chris, 284
Berra, Dale, 232
Berra, Yogi, 90
Bibby, Jim, 32
Bierbauer, Lou, 268
Bigbee, Carson, 72, 83
Blass, Steve, 28, 116, 125, 182, 214,
    219–220, 265, 299–304
Bloomquist, Willie, 274
Bluege, Oscar, 141
Blyleven, Bert, 181
Bonds, Barry, 2, 49–55, 78, 132–133,
    156–157, 179, 198, 227, 284
Bonilla, Bobby, 158, 194, 225–228
Boswell, Ken, 17
Boswell, Tom, 226
Bottomley, Jim, 262
Bouchee, Ed, 117
Boudreau, Lou, 107
Boyer, Ken, 162
Boyle, Harvey J., 102
Bradley, Bobby, 272
Bragan, Bobby, 89
Brail, British Columbia, 306
Brain, Dave, 210
Bream, Sid, 52, 195
Brecheen, Harry, 125
Breining, Fred, 230
Bresnahan, Roger, 107
Brett, George, 64, 67
Brett, Ken, 320
Briles, Nellie, 244
Brock, Lou, 214
Brodie, Steve, 279, 312
Brown, Eddie, 279
Brown, Joe L., 215, 242, 244, 289, 311,
    314, 320
Brown, Mike, 206
Brunet, George, 244
Buford, Don, 303
Buhner, Jay, 321
Bullington, Brian, 76, 272
Bumgarner, Madison, 125

Burdette, Lew, 125, 164
Burgess, Bill, 67
Burgess, Smoky, 289, 313
Burke, Jimmy, 187
Burnett, Sean, 76
Burns, George, 262
Bush, Donie, 132, 134, 318
Butcher, Max, 280
Byrne, Bobby, 105, 230, 256

Cabrera, Francisco, 52
Callahan, Nixie, 9
Camnitz, Howie, 70–71, 253–257
Canaan, Connecticut, 299–300
Candelaria, John, 32, 203–207, 286
Candiotti, Tom, 150
Candlestick Park, 222
Capilla, Doug, 284
Cardwell, Don, 164
Carey, Max, 65, 72, 81–85, 110, 135,
    297
Carlton, Steve, 205, 302
Carnegie, PA, 5
Carolina, Puerto Rico, 14
Carroll, Fred, 110
Carroll, John, 102
Carter, Gary, 45, 47
Carty, Rico, 215
Cash, Dave, 88, 182
Castilione, Pete, 288
Cecil County, Maryland, 209
Centre College, 254
Chance, Frank, 107–108
Chartiers Valley, 6
Chautauqua Sports Hall of Fame, 176
Chesbro, Jack, 7, 119–120, 122, 185–187,
    254, 321
Chiles, Pearce, 170
Christopher, Joe, 147
Chronicle Telegraph Cup, 126, 188
Chylak, Nestor, 303
Citi Field, 308
Clark, Jack, 222
Clarke, Fred, 7, 11, 71–72, 82, 83,
    105–111, 126–128, 167, 168, 173–175,
    185, 188, 211–212, 260, 314, 318
Clarkson, Buzz, 138

Clemente, Roberto, 2, 13–19, 21, 24, 28, 30, 33, 43, 46, 57, 102, 115, 125, 144, 150, 156, 162–163, 182, 216, 225, 242, 267, 284
Clements, Pat, 192, 206
Clifty, Arkansas, 57
Clines, Gene, 17
Cobb, Ty, 8–9, 31, 64, 107, 133
Cochrane, Mickey, 108
Cole, Gerrit, 71, 315
Cole, King, 175
Coleman, John, 265–266
Colon, Bartolo, 103
Comorosky, Adam, 67
Concordia College, 81
Concordia Seminary, 82
Connie Mack Stadium, 244
Considine, Bob, 64
Cooley, Duff, 171
Coombs, Jack, 125
Cooney, Jimmy, 262
Cooper, Mort, 237
Cooper, Wilbur, 101–106, 109, 207, 294
Cooperstown, 14, 24, 46, 91, 98, 102–103, 119–120, 153, 174, 179, 209, 232, 319
Coscarart, Pete, 59
County Stadium, 164
Courter Tech High School, 43
Coury, Dick, 220
Coveleski, Stan, 125
Covington, Kentucky, 253–255
Crawford, Jerry, 231
Crawford, Sam, 173
Cronin, Joe, 318
Crosby, Bing, 145
Crosley Field, 290
Cross, Monte, 170
Crowley, Terry, 220
Cuellar, Mike, 16, 119
Cunningham, Bert, 7
Cuyler, Hazen "Kiki," 2, 125, 131–135
Cy Young Award, 16, 143–144, 146, 148, 150, 152, 154, 168, 191–195, 204–205, 207, 221, 223, 237, 302, 304–305

Damon, Johnny, 179
Darling, Ron, 119

Dauer, Rich, 32
Davalillo, Vic, 244
Davis, J. J., 76, 272
Davis, Ralph, 121
Dawson, Andre, 180
Dawson, H.P., 64
Dayton, Kentucky, 185–186
Debayle, Anastasio Somoza, 14
Del Greco, Bobby, 288, 314
DeLeon, Jose, 226
Diaz, Elias, 283
Diaz, Robinzon, 317, 320
Dickey, Bill, 238–239
Dilello, Eddie, 2
Dilone, Miguel, 216
DiMaggio, Joe, 250, 271
Dineen, Bill, 125
Dobson, Pat, 119, 150
Dodgers Stadium, 27, 31
Doheny, Ed, 122
Dolan, Cozy, 256
Donnelly, Jim, 312
Donovan, Patsy, 7, 168, 186, 250, 268
Downing, Brian, 45–47
Doyle, Larry, 73
Drabek, Doug, 191–195, 204
Dreyfuss, Barney, 7, 9, 22, 65, 72, 82, 109–110, 122, 126, 134, 138–139, 167–169, 174–175, 187–188, 210–212, 254–256, 259–260, 279, 294, 296, 321
Drysdale, Don, 119, 300
Duke University, 163
Dunne, Mike, 155, 305–306
Durocher, Leo, 59, 107, 300

Earlsboro, Oklahoma, 28
Easley, Logan, 193
East Central State Teachers College, 21
Edwards, Mike, 216
Eephus pitch, 235–239
El Cajon, California, 199
Elliott, Bob, 23, 157, 307, 321
Ellis, Dock, 180, 320
Encinal High School, 28
Ens, Jewel, 66
Euclid Hotel, 9
Evans, Darrell, 222

Evans, Dwight, 199
Exposition Park, 111, 206, 212, 256

Faber, Urban "Red," 125, 319
Face, Roy, 113–117, 225
Farrell, Charley "Duke," 248
Farris, Mark, 76, 272
Federal League, 103, 128, 256
Fernandez, Sid, 119
Fingers, Rollie, 153, 221
Fisher, Brian, 193
Flagstaff, Arizona, 294
Flaherty, Patsy, 169
Flick, Elmer, 171
Foli, Tim, 231–233
Forbes Field, 8, 10,11, 27, 29, 31, 37–38,
    70, 82, 84, 88, 91, 99, 117, 134–135,
    140, 211–212, 219, 255, 279, 287, 314
Fort Eustis, 145
Fort Meade High School, 76
Fort Meade, Florida, 79
Fox, George, 7
Framingham, Massachusetts, 64
Fraser, Chick, 170
Freese, George, 38
French, Larry, 99
Friend, Bob, 91, 149–153, 163, 193
Frisch, Frankie, 59–60, 237
Fryman, Woody, 150
Fullerton High School, 57
Fullerton, California, 57

Galbreath Family, 37
Galena, Kansas, 294
Galvin, Pud, 313
Garagiola, Joe, 38, 288
Garber, Gene, 321
Garner, Phil, 217, 231–232, 313
Garvey, Steve, 44, 278
Gehrig, Lou, 18, 33, 148, 165, 261, 278
Gibbon, Joe, 243
Gibson, Bob, 15, 125, 206
Gibson, George, 65–66, 279
Giles, Brian, 77, 197–201, 271, 294,
    305–306
Giusti, Dave, 312–313
Glavine, Tom, 119

Gleason, Kid, 123, 265–266
Gonzaga University, 145, 306
Gonzalez, Alex, 308
Good, Bill, 259
Gooden, Doc, 119
Goshen, Ohio, 119, 122
Goslin, Goose, 135, 141, 180, 220
Gossage, Goose, 221
Gotay, Julio, 164
Gott, Jim, 158
Grantham, George, 104, 293–297, 318
Gray, Bill, 168, 267
Gray, Dick, 230
Gray, Dolly, 71
Green, Shawn, 168
Greenberg Gardens, 37
Greenberg, Hank, 37, 40, 236
Greene, Khalil, 307
Griffey, Ken, 179
Griffin, Frankie, 221
Grimes, Burleigh, 314
Grimm, Charlie, 104, 260, 294–295
Groat, Dick, 16, 143–144, 146, 161–165,
    288
Grodzicki, Johnny, 40
Gruber, John, 167
Guante, Cecilio, 192
Gubicza, Mark, 150
Guillen, Jose, 321
Gustine, Frankie, 40

Haak, Howie, 214
Haddix, Harvey, 91, 164, 284, 289, 313
Hall, Dick, 321
Hamlin, Luke, 59
Haney, Fred, 151
Hansen, Craig, 307
Hansen, Snipe, 67
Harding, Warren G., 103
Harper, Tommy, 28
Harrah, Oklahoma, 21
Harris, Bucky, 107
Harrisville, Michigan, 132
Hart, Bill, 168
Hartnett, Gabby, 59
Hawley, Pink, 267
Hebner, Richie, 2, 176, 180, 182

Hendrick, George, 206
Herman, Billy, 37
Hermansen, Chad, 76, 272
Hermanski, Gene, 38
Hernandez, Keith, 31
Heydler, John, 71
Hill, Bobby, 294
Hines, Paul, 262
Hoak, Don, 16, 117, 144, 146, 162–163, 289, 313
Hoban, Mike, 103
Hofman, Solly, 175
Holland, Al, 206, 221, 230
Hollander, Zander, 216
Honey Creek, Wisconsin, 170
Horner, Bob, 305
Hornsby, Rogers, 64, 107, 134, 261–262
Hostetler, Chuck, 138
Housatonic High School, 299
Howard, Del, 210
Howell, Ken, 228
Huntingdon Avenue Baseball Grounds, 127, 169
Huntington, Neal, 307
Hurdle, Clint, 312

Jackson, Grant, 222
Jackson, Reggie, 46
Jacobs Field, 285
Jaffe, Jay, 199
James, Bill, 46, 60, 64, 67, 96, 102, 119, 179, 296
Javier, Julian, 88, 230, 321
Jefferson-Morgan High School, 230
Jennings, Hughie, 65
Jeter, Derek, 6, 179
Jeter, Johnny, 230
John, Tommy, 205
Johnson, Ban, 187
Johnson, Clint, 76
Johnson, Harold, 108
Johnson, Jerry, 183
Johnson, Randy, 125
Johnson, Walter, 65, 116, 131, 134–135
Jones, Davy, 11
Jones, Randy, 150
Jones, Tom, 220

Keeler, "Wee" Willie, 249–250
Keen, Vic, 261
Kelley, Joe, 319–320
Kelley, Mike, 7
Kelly Pat, 220
Kelly, George "High Pockets," 319
Kendall, Fred, 271
Kendall, Jason, 76–77, 201, 271–275, 305–306, 308
Kent State, 180
Kent, Jeff, 274
Keppinger, Jeff, 320
Killen, Frank, 247–251
Kiner, Ralph, 35–41, 288–289, 307–308
King, Jeff, 312
King, Nellie, 15
Kingdome, 45–46
Kingman, Arizona, 295
Kipper, Bob, 206
Kison, Bruce, 217
Klaus, Bobby, 147
Klobedanz, Fred, 210
Knabe, Oscar, 259
Knell, Phil, 248
Koufax, Sandy, 119, 164, 205
KQV, 67
Kramer, Jack, 239
Kranepool, Ed, 147
Kremer, Ray, 137–141

Laboy, Cocoa, 181
Lachima, Jim, 51
Lacy, Lee, 286
Lafayette, Indiana, 151
Lajoie, Nap, 107, 173
Lally, Daniel, 249
Laloosh, Nuke, 302
Lansford, Carney, 231
LaRoche Brothers, 98
LaRoche, Andy, 307
Latimer, Tacks, 7
Lavagetto, Cookie, 321
LaVallierre Mike, 155, 158
Law, Vern, 2, 16, 143–147, 152, 162–163, 192, 204
Leach, Tommy, 7–8, 11, 109, 126, 128, 168, 173–177, 257, 314

Leever, Sam, 119–123, 126, 173, 185–186, 254
Leifield, Lefty, 70, 254
Leigh, Janet, 37
Lemmon, Jack, 37
Lewis, Ted, 210
Leyland, Jim, 51–52, 156–157, 194, 227
Lieb, Frederick, 59, 121, 139, 260, 267
Lind, Jose, 195
Lindaman, Vive, 210
Little League World Series, 307
Littlefield, Dick, 314
Littlejohn, Dennis, 222
Lobert, Hans, 321
Lolich, Mickey, 125
Lopes, Davy, 207
Lopez, Al, 237
Lucas, Red, 279
Luzinski, Greg, 44

MacFarlan, Claude, 7
Mack, Connie, 64, 107, 168, 267
Mackowiak, Rob, 308
Maddox, Nick, 70, 206, 254
Maddux, Greg, 119
Madison, Art, 7
Madlock, Bill, 217, 229–233
Maholm, Paul, 76, 272
Manhattan Beach, California, 271
Mantle, Mickey, 288
Maranville, Rabbit, 104, 259, 294
Marietta College, 220
Maris, Roger, 29, 199
Markeson, Bruce, 14
Marquard, Rube, 71, 73, 115
Mathewson, Christy, 8, 125
Matlack, Jon, 17, 150
Mauch, Gene, 290
May, Jerry, 245
Mays, Willie, 50, 162, 267, 288–289, 296
Mazeroski, Bill, 17, 24, 87–93, 125, 131, 134, 147, 156, 163, 284
McCarthy, Jack, 171, 267
McCarthy, Joe, 107
McClatchy, Kevin, 24
McClendon, Lloyd, 157
McCloud High School, 96

McClouth, Nate, 77
McCovey, Willie, 227, 243
McCreery, Tom, 168, 188
McCutchen, Andrew, 2, 75–79, 132–133
McDaniel, Lindy, 162
McGraw, John, 21, 65, 107, 242
McGregor, Scott, 32
McKechnie, Bill, 65, 72, 83, 107, 110, 139–140, 294–296, 318
McMurtry, Craig, 54
McNally, Dave, 119
Meares, Pat, 201
Medich, George "Doc," 320
Meine, Heinie, 67
Memorial Stadium, 16, 32, 220
Memphis, Tennessee, 229, 231
Meridian High School, 145
Meridian, Idaho, 145
Merson, Jack, 288
Messitt, Tom, 7
Metkovich, Catfish, 38
Middlebrook, Jason, 306
Mikklesen, Pete, 153
Miller, Bob, 230
Miller, Dots, 21
Millwood, Kevin, 119
Milner, John, 181
Minaya, Oscar, 306
Mitchell, Keith, 52
Mize, Johnny, 35–37, 60
Mizell, Wilmer "Vinegar Bend," 229–230
Money, Don, 321
Monte Cristi, Dominican Republic, 283–284
Moore, Eddie, 141
Morandini, Mickey, 321
Morgan, Joe, 44, 88
Morris, Bryan, 307
Morris, Jim, 138
Morrison, Jim, 286
Moss, Brandon, 307
Mota, Manny, 243–244
Motton, Curt, 28
Mount Carmel College, 287
Mount Moriah, Missouri, 72
Mount Rushmore, 24

Muehlebach, George, 259–260
Mulcahy, Hugh, 150
Murcer, Bobby, 230
Murray, Eddie, 45, 217, 219–220
Murray, Red, 73
Murtaugh, Danny, 89, 108, 115, 117, 146, 152, 303, 312
Musial, Stan, 37–38, 238, 278, 280

NBA, 161, 163
Neagle, Denny, 119
Nettles, Graig, 46
New York Baseball Writers Association of America, 90
Newcombe, Don, 116
Nicaragua Earthquake, 13–14, 216
Nichols, Kid, 210
Niehaus, Al, 104, 230, 294–295
Nitcholas, Otho, 138
Northern Exposure, 302

O'Brien, John, 7
O'Conner, Jack, 187
O'Day, Hank, 153
O'Doul, Lefty, 67
Ojeda, Bob, 119
Oldham, Red, 219–220
Oliva, Tony, 199
Olivo, Diomedes, 138, 164
Oquendo, Jose, 158
Orosco, Jesse, 222
Osborne, Don, 299
Osteen, Claude, 119
Ott, Ed, 217

Padgett, Ernie, 262
Page, Joe, 115
Pagliaroni, Jim, 147, 285
Paige, Satchel, 138, 153
Palmeiro, Rafael, 179
Palmer, Jim, 119
Parker, Dave, 43–47, 156, 199, 207, 220, 232, 284
Pena, Alejandro, 52
Pena, Tony, 155–157, 283–286
Pendleton, Terry, 51
Perez, Oliver, 200, 306

Perez, Tony, 46, 180
Peterson, Charles, 76, 272
Peterson, Harding, 220, 229, 231
Peterson, Matt, 320
Petty, Jesse, 261
Phelps, Babe, 59
Phillippe, Deacon, 7, 70, 109, 119–120, 122, 125–129, 173–174, 185–187, 254, 314
Piazza, Mike, 273
Pinson, Vada, 179–180
Pittsburgh Dispatch, 127
Pittsburgh Post-Gazette, 66, 102
PNC Park, 10, 11, 18, 21, 32, 39–40, 78–79, 92, 200–201, 212, 217, 203, 308–309
Pollet, Howie, 38
Polo Grounds, 96, 280
Polytechnic High School, 278
Portsmouth, Ohio, 64, 180, 182
Posedel, Bill, 151
Powell, Boog, 303–304
Pre-Integration Era Committee, 102
Price, Joe, 286
Pulliam, Harry, 7
Purdue University, 151
Purkey, Bob, 321

Quay, Luke, 17

Ramirez, Aramis, 321
Randle, Lenny, 230
Randolph, Willie, 320
Ranier, Bill, 1, 2
Ray, Johnny, 286, 305–306
Reach Guide, 133
Redman, Mark, 273
Redus, Gary, 195
Reed, Steve, 306
Rettenmund, Merv, 220
Reuschal, Rick, 205
Reynolds, Mark, 96
Rhines, Billy, 186, 267
Rhoden, Rick, 192
Rhodes, Arthur, 273
Rice, Andy, 76
Rice, Jim, 46

Richardson, Bobby, 90, 243
Rickey, Branch, 15, 28, 89, 114, 145, 163, 288
Riconda, Harry, 261
Riley, Leon, 138
Ripken Jr., Cal, 6, 278
Ritchey, Claude, 7, 109, 169, 188, 314
Riverside, California, 51
Rizzo, Johnny, 307
Roberts, Dave, 230
Robertson, Bob, 43, 180–181
Robinson, Bill, 32, 207
Robinson, Don, 217, 305–306
Robinson, Jackie, 38, 138
Robinson, Kirk, 302
Robinson, Wilbert, 99
Rochester, Wisconsin, 168
Rodriguez, Alex, 179
Rodriguez, Ivan, 179
Rohwer, Ray, 84
Rollins, Jimmy, 28
Rooker, Jim, 32, 150, 232
Rose, Pete, 88, 179, 286
Route 136, 72
Rural Retreat, Virginia, 126
Russell, Bill, 207
Ruth, Babe, 6, 18, 29, 39, 90, 92, 114, 261, 265–266

San Leandro, California, 28
Sanguillen, Manny, 180, 213–218
Santa Rita, New Mexico, 36
Santo, Ron, 67
Scantlebury, Pat, 138
Scherzer, Max, 116
Schmidt, Mike, 64, 67
Schriver, Pop, 267
Schuerholz, John, 52
Schultz, Bob, 38
Scott, Everett, 64, 278
Scott, Pete, 134–135
Seaver, Tom, 205
Sebring, Jimmy, 128
Sewell, Joe, 236, 278
Sewell, Luke, 236
Sewell, Tommy, 236
Sewell, Truett "Rip", 235–239

Seymour, Cy, 6, 265–266
Sheehan, Tom, 230
Shepard, Larry, 29
Show, Eric, 226
Simmons, Ted, 181
Singer, Bill, 150
Singleton, Ken, 199, 220
Sizemore, Ted, 207
Skinner, Bob, 165, 290
Slaughter, Enos, 60, 199
Smiley, John, 194
Smith, Elmer, 265–269
Smith, Hal, 91–92
Smith, Lonnie, 231
Smith, Ozzie, 88, 305
Smith, Zane, 150
Smoltz, John, 119
Society of American Baseball Research (SABR), 333
Sosa, Elias, 216
Sosa, Sammy, 198
Spahn, Warren, 39, 152
Sparks, Tully, 123
Sporting News, 8, 22,33, 90, 92, 108, 121, 157–158, 195, 272, 285, 305–306, 309
Sports Illustrated, 33, 199, 302
Stahl, Chick, 168
Stairs, Matt, 308
Stargell, Willie, 24, 27–33, 43–44, 83, 125, 147, 182, 200, 219,220, 227, 231–232, 245
Stearnes, John, 44
Stenzel, Jake, 312
Stephens, Vern, 239
Stephentown, New York, 114
Steve Blass Disease, 265, 299, 302
Stewart, Ace, 267
Stewart, Cory, 200, 306
Storke, Alan, 230
Strawberry, Daryl, 199
Strincevich, Nick, 98
Stuart, Dick, 117, 165, 290
Suhr, Gus, 277–281
Suhr, Gus Jr., 280
Sutter, Bruce, 153
Sutton, Don, 119
Suzuki, Ichiro, 179

CONTENTS

Tannehill, Jesse, 119, 122, 185–189, 254
Tanner, Chuck, 206, 216–217, 222, 231
Taylor, Elizabeth, 37
Tebeau, Patsy, 249
Tejada, Miguel, 278
Tekulve, Kent, 219–223
Terre Haute, Indiana, 81–83
Terry, Ralph, 90
Thevenow, Tommy, 57
Thomas, Frank (Pirates), 200, 287–291
Thomas, Frank (White Sox), 287–288
Thornley, Stew, 15
Three Rivers Stadium, 10, 18, 27, 29,
    31–32, 50, 158, 182, 200, 206, 221,
    226, 232, 273–274
Thrift, Syd, 155–156, 192–193, 195
Thurman, Bob, 138
Tiltonsville, Ohio, 89
Tipton, Indiana, 70
Tolan, Bobby, 321
Topps, 272, 284
Torrance High School, 271
Torre, Joe, 30, 107, 215, 274
Traynor, Harold "Pie," 63–67, 83, 125,
    141, 176
Tronzo, Joe, 21
Trouppe, Quincy, 138
Trujillo, Rafael, 243
Turley, Bob, 152

Ueberroth, Peter, 232
United Press International, 102, 152,
    154, 284
University of Delaware, 211
University of Houston, 192
University of Missouri, 259
University of Pittsburgh, 164
USA Today, 309
Utica, New York, 156

Valenzuela, Fernando, 228
Van Benschoten, John, 76, 265, 272
Van Haltren, George, 319
Van Robays, Maurice, 236
Van Slyke, Andy, 50, 52, 155–159, 195,
    284–285
Vance, Dazzy, 319

Vanderbilt University, 236
Varsho, Gary, 157
Vaughan, Greg, 321
Vaughan, Joseph "Arky," 57–61, 70, 111
Veale, Bob, 312
Victoria, Texas, 192
Virdon, Bill, 51, 91, 117, 216, 311, 314
Virgil, Ozzie, 243
Vizquel, Omar, 179

Waddell, Rube, 7, 109, 318
Wadsworth, Jack, 7
Wagner, Albert, 6
Wagner, Billy, 201
Wagner, Honus, 5–11, 14, 21, 24, 58, 60,
    73, 82, 109, 117, 123, 126–127, 161,
    167–169, 173–176, 256, 259–260, 314,
    318–319
Wakefield, Dick, 237
Wakefield, Tim, 71, 320
Walker, Harry, 241–244, 300
Walker, Neil, 90, 272
Walker, Shon, 76
Walling, Denny, 195
Wambsganss, Bill, 262
Waner, Lloyd, 22, 25, 95–99
Waner, Ora, 96
Waner, Paul, 21–25, 64, 95–96, 98, 156,
    200
Waner, Paul III, 24
Ward, Daryl, 225
Ward, John, 266
Ward, Preston, 38
Wasdell, Jimmy, 59
Watkins, William, 168
Weaver, Earl, 301, 303–304
Welker, Herman, 145
West Coast Conference, 306
West Creek, New York, 174
West Lafayette High School, 151
Westlake, Wally, 111
Wheeling, West Virginia, 88, 90–91
Whitfield, Terry, 222
Whitson, Ed, 230
Wigginton, Ty, 320
Wilhelm, Hoyt, 163
Williams, Bernie, 28

Williams, Billy (Pilots), 138
Williams, Billy Leo (Cubs, A's), 46,
    278
Williams, Jimmy, 168, 174
Williams, Ted, 61, 238–239
Willis, Dontrelle, 28
Willis, Vic, 70, 13, 209–212, 254
Wills, Les, 138
Wills, Maury, 114
Wilson, Chief, 105
Wilson, Jack, 308
Wilson, Parke, 249
Wilton Consolidated High School, 89

Winfield, Dave, 199
Winfield, Kansas, 110
Winterset, Iowa, 109
Wood, Joe, 125
Wood, Wilbur, 321
Woodling, Gene, 321
Wright, Glenn, 259–263

Yost, Eddie, 278
Young, Kevin, 201

Zimmer, Chief, 7
Zisk, Richie, 43, 207

ABOUT THE AUTHOR

David Finoli is a sportswriter and sports historian who has written 19 books focusing mostly on the history of sports in Western Pennsylvania, the majority of them dealing with the team he is most passionate about, the Pittsburgh Pirates. Growing up in nearby Greensburg, Pennsylvania, he has closely followed the exploits of the Bucs for the past six decades, experiencing both the greatest moments and the lows of a historical 20-season run of losing baseball between 1993 and 2012. Finoli attended Duquesne University in Pittsburgh starting in 1979, the year the Bucs won their last world championship to date, and graduated with a bachelor of arts in journalism. Contributing to several books, as well as writing for *Pittsburgh Magazine* and the *Pirates Game Day* program, Finoli, who has been a member of the Society of American Baseball Research for 17 years, has also worked in retail management for the past 31 years and currently lives in Monroeville, Pennsylvania, with his wife Vivian and three children, Cara, Matthew, and Tony.